Organizational Strategy, Structure, and Process

McGraw Hill-Series in Management

Keith Davis and Fred Luthans, Consulting Editors

Organizational Strategy, Structure, and Process

Raymond E. Miles

School of Business Administration
University of California, Berkeley

Charles C. Snow

College of Business Administration
The Pennsylvania State University

in collaboration with
Alan D. Meyer

and with contributions by
Henry J. Coleman, Jr.

McGraw-Hill Book Company

New York   St. Louis   San Francisco   Auckland   Bogotá   Düsseldorf
Johannesburg   London   Madrid   Mexico   Montreal   New Delhi   Panama
Paris   São Paulo   Singapore   Sydney   Tokyo   Toronto

Library of Congress Cataloging in Publication Data

Miles, Raymond E.
    Organizational Strategy, Structure, and Process

    (McGraw-Hill series in management)
    Bibliography: p.
    Includes index.
    1. Industrial management.   I.   Snow, Charles Curtis,
(date)   joint author.   II. Title.
HD31.M437   658.4   77-26102
ISBN 0-07-041932-9

ORGANIZATIONAL STRATEGY, STRUCTURE, AND PROCESS

567890 DODO 897654

This book was set in English Times by Allen Wayne Technical Corp.
The editor was William J. Kane
and the production supervisor was Milton J. Heiberg.
R. R. Donnelley & Sons Company was printer and binder.

Contents

2

INDUSTRY STUDIES

3

OVERVIEW OF THE LITERATURE

Preface

Interest in the concept of organization strategy and its relation to structure and management processes has increased rapidly over the past few years. In an earlier work dealing with the impact of managers' theories on organizational structure and process, we rather blandly announced that "economic or entrepreneurial actions and decisions . . . although crucial areas of concern . . . fall outside the scope of this book" (Miles, 1975, p. 5). The decision to treat an organization's strategic or market orientation as simply a fixed part of the environment in which all other managerial decisions are made was, in part at least, a concession to the constraints of space and to the existing lines of scholarly demarcation in the area of organization and management theory. However, a reason far more important than space limitations or disciplinary boundaries led to the decision to view strategy as, at best, a moderating variable. Neither we—nor anyone else judging from the literature to that point—had a clear understanding of the ways in which strategy, structure, process, and management theory were intertwined.

Now, only a few years later, we are offering a theoretical framework that was "outside the scope" of the earlier book. In the intervening period we have become increasingly convinced that it is not only internal organizational processes that follow recognizable, even predictable patterns; the organization's relationship with its task environment also follows such patterns. The intent of this book is to draw these two spheres of behavior together into a single overall pattern amenable to description and analysis.

The framework presented here did not emerge full-blown. Instead, as noted in Chapter 1 and in the chapters describing our industry studies, the framework was developed sequentially. While in no sense do we consider the empirical research reported here to supply "proof" of the validity of our conceptual approach, our first study suggested that organizations within one industry or grouping develop over time a strategy of relating to their market or constituency that is recognizable to industry observers (and to their competitors). Subsequently, it became clear that a given market strategy was best served by a particular type of organizational structure, technology, and administrative process—an internal pattern that not only supported the existing strategy but also tended to perpetuate it. With the basic framework then in place, it was relatively easy to fill in many of the missing pieces. For example, chronological similarities in the development of management theory and of organizational strategy and structure took on new meaning and became a major target of our later research. Finally, we became convinced that if present patterns in strategy, structure, and process were recognizable, it was not unreasonable to speculate about future forms.

Early on we presented portions of the evolving framework in articles (Miles, Snow, and Pfeffer, 1974) and papers (Darran, Miles, and Snow, 1975; Snow, 1976). The usual procedure at that point would have been to write more papers and articles, gradually accumulating these into a complete theory. In fact, several working papers were begun and then abandoned as new data and insights emerged.

During the course of this process, it became clear that we could not compress the entire framework and its related research evidence into a single article or monograph. Therefore, we decided that a book would be much more appropriate than a series of fragmented presentations, particularly since the primary purpose was a synthesis of the relevant theory and research.

Obviously, we now believe that this decision was correct. By giving ourselves the space to develop our ideas fully, we discovered how sparse they were at numerous points, and we were forced to return to the literature, the data, and our colleagues in order to expand and strengthen the framework. Moreover, by striving for consistency in reasoning and presentation across the several chapters of a book, we had to rethink and clarify wisps of thought that had appeared to be quite logical and useful at some earlier point in time. Then, as the book took shape, linking our ideas back to our previous treatment of management theory and forward toward new organizational forms became a clear obligation that we might otherwise have been tempted to slight.

That the time was ripe for this effort is evidenced, we believe, by the fact that, once begun, the book took shape remarkably quickly. It appears to us that the study of organizations has been converging toward the sort of synthesis presented here and that our research efforts have helped us ride with and hopefully accelerate this trend. Further evidence that a theoretical treatment of organizational strategy, structure, and process was genuinely needed has been provided by the response of students and managers to the manuscript at its several stages of development. We have used all or portions of these materials in classes at several universities, with managers in university executive-development programs, and in private consulting activities with top-management groups. The verbal and written responses of these individuals were more than adequate encouragement to keep us at our task.

However, even as the book took final form, we were not without concerns, most of which were focused on the incompleteness of our effort. As is the case with any attempt at synthesis, we have not portrayed all of the forces shaping organizational behavior, and our efforts to categorize inevitably masked some of the richness and diversity of organizational strategies and structures. Of even more concern was the fact that as this book moved toward press, new topics and insights were emerging (e.g., additional relationships between our framework and organization development, links to governance issues in representational bodies, etc.). However, for a variety of reasons we decided to stop revising the manuscript and to offer it to students, managers, and scholars for their use and comment.

ATTRIBUTIONS AND ACKNOWLEDGMENTS

We wish to share with our readers the process by which we wrote this book and to acknowledge the sources of many of our ideas.

Although the initial insights concerning the process of organizational adaptation and the various ways in which organizations move through this process were provided by Miles and Snow, the complete theoretical framework emerged from group discussions of the literature and the three studies reported in Chapters 11, 12, and 13. These studies were conducted by Snow (publishing industry), Coleman (food processing and electronics), and Meyer (hospitals). Principal authorship of the first six chapters of the book can be claimed by Snow, Miles, and Meyer (in approximately that order) with important case study contributions by Coleman. Ownership of the ideas offered in this portion of the book, however, is clearly shared across the entire group.

By the time the second half of the book was seriously under way, the group was geographically dispersed, and much of the beginning material for Chapters 7, 8, 9, and 10 was provided by Miles, again drawing in part on earlier group discussions. However, the final drafts of these chapters reflect close creative partnership with Snow, crucial conceptual and editorial collaboration with Meyer, and more limited but important contributions from Coleman. Again, ownership of ideas in their final form is widely shared.

Finally, the literature summary and review (Chapter 14) was initiated by Snow, but the final product was more nearly a joint effort with Meyer supported by contributions and insights from Coleman and Miles.

In sum, virtually every page of the finished manuscript can be viewed as a joint product of two or more members of our group. Thus, the collaboration and contribution pattern indicated on the title page reflects only the group's judgment of the volume of contributions to the book and not their individual value.

We have acknowledged in the Introduction and in the overview of the literature individuals whose insights and research we have found to be useful. In addition, we have benefited directly from the comments and suggestions of many colleagues. George Strauss of the University of California, Berkeley, read the bulk of the manuscript and, as always, spotted innumerable conceptual and stylistic problems. Professors John W. Hennessey, Jr., Robert Guest, and Brian Quinn of the Amos Tuck School, Dartmouth College, and Chris Argyris and Charles Christenson of Harvard University, made many valuable suggestions throughout the manuscript. J.B. Ritchie, regularly on the faculty at Brigham Young University, used the manuscript in an advanced MBA course he taught at Berkeley and provided us with many useful comments. Suggestions and encouragement were also provided by Roy Lewicki of Duke University and Marianne Jelinek at Amos Tuck, and by John Slocum, Robert Pitts, Max Richards, and R. William Millman at The Pennsylvania State University. Particularly in the early stages of this effort, Jeffrey Pfeffer at Berkeley was a source of ideas and useful criticism. While we acknowledge directly in the text several concepts borrowed from Robert Biller, Dean of the Graduate School of Public Administration at the University of Southern California, our conceptual debt to him goes well beyond those citations.

In the latter stages of the book, Frank Heller of the Tavistock Institute of Human Relations, London, and Bernhard Wilpert of the International Institute of Management, Berlin, provided support for and constructive criticism of our efforts.

Many students and managers have assisted us through their comments and criticisms and, in some instances, by providing examples that illustrate concepts in the book. While we cannot thank them all individually, six deserve special recognition: Douglas Darran, Donald Hambrick, M.C.G. Lardge, Richard W. Matselboba, Edward E. Pollack, and Milton Steele. Special thanks are also due to the many managers of the organizations that participated in our research.

Finally, as every author knows, no book can be completed satisfactorily without skillful secretarial assistance. We deeply appreciate the help, sometimes under very trying conditions, of Lorraine Fies, Tricia Harrison, Barbara Porter, and Ildiko Takacs.

Raymond E. Miles
Charles C. Snow

Part One

Theory and
Applications

Chapter 1

Introduction

An organization is both an articulated purpose and an established mechanism for achieving it. Most organizations engage in an ongoing process of evaluating their purposes—questioning, verifying, and redefining the manner in which they interact with their environments. Effective organizations carve out and maintain a viable market for their goods or services. Ineffective organizations fail at this market alignment task. Organizations must also constantly modify and refine the mechanism by which they achieve their purposes—rearranging their structure of roles and relationships and their decision making and control processes. Efficient organizations establish mechanisms that complement their market strategy. Inefficient organizations struggle with these structure and process mechanisms.

For most organizations, the dynamic process of adjusting to environmental change and uncertainty—of maintaining an effective alignment with the environment while efficiently managing internal interdependencies—is enormously complex, encompassing myriad decisions and behaviors at several organization levels. Nonetheless, we believe that the complexity of the adjustment process can be penetrated: by searching for patterns in the behavior of organizations, one can describe and even predict the process of organizational adaptation. This book, which is based on our interpretation of the existing literature and continuing studies in four industries, provides a theoretical framework for portraying the adjustment or adaptive process, identifying its key variables, and defining their interrelationships.

More specifically, the framework presented in this book suggests some tentative answers to the following organizational and managerial questions:

To what extent and why do organizations within the same industry differ in their strategy, structure, and process? That is, what factors influence the decision to offer a narrow or broad line of products or services, to structure the organization around functions or products, to centralize or disperse decision making and control, and so forth?

How is an organization's market strategy related to the structures and processes that management selects to pursue this strategy?

To what extent and why do organizations develop typical ways of responding to environmental change and uncertainty? Within a given industry, can persistent types of organizational behaviors be identified?

Can an organization's type be diagnosed and changed? What key variables, relationships, and characteristics must be altered if change is to be effective?

Does a particular type or form of organization require a specific style of management? How does the theory of management held by an organization's leaders enhance or inhibit the organization's ability to adapt to its environment?

Are existing models of organization strategy, structure, and process able to meet all environmental conditions? If not, can new organizational forms be constructed? What characteristics will these new forms have?

The answers we offer in this book are tentative in that we have no final proof of the validity of our theoretical framework, nor is such proof likely to become available. Any attempt to examine organizational adaptation is difficult since the process is both highly complex and changeable. Nevertheless, we believe it is important to develop conceptual models of the adaptive process and to examine empirically the behaviors employed by organizations as they adjust to their environments. Managers and students of management need a theory and vocabulary that deal with the organization as an integrated and dynamic whole—a model that takes into account the interrelationships among strategy, structure, and process.

The theoretical framework proposed in this book has two major elements: (1) a general model of the process of adaptation that describes the decisions needed by the organization to maintain an effective alignment with its environment, and (2) an organizational typology that portrays the different patterns of adaptive behavior used by organizations within a given industry or other grouping. The framework is used to describe and diagnose existing organizational behaviors and to prescribe alternative directions for change where necessary. Successful organizational change, however, requires another important element to be added to the framework—management theory. Organizations are limited in their choices of adaptive behavior to those which top management believes will allow the effective direction and control of human resources. Therefore, at several points, managers' theories about how people can and should be managed are brought into our discussion.

THEORY AND RESEARCH FOUNDATIONS

The cornerstones of both the research summarized in this book and our ongoing studies consist of three pivotal ideas that were introduced and developed by a number of other authors. Although these ideas did not necessarily grow out of studies of organizational adaptation, we have nonetheless found them useful in our own research.

Organizations act to create their environments. Until recently, much organizational research has been based on the assumption that organizations *respond* in predictable ways to the conditions which surround them, adjusting their purpose and shape to meet market and other environmental characteristics. As a result, researchers have tended to search for those environmental factors which shape organizational behavior. Over the past several years, however, organizational scholars have become increasingly disenchanted with this mechanical, deterministic conception of the organization-environment relationship. Child (1972) and others argue for a less rigid view of the interaction between organizations and their environments that takes into account the dynamic interchange between the two forces. Child has called for a *strategic-choice* approach to organization-environment relations— recognition that major decisions made by management serve to define the organization's relationship with the broader environment.

Weick (1969, 1977) introduced a similar concept which he calls *environmental enactment.* He argues that organizations do not respond to preordained environmental conditions but instead create their own environments through a series of choices regarding markets, products, technologies, desired scale of operations, and so forth. Given the range of choice regarding each of these factors, the number and kinds of different environments which might be enacted are theoretically limited only by man's imagination. Indeed, much of what is taken for granted in organizations today was, in some earlier time, seen as novel.

In fact, however, the type of environment which managers can enact is severely constrained by two broad factors: existing knowledge of alternative organizational forms and managers' beliefs about how people can and should be managed. The ability to enact a new or different environment is significantly constrained by what is known about allocating, structuring, and developing resources in the form of organizations. Since their appearance as a social invention, organizations have evolved through several distinct forms. Each of these new or modified forms has enabled managers to accomplish objectives previously considered unattainable. However, as Stinchcombe (1965) has indicated, each new form has also suffered from the "liability of newness"—managers may be reluctant to adopt new structures and processes unless environmental demands are especially strong. Therefore, environmental enactment is likely to proceed cautiously and incrementally until new organizational forms are clearly articulated.

Furthermore, each new form of organization has also required a new, or at least expanded, theory of management before it became practically useful. If managers believe that people cannot be properly guided, coordinated, and controlled within a new type of organization, then they are unlikely to behave in a way that will allow the system to become fully operational. As Argyris (1973) has argued, changes in managerial attitudes and behavior must usually precede changes in organization design.

In sum, the enactment of an organizational environment cannot readily occur outside the boundaries of present knowledge concerning organizational form and management theory. Nevertheless, it is clear, as Child, Weick, Argyris, and others have argued, that managers enjoy substantial freedom to create, shape, and manage the environments in which their organizations exist.

Viewing organizations from an organic rather than a mechanical perspective requires that theories of organizational behavior place considerable emphasis on those individuals who make strategic choices, the organization's top managers. From its vantage point, top management has both the opportunity and the requirement to view the organization as a total system—a collection of people, structures, and processes that must be effectively aligned with the organization's chosen environment. Thompson (1967) emphasized the importance of this administrative role and discussed certain structure-process arrangements associated with different organizational environments. We have sought to extend Thompson's thinking in our research, particularly in examining how organizations develop means for *consistently* responding to the environments which they have enacted.

Management's strategic choices shape the organization's structure and process. To many observers, the development of a consistent organization strategy is a highly situational art characterized by insightful managerial decisions which dramatically redirect the organization's resources toward environmental opportunities. However, in Mintzberg's (1976) view, and in ours, strategy is more of a *pattern* or *stream* of major and minor decisions about an organization's possible future domains. Further, these decisions take on meaning only as they are implemented through the organization's structure and processes. In other words, an organization's strategy can best be inferred from its behavior, though one can conceptually associate strategy with *intent* and structure with *action*.

Two of the most influential proponents of this link between strategy and structure have been Drucker (1954, 1974a) and Chandler (1962). Chandler defined strategy as ". . . the determination of the basic long-term goals and objectives of the enterprise and the adoption of courses of action and the allocation of resources necessary for carrying out these goals" (p. 13). In his study of 100 U.S. companies (including an intensive investigation of the development of four large firms), Chandler cogently discussed the impact of strategy on organization structure. He discovered that "a new strategy required a new or at least refashioned structure if the enlarged enterprise was to be operated efficiently" (p. 15). However, it is clear from both Chandler's and Drucker's descriptions that no simple causal linkage exists between strategy and structure. Pioneering companies which they both studied, such as General Motors and Sears, spent years developing and clarifying the structures required to implement their strategies. Following the early work of Drucker and Chandler, other authors such as Thompson (1967), Lawrence and Lorsch (1967), Perrow (1967), and Galbraith (1973) have attempted to develop frameworks and criteria for making choices about organizational structure and processes given the nature of the environment and management's choice of strategy. We have attempted in this book to point out the advantages and disadvantages of these alternative choices concerning strategy and structure.

Structure and process constrain strategy. Once an organization has developed a particular strategy-structure arrangement, it may have difficulty pursuing activities outside its normal scope of operations. For example, Fouraker and Stopford (1968), who sought to extend Chandler's findings to multinational companies, found that diversified organizations made up of semiautonomous divisions were far more likely, and presumably far more able, to move into foreign operations than centralized, functionally structured companies.

March and Simon's (1958) discussion of how individuals make decisions provides a perspective on why such constraints on strategy might arise. They concluded that because human beings are limited in their ability to make completely rational decisions, organizational structure and process evolve so as to prevent uncertainty from overwhelming these limited capacities. Thus, the development of rules, programs, and other repertoires of action serve to break down large and complex problems into more manageable units for human decision makers. In effect, then, organizations can put boundaries around the areas in which rational decisions are needed.

However, in reducing uncertainty in this manner, organizations encourage, if not demand, that individual decision makers be parochial in their perceptions and felt responsibilities. Based on their studies, Cyert and March (1963) concluded that managers searched only in the "neighborhood" of familiar alternatives in attempting to develop solutions to the organization's problems. Essentially, then, the structure and processes of the organization influenced the scope of the scanning mechanisms available to top management. Over time, this *limited search* activity tends to become routinized in any organization, so that the organization may do some things very well (such as manufacture products efficiently) but lack capabilities in other areas (such as developing new products).

As these studies suggest, the interactions between strategy and structure become highly complex. On one hand, Drucker's, Chandler's, and Perrow's research shows that structure tends to follow strategy and that the two must be properly aligned for an organization to be effective. On the other hand, investigators like Fouraker, Stopford, March, Simon, and Cyert have demonstrated that structure constrains strategy; an organization is seldom able to veer substantially from its current course without major structure-process alterations. In our research and in this book, we have attempted to take these strategy-structure interactions into account. We have looked not only for consistencies in the alignment of strategy, structure, and process, but also for the structural constraints on strategy.

DEVELOPMENT OF THE THEORETICAL FRAMEWORK

As indicated, the theoretical framework presented in this book draws not only on the authors mentioned above (and others to be cited later) but also on our own ongoing research in four industries. Our studies have emerged, in part fortuitously, in a loose but logical sequence which has given us the opportunity to construct and at least partially test a dynamic model of the adaptive process—a model which we believe synthesizes, extends, and gives operational meaning to much of the existing literature. In our opinion, it now appears possible to classify organizations according to their strategic orientation and to predict with some reliability the structural and process characteristics associated with a chosen strategy. To a lesser extent it is also possible to predict the future development of an organization given management's choice of strategy and to point out the strengths and weaknesses inherent in this pattern of evolution. Lastly, we have a preliminary indication that some types of organizations require specific styles of management whereas other types permit a broader range of managerial philosophies and practices.

College Textbook Publishing

Our first study, which took place within 16 firms in the college textbook publishing industry, broadly explored the question, "Does an organization's form of enactment—its selection and development of a particular domain within the larger environment—produce predictable patterns in organizational structure and processes?" The college textbook publishing industry was chosen for this research because at the time (1972) the industry was, and had been, undergoing significant changes, and we believed that these changes would elicit a variety of responses from the industry's major participants. This indeed turned out to be the case, as many firms were experiencing some form of organizational adjustment: entering or dropping certain markets, modifying technologies for producing textbooks, altering organization structure, and so forth. In company after company, management had recently made a major decision concerning company policy or structure or was on the verge of doing so. As researchers, caught in the middle of what appeared to be an ongoing and sometimes rushing stream of adjustment, we were often reluctant to stop studying a particular organization for fear that it would change as soon as we left.

Faced with the disconcerting prospect that our information was becoming outdated almost as fast as we could collect it, we decided that the best way to make sense of this shifting information base was to try to learn as much as possible about the history of each company, the most critical events at various stages of its development, the perceptions of high-level executives concerning current conditions in the industry, and the general plans which these executives had for the future. In short, we tried to determine each organization's strategy for responding to the changing conditions in the publishing industry. Our subsequent contacts three years later with several of the original 16 firms indicated that each organization's strategy was a powerful determinant of the organization's structure and method of operation.

Although it was clear that there were different patterns of organizational behavior in this industry and that these patterns appeared to be persistent, it was also clear that there was no available framework for describing what we had found. Furthermore, we had generated a long list of adaptive behaviors—mergers, acquisitions, improved planning systems, management changeovers, and many others—for which there was no adequate classification scheme. We therefore concluded the publishers study by developing a typology of four relatively distinct organizational forms (based on patterns of response to market conditions and complementary structure-process characteristics) and by formulating a dynamic model of the adaptive process.

Electronics and Food Processing

The second study, involving 49 organizations in the electronics and food-processing industries, provided an opportunity for further development of the theoretical framework. To permit a more comprehensive examination of the linkage between the form of domain enactment and key aspects of organizational structure and process, we chose the electronics and food-processing industries for their wide variation in technological change and market uncertainty. In each firm in these industries, executives were asked to indicate sources and levels of environmental uncertainty, to specify which functional areas of the organization had the greatest strategic importance, and to describe major structure and process characteristics. In addition, executives were asked to use descriptions of the four organization types to classify the firms in their industry. In this larger and more complex sample, however, executives were not always able to describe or evaluate other companies in their respective industries, and while the typology was generally supported, it could not be definitively concluded that it was a valid means of classifying organizations.

Within a particular company, however, patterns of structure and process similar to those found in textbook firms were evident. For example, depending on whether the organization had created a stable or changing domain, it appeared possible to predict the most influential members of the top-management group, which functional areas would receive the largest share of current budget allocations, and where additional personnel and financial resources would be applied were they available. Moreover, while the above relationships were typically stronger in the food-processing industry than in the electronics industry, adjustment patterns similar to our four types of organizations were found in both industries and their structure-process characteristics were in line with our model. Thus, it appeared that the framework potentially had useful descriptive and predictive value.

Hospitals

The third study, conducted in 19 voluntary hospitals, was a more rigorous attempt to test all of the major features of the theoretical framework. In this study, hospital administrators and other health care experts characterized sample hospitals according to strategic type. Chief administrators reported changes in hospital structure, process, and programs over the previous year; described the configuration of influence within the hospital; and completed an instrument-measuring management theory. Because of the small, tightly knit nature of this sample of hospitals, raters were usually able to evaluate a substantial portion of the sample according to strategic type. The results of this study indicated that there was relatively strong external agreement about a particular hospital's strategy, thus confirming our typology. Moreover, organizations judged by their competitors to be a given type tended to have the structure-process characteristics suggested by our model. Further, the adaptive changes made during the previous year were substantially those that would be expected given the hospital's strategy. Finally, there was some initial evidence that certain managerial philosophies and practices were appropriate for some types of organizations but not for others.

As is the case with the existing literature, this series of studies is most meaningful when viewed as a whole. The evidence, although incomplete, appears to converge toward support for our framework. Similarly, the theoretical and practical content of our framework is greatest when it is presented in full and illustrated with case examples. Not surprisingly, this is the purpose of our book.

OBJECTIVES AND CONTENT

As stated and implied in the preceding pages, this book has five major objectives. The first objective is to develop an understanding of the process by which organizations continually adjust to their environments. A dynamic model of this process, which we call the *adaptive cycle,* is discussed and illustrated in Chapter 2. The intent of the model is to portray the nature and interrelationships of the key problems that organizations must solve in order to achieve an effective position within their chosen environment.

Our second objective is to provide an explanation for the alternative forms of adaptive behavior which exist in the industries we have studied and which are probably present in most other industries. A typology of these forms of organization, which we call *strategic types,* is briefly presented in Chapter 2 and elaborated in Chapters 3–6. Three of the four strategic types have their own unique, viable pattern of adaptation. The fourth is a form of organization that occurs when management fails to align strategy, structure, and process in a consistent fashion.

In Chapter 7 we pursue our third objective, the development of an approach for diagnosing the relationship between organizations and their environments that utilizes the adaptive cycle and the four strategic types. Diagnosis is the first step in refining or changing an organization's adaptive behavior. We offer a diagnostic checklist that poses a series of questions to aid management in maintaining an existing strategy or moving the organization to another strategy.

Our fourth objective is to create a heightened awareness of the degree to which successful organizational diagnosis and change hinges on managers' theories about how people can and should be managed. Thus, in Chapter 8 we trace the parallel development of management theory and organizational forms as we link alternative theories of management to the types of organizations described in the earlier chapters.

The fifth and final objective of this book is to create a conceptual foundation for the examination of emerging organizational forms. The first eight chapters discuss the process of organizational adaptation, four alternative types of adaptation, linkages among these organization types and management theory, and issues associated with diagnosing and changing an organization's strategic orientation. All of this discussion is based on existing patterns of organizational behavior. In Chapter 9, we discuss future patterns of organizational behavior, projecting current and emerging environmental conditions and discussing the organizational forms and management theories needed to cope successfully with these conditions.

In Chapter 10, we present our conclusions and speculate further about future organizational forms and management theories.

The final four chapters are included to support our previous discussions by supplying more detailed descriptions of our research and our interpretation of the literature. Chapters 11, 12, and 13 provide, respectively, descriptions of the three research studies in college textbook publishing, electronics and food processing, and hospitals. Chapter 14 is a nontechnical overview of the literature related to organization-environment relations and is intended for those readers who desire a more complete discussion of relevant theories and research.

Chapter 2

The Process of Organizational Adaptation

We have indicated that organizational adaptation is a topic of major managerial concern that has received only limited and fragmented theoretical treatment. In this chapter, we develop our own view of the process of adaptation. First, as an example, we discuss the adaptive problems encountered by a subsidiary of one of the companies in our studies. At the suggestion of corporate management, this subsidiary made substantial changes in its products, markets, and methods of operation. We present this case to illustrate the difficulties in analyzing organizational adaptation, and we briefly characterize the major perspectives relevant to this problem.

Following the discussion of this case, we examine three alternative views of the process of organizational adaptation, each of which assigns management a different role. When each of these views is applied to the case example, the *strategic-choice* approach, discussed in Chapter 1, appears most relevant. This approach underlies our discussions throughout the book.

The third section presents our model of organizational adaptation which we call the *adaptive cycle.* Although we recognize that adaptation is a complex and ongoing process, we believe nevertheless that it can be broken apart, for purposes of analysis, into three major problems requiring top-management attention and decisions: the entrepreneurial problem, the engineering problem, and the administrative problem. Each of these problems is, of course, interrelated, but each must be considered fully by management before an effective adaptive cycle is completed.

Finally, we describe four types of organizations which, our research indicates, represent alternative ways of moving through the adaptive cycle. Three of these *strategic types*—which we label the *Defender,* the *Analyzer,* and the *Prospector*—are "stable" forms of organization. That is, if management chooses to pursue one of these strategies, and designs the organization accordingly, then the organization may be an effective competitor in its particular industry over a considerable period of time. On the other hand, if management does not choose to pursue one of these "pure" strategies, then the organization will be slow to respond to opportunities and is likely to be an ineffective performer in its industry. We call these latter organizations *Reactors* and argue that they are essentially "unstable." A more complete discussion of each of the four strategic types will follow in Chapters 3–6.

Porter Pump and Valve (PPV) is a semiautonomous division of a medium-sized equipment-manufacturing firm, which is in turn part of a large, highly diversified conglomerate. PPV manufactures a line of heavy-duty pumps and components for fluid-movement systems. The company does most of its own castings, makes many of its own parts, and maintains a complete stock of replacement parts. PPV also does special-order foundry work for other firms as its production schedule allows.

Until recently, Porter Pump and Valve had defined its business as providing quality products and service to a limited set of reliable customers. After an initial growth spurt in the late forties and early fifties, the company had remained approximately the same size through the sixties and early seventies. Portions of the 30-year-old foundry facilities had become increasingly unreliable and occasionally unsafe, so four years ago PPV invested $850,000 replacing equipment and refurbishing the plant. PPV's general manager, a first-rate engineer who spent much of his time in the machine shop and foundry, personified the company's image of quality and cost efficiency. He believed the recent capital expenditures considerably strengthened the firm's ability to manufacture efficiently and cheaply the products required by current customers.

In the mid-seventies, however, corporate management became concerned about both the speed and direction of PPV's growth. The management and staff at corporate headquarters began considering two new product and market opportunities, both in the energy field. Fluid-movement systems required for nuclear power generation provided one of these opportunities, and the development of novel techniques for petroleum exploration, well recovery, and fluid delivery provided the second. PPV had supplied some components to these markets in the past, but it was now clear that opportunities for the sale of entire systems or large-scale subsystems were growing rapidly. Moreover, top management strongly believed that PPV's current markets were in a state of steady, if only gradual, decline. Management decided that it was time to revamp the operations of its subsidiary.

Relying on the advice of its own internal specialists, corporate management began the process of redirecting PPV toward the perceived opportunities in the energy field. PPV's initial move toward these new opportunities were tentative. The general manager discovered that contract sales required extensive planning, field contact work, and careful negotiations—activities not within his primary areas of interest or experience. Finally, in an effort to foster more rapid movement into these new markets, executives in the parent organization transferred the general manager to the head office and moved into the top spot at PPV a manager with an extensive background in both sales and engineering who was adept at large-scale contract negotiations.

Within a year of the changeover in general managers, PPV landed several lucrative contracts, and more appeared to be in the offing. The new business created by these contracts, however, placed heavy coordination demands on company management, and while the organization's technology (production and distribution system) has not been drastically revised over the past 2 years, work flow processes and the operational responsibilities of several managers have changed markedly. Materials control and scheduling, routine tasks in the past, are now crucial activities, and managers of these operations meet regularly with the executive planning committee. Moreover, a rudimentary matrix structure has emerged in which various line managers undertake specific project responsibilities in addition to their regular duties. Key personnel additions have been made to the marketing department, and more are planned, with particular emphasis on individuals who are capable of performing field planning and supervising and who can quickly bring new fluid systems to full operation. Budgets of some of the older departments are being cut back, and these funds are being diverted to the new areas of activity.

These changes appear to have brought PPV's structure and management processes more fully into line with its new strategy. However, the changes were not accomplished without cost. In retrospect, corporate management can now see more clearly areas where it would have benefitted from more guidance. For example, management now wishes that it had a more efficient means of scanning the environment to locate new areas of opportunity, not only for PPV but also for its other subsidiaries as well. If PPV's new product and market opportunities had been spotted and acted upon earlier, the costs of refurbishing the plant to conduct what is now largely old business would have been saved.

Secondly, management now believes that the conversion could have been accomplished more rapidly had the headquarters group seen that the technology required to produce and distribute PPV's new products was different in several respects from the previous technology. For example, in the past, PPV's customers provided the company with a largely predictable stream of orders for heavy-duty pumps and other related products. Many of these parts had already been produced and were simply pulled out of stock and shipped to the customer. Today, however, PPV must actively search out new customers, bid on projects according to a set of usually unique customer specifications, and then produce the required components. In addition, PPV has had to hire and quickly train a staff of field specialists to supervise the installation of these systems.

Thirdly, top management has watched PPV management solve one set of difficult problems only to have another, and usually different, set of problems arise. For example, in the process of solving its market and technological problems, PPV found itself faced with a number of thorny administrative issues, matters in which the company had previously had no major difficulties. The transformation from what was previously a stable manufacturing operation to a job-shop operation with extensive field duties left management with many new planning, coordination, and control problems for which solutions had to be developed.

Finally, corporate management now realizes that several years may pass before these changes are completely assimilated into the day-to-day operations of the organization. Had corporate management been able to visualize the entire process of adjustment at PPV, it might have been able to reduce the amount of time and resources that were—and continue to be—devoted to this subsidiary's adaptive problems.

Alternative Analytical Perspectives

Over time, experts from several fields have developed knowledge and techniques useful for analyzing and assisting organizational changes such as those undertaken by Porter Pump and Valve. However, specialists in each of these fields, while acknowledging the broader process of adaptation, have tended to focus their attention on only limited aspects of adaptation. Models developed by *economists,* for example, provide tools for evaluating alternative allocations of organizational resources through estimates of market demand, levels of output, and product prices. Most likely, however, these models would not have aided PPV's corporate staff in identifying new markets nor would they have suggested the mechanisms by which the organization's goal and technological changes should be achieved.

Marketing specialists and business-policy analysts devote major attention to the methods by which organizations scan their environments for opportunities and decide which among these should be pursued and how. Typically, however, experts in these areas have dealt less extensively with the full range of internal changes which an organization such as PPV would require to reach newly chosen product-market goals. That is, the behavioral ramifications of change in terms of training and reorienting personnel, designing information and reward systems, etc., are usually not highlighted in their models.

The domain of work flow design (or redesign) in response to new product or service goals has been historically claimed by *industrial engineers.* To some extent, the industrial engineer's view of the adjustment process is the converse of that of the marketing specialist or the business-policy analyst. Whereas these latter experts tend to focus on choices among alternative market goals, the industrial engineer has historically entered the scene after the direction of change has been established. The industrial engineer's skills have been most helpful in revamping the organization's technology to fit new market objectives.

In recent years, industrial engineers have added to their traditional concern for the design of least-cost systems of production, scheduling, and control by taking into account concepts and techniques from the field of Organizational Behavior. Experts in *Organizational Behavior* (OB) have focused major attention on managerial problems such as leadership, motivation, job design, and reward systems in an effort to reduce the "people" barriers to efficient systems operation. To some extent, the field of Organizational Behavior has begun to focus on the adaptive process but not yet in a fully integrated manner. A subset of OB experts, *Organization Development* (OD) specialists, profess a concern with the process of change throughout the entire organizational system, but they have argued that they are not concerned with the targets of change. That is, they have claimed dominion over the managerial skills necessary to create and maintain new organizational forms but have assumed the prime impetus for change—the organization's response to its external environment—to be given. At PPV, organizational behaviorists would have been alert to the strains placed on the human system by the new goals and process changes. Their orientation would have called attention to the behavioral implications of alterations in work roles, authority, and responsibility, and they could have offered advice to PPV's general manager about job design, communications and control systems, and so on. Organization Development specialists would have begun working with the top executives at PPV in an effort to increase their awareness of the human implications of their marketing and engineering decisions and to help them recognize the inhibiting factors in their own decision-making processes. Subsequently (in rare instances, simultaneously), they would have begun similar activities with work groups throughout the organizational hierarchy. In virtually all cases, however, the OD expert's orientation would have been toward the process of implementing change rather than toward the more substantive question of why change was taking place at all.

Thus, none of these basic approaches—economic, marketing, policy, industrial engineering, or behavioral—appears to address all of the problems and issues associated with the changes which occurred at Porter Pump and Valve. PPV experienced changes in its products and markets, in the technological processes needed to make new products and serve new markets, and in the administrative structure and processes required to plan, coordinate, and control the company's new operations. Therefore, how can the adaptive process which occurred at PPV be described in its entirety? To answer this question requires discussion of the major ways in which organizational adaptation has been conceptualized.

ORGANIZATIONAL ADAPTATION: THREE GENERAL PERSPECTIVES

It is true, but not terribly profound, to say that every organization is embedded in a network of external influences and relationships which can be labeled as its *environment*. However, more specifically, the environment is not a homogeneous entity but rather is composed of a complex combination of factors such as product and labor market conditions, industry customs and practices, governmental regulations, and relations with financial and raw materials suppliers. Each of these factors tends to influence the organization in its own unique way: the behavior of certain environmental elements can be reliably predicted while that of others cannot; the impact of some conditions can be buffered while the impact of others cannot; and some factors are critical to the organization's operations while others are only incidental.

Top management, as noted in Chapter 1, is charged with the dual responsibility of aligning the organization with its environment and of managing the internal interdependencies thereby created. Organizational survival may be said to rest on the quality of the "fit" which management achieves among such major variables as the organization's product-market domain, its technology for serving that domain, and the organizational structures and processes developed to coordinate and control the technology. Maintaining and improving this coalignment of environmental and organizational variables is obviously a difficult task, primarily because each set of variables changes according to its own dynamics, and each change places new or different demands on the administrative group. Thus if, as Thompson (1967, p. 148) has pointed out, top managers are continually "shooting at a moving target of co-alignment," how does this alignment process occur?

Natural Selection

This question has been answered several ways. The first answer clearly minimizes management's role in the alignment process. One can imagine, as Alchian (1960) has illustrated, a *natural selection* process of alignment. That is, within a given group of organizations, some by chance alone will develop characteristics more compatible with emerging environmental conditions than will their counterparts. Those organizations fortunate enough to have the "right" structure at that time will perform best, forcing their competitors to emulate these structures or to cease to exist. Thus, in the case of Porter Pump and Valve described above, management would have been forced to look at how its successful competitors operated and then simply to have copied important aspects of their structure and process.

Rational Selection

Conversely, one can, taking the economic theory of the firm at face value, imagine a *rational selection* process of alignment. The rational selection approach asserts that while environmental conditions largely determine the efficacy of different organizational structures and processes, the managers of successful organizations efficiently select, adopt, and discard structural and process components to maintain the organization's equilibrium with its environment. Therefore, according to this approach, the management of Porter Pump and Valve would have determined that changes in the company's market were occurring, that the firm's ability to cope with these changes was inadequate, and that certain adjustments were required to bring PPV into an optimal alignment with these new environmental conditions.

As we have seen, the process did not work exactly that way, in fact, division management, if left alone, might not have spotted the environmental opportunities for some time. Moreover, even when top management intervened to change PPV's market strategy, the accompanying structure and process requirements were neither fully foreseen nor efficiently implemented. Indeed, many of the adjustments ultimately made by PPV management were in response to problems created by its own previous decisions. Thus, in retrospect, the bulk of the rationality present in PPV's alignment process was simply the "intended" rationality with which management approached each major decision.

Neither the natural selection nor the rational selection view of the alignment process appears to fit the PPV experience—or that of most organizations. It seems highly implausible that organizational survival stems from environmental fluctuations which are seldom influenced by managers' responses to these conditions. Similarly, based on what is known about the cognitive limits of individual and group decision making, the argument that managers select appropriate organization structures with consummate rationality is also questionable. A more palatable position is that both approaches are partially correct in that managers usually *attempt* to make rational choices based on their imperfect perceptions, and some of these choices are more *fortuitously* in line with reality than others.

Strategic Choice

If the natural and rational selection views of the alignment process are not accurate, how then *do* organizations align themselves with their environments? Probably the most accurate way of conceptualizing this process is the *strategic-choice* approach (Child, 1972) discussed in Chapter 1. This approach argues that organization structure is only partially preordained by environmental conditions, and it places heavy emphasis on the role of the top decision makers who serve as the primary link between the organization and its environment. These managers are viewed as being in a position not only to adjust organization structure and process when necessary but also to attempt to manipulate the environment itself in order to bring it into conformity with what the organization is already doing. The particular strategic-choice approach which we have used in our research has several important features which will be referred to throughout our discussions in subsequent chapters:

1   *Dominant coalition*—every organization has a group of decision makers whose influence on the system is greatest. This group of executives has problem-finding as well as problem-solving responsibilities.

2   *Perceptions*—the dominant coalition largely enacts or creates the organization's relevant environment. That is, the organization responds largely to what its management perceives; those environmental conditions that go unnoticed or are deliberately ignored have little effect on management's decisions and actions.

3 *Segmentation*—the dominant coalition is responsible for partitioning the environment and assigning its components to various organizational subunits. Resources are allocated to these subunits according to their strategic importance.

4 *Scanning activities*—the dominant coalition is responsible for the surveillance of those environmental elements deemed most critical to the organization. It has the choice of being reactive (waiting for events to take shape clearly before responding) or proactive (anticipating the shape of events and acting quickly) with respect to the information it gathers.

5 *Dynamic constraints*—the dominant coalition's adaptive decisions are constrained by the organization's past and current strategy, structure, and performance. Existing constraints can be relaxed or removed by major alterations of strategy, but any new direction chosen will have its own set of constraints.

THE ADAPTIVE CYCLE

The strategic-choice approach essentially argues that the effectiveness of organizational adaptation hinges on the dominant coalition's perceptions of environmental conditions and the decisions it makes concerning how the organization will cope with these conditions. As indicated at the beginning of this chapter, we believe that this complex and dynamic process can be broken apart into three major problems which management must continually solve: entrepreneurial, engineering, and administrative problems. In mature organizations, each of these three problems typically occurs more or less simultaneously, but they will be discussed here, for explanatory purposes, as sequential.

The Entrepreneurial Problem

The adaptive cycle, though evident in all organizations, is perhaps most visible in new or rapidly growing organizations (and in organizations which recently have survived a major crisis). In a new organization, an entrepreneurial insight, perhaps only vaguely defined at first, must be developed into a concrete definition of an organizational domain: a specific product or service and a target market or market segment. In an ongoing organization, the entrepreneurial problem has an added dimension. Because the organization has already obtained a set of "solutions" to its engineering and administrative problems, its next attempt at an entrepreneurial thrust may be difficult. In the earlier example of Porter Pump and Valve, the company's attempt to modify its products and markets was constrained by its existing production process and by the fact that the general manager and his staff did not possess the needed marketing orientation.

In either a new or ongoing organization, the solution to the entrepreneurial problem is marked by management's acceptance of a particular product-market domain, and this acceptance becomes evident when management decides to commit resources to achieve objectives relative to the domain. In many organizations, external and internal commitment to the entrepreneurial solution is sought through the development and projection of an organizational image which defines both the organization's market and its orientation toward it (e.g., an emphasis on size, efficiency, or innovation).

Although we are suggesting that the engineering phase begins at this point, the need for further entrepreneurial activities clearly does not disappear. The entrepreneurial function remains a top-management responsibility, and time and other resources must be committed to it.

The Engineering Problem

The engineering problem involves the creation of a system which puts into actual operation management's solution to the entrepreneurial problem. The creation of such a system requires management to select an appropriate technology (input-transformation-output process) for producing and distributing the chosen products or services and to form new information, communication, and control linkages (or modify existing linkages) to ensure proper operation of the technology.

As solutions to these problems are reached, initial implementation of the organizational system takes place. However, there is no assurance that the configuration of the organization, as it begins to emerge during this phase, will remain the same when the engineering problem finally has been "solved." The actual form of the organization's structure will be determined during the administrative phase as management solidifies relations with the environment and establishes processes for coordinating and controlling internal operations. Referring again to the case of Porter Pump and Valve, the company's redefinition of its domain required concomitant changes in its technology from a pure mass-production technology to a unit or small-batch technology (Woodward, 1965, 1970).

The Administrative Problem

The administrative problem, as described by most theories of management, is primarily that of reducing uncertainty within the organizational system, or, in terms of the present model, of rationalizing and stabilizing those activities which successfully solved problems faced by the organization during the entrepreneurial and engineering phases. Solving the administrative problem, however, involves more than simply rationalizing the system already developed (uncertainty reduction); it also involves formulating and implementing those processes which will enable the organization to continue to evolve (innovation). The conception of the administrative problem as a pivotal factor in the cycle of adaptation deserves further elaboration.

Rationalization and articulation   In the ideal organization, management would be equally adept at performing two somewhat conflicting functions: it would be able to create an administrative system (structure and processes) that could smoothly direct and monitor the organization's current activities without allowing the system to become so ingrained that future innovative activities would be jeopardized. Such a perspective requires the administrative system to be viewed as both a *lagging* and *leading* variable in the process of adaptation. As a lagging variable, the administrative system must rationalize, through the development of appropriate structures and processes, the strategic decisions made at previous points in the adjustment process. As a leading variable, on the other hand, the administrative system will facilitate or restrict the organization's future capacity to adapt depending on the extent to which management articulates and reinforces the paths along which such activity can proceed. At Porter Pump and Valve, for example, management revamped its planning, coordination, and control processes completely in order to pursue the company's newly chosen areas of business (the lagging aspect of administration). At the same time, key personnel were added to the marketing department whose duties included product development, market research, and technical consulting. These activities were designed to keep PPV at the forefront of new product and market opportunities (the leading aspect of administration).

The entire adaptive cycle is portrayed in Figure 2-1.

Examples of Adaptive Failure

When management embarks on a program of organizational change without considering the entrepreneurial, engineering, and administrative problems as interrelated aspects of the adaptive process, the results are frequently undesirable, as the following examples from our research suggest.*

> *Example 1* (New domain). In 1967, American Electronics (AMEL) was a well-established manufacturer of high-quality electrical components used by firms in the aerospace industry. Users of AMEL equipment regarded it as

---

*The examples used throughout this book come primarily from our research. However, at management's request, we have masked each organization's identity and, in some instances, its industry setting. In addition, some examples have been brought to our attention by managers with whom we have discussed our research and theoretical framework.

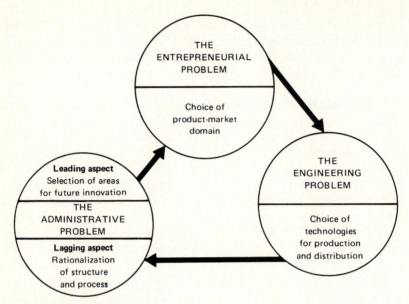

Figure 2-1   The adaptive cycle.

among the best available. The company's four product divisions mostly designed equipment to customer specifications, and AMEL was widely respected as an industry leader in research and development. The firm's marketing effort was relatively small and was mainly limited to specific types of industrial customers.

Although many competitors and customers regarded AMEL as one of the foremost companies in the industry, the firm had not generated large profits. Consequently, top management decided to exploit the company's reputation and expertise by moving into the manufacture of consumer products utilizing its existing technology. Two divisions were added, and product-management personnel were assigned to them.

By 1971, it had become apparent that the consumer divisions not only were failing to perform up to expectations but also were, in fact, siphoning off overall corporate profits. Consumer sales were sluggish, mass-production economies of scale were never achieved, and it was clear that AMEL's image of quality had not carried over to the consumer market. The board of directors concluded that the company was overextended, and it moved quickly to appoint a new president. He immediately sold the two consumer divisions and essentially returned the company to its previous industrial business. In addition, he hired a first-rate controller whose mandate was to enhance profits through aggressive efforts to control costs. To date, American Electronics has not attempted to reenter the consumer market.

In terms of the adaptive cycle, management extended the organization's product-market domain, but it seemed unwilling to make the engineering and administrative changes necessary to serve this expanded domain. A major requirement for success in the consumer market—high-volume, low-cost production—was never achieved by AMEL. Instead, the company tried to use its existing technology, well suited for the custom-made equipment desired by industrial users, to make products that were being cheaply manufactured by competitors on a mass-production basis. Moreover, the company did not attempt to launch an aggressive marketing campaign to extend the firm's image of quality to the consumer market. As a result, AMEL's products were viewed as overpriced.

> *Example 2* (New technology). In the late sixties, the New Publishing Company was formed by a nucleus of individuals who had developed an innovative way of putting together a college-level textbook. Eschewing the standard procedure of contracting with a particular author to write a textbook, this company asked as many as 40 respected researchers and teachers in a particular field to put down in any form (written chapters, outlines, cassettes, etc.) their thoughts about their respective areas of interest.
>
> After these materials had been collected, a professional writer was hired to incorporate all of the information into a single, well-written book. In addition, a professional photographer was hired to make color photographs of important illustrative material, and the overall design and styling of the book was highly elaborate. The result of this publishing effort, at least in terms of sales, was spectacular. Using this same mode of production, the company went on to publish several other textbooks, most of which were also well received.
>
> Once the novelty of producing books in this manner had worn off, several key individuals left the company, and nearly all of the engineering expertise left with them. The firm has since been merged with a larger, more traditional publishing house; most of the original people have gone their separate ways; and to this day the new owners have not been fully able to develop this type of publishing.

In this company, management developed a substantially new solution to the engineering problem of creating a college textbook. Performing the *leading* aspect of the administrative process admirably, management articulated a promising new direction for the organization. The new productive, or engineering, capability created an opportunity of considerable magnitude, and each successive book, though not as successful as the first, was nevertheless profitable. However, management gave no consideration to the *lagging* aspect of administration, that is, formalizing this publishing process so that it could be performed on a larger and more efficient scale. Because of management's failure to preserve the newly developed expertise, the engineering breakthrough was short-lived.

Example 3 (New structure). Valley Community Hospital's chief administrator was concerned about both rising costs in the hospital's nursing units and recent indications that the quality of patient care given by the nurses was declining. In an informal survey, floor nurses frequently complained that their nursing supervisors forced them to place more emphasis on rules and procedures than on providing good patient care. Head nurses, in turn, appeared to be frustrated by increases in the amount and complexity of their administrative duties.

In hopes of alleviating both problems, Valley's chief administrator introduced a change in the hospital's structure. The head nurse's patient care and administrative responsibilities were separated, and a new position, administrative coordinator, was established in each ward to assume staffing, budgeting, and other administrative duties. It was anticipated that current inefficiencies and operating costs could be better contained by individuals with a background in administration. Moreover, once relieved of the burden of these duties, head nurses could devote their time and expertise to training less experienced nurses and to supervising direct patient care activities.

The reorganization achieved one of its intended purposes. Nursing budgets became more timely and more sophisticated, leading to considerable cost savings. Efficiency and standardization in staffing patterns and in shift scheduling increased. However, instead of using their new freedom to work on behalf of patient care as hoped, many head nurses completely abandoned these activities to dedicate their full attention to resisting what they viewed as unprecedented administrative interference in the nursing profession and a direct assault on their own status and authority.

Complaints were lodged by the administrative coordinators as well as the nurses, and vigorous conflict broke out in several wards. Nurses claimed that the coordinators were pursuing cost savings with such single-mindedness that the quality of patient care suffered, while the coordinators accused nurses of withholding critical information and of other forms of deliberate subversion. Within a year of the reorganization, many of the newly hired coordinators and over half of the head nurses had left the hospital; signs of suppressed hostility were evident among those remaining. Moreover, Valley's chief administrator was beginning to receive complaints from doctors who felt that the increasing hostility between nurses and coordinators made it difficult for them to suggest Valley Hospital to their patients.

In this case, a particular structural reorganization was seen as the solution to the nursing units' problems (although alternate solutions might also have been considered, such as eliminating unnecessary administrative procedures and changing the criteria for evaluating nursing performance to take into account quality of care as well as adherence to rules). The change in structure produced a major outcome desired by management: costs were reduced and operating efficiency increased. However, patient care was not directly improved, and other undesirable technological and individual outcomes resulted: not only were many head nurses unwilling or unable to adapt to an exclusive emphasis on patient care, but they also interpreted the change as a personal as well as professional affront. As a consequence of the discord which ensued, the hospital was forced to bear the expense of a great deal of turnover among its professional employees and a decline in its market image.

What causes organizations to fail to adapt successfully? Chandler's (1962, pp. 15–19) research has identified at least three important reasons. First, top managers may become too involved in day-to-day operations to appreciate or understand the longer-range needs of their organizations. At New Publishing, management did not stop to consider how its innovative publishing program could be maintained when or if key individuals left the organization. Second, the training and education of top executives may have failed to sharpen their perception of administrative problems or failed to develop their ability to handle them. The unilateral and unheralded manner in which Valley Hospital's administrator modified the structure of nursing units indicates that he failed to anticipate potential resistance to the change. Opposition might have been reduced had nursing personnel been included in the design phase, and perhaps their input could have yielded a simultaneous solution to both the patient care and operating cost problems. Finally, Chandler argues that required changes in organizational structure and process may be hindered if they promise to threaten managers' personal positions, power, or psychological security. Indeed, in the companies studied by Chandler, major alterations of the organizational system typically occurred only after the replacement of one or more top executives.

Summary of the Model

We have argued that although organizational adaptation is a complex and dynamic process, it can be broadly conceptualized as a cycle of adjustment potentially requiring the simultaneous solution of three major problems: entrepreneurial (domain definition), engineering (technology), and administrative (structure-process and innovation). Important features of the adaptive cycle are the following:

1 *The adaptive cycle is a general physiology of organizational behavior.* By dealing with the organization as a whole, the adaptive cycle provides a means of conceptualizing the major elements of adaptation and of visualizing the relationships among them. Further, the model specifies the areas where prescriptions from basic disciplines such as economics, marketing, etc., are most relevant.

2 *The three adaptive problems—entrepreneurial, engineering, ad-*

ministrative—are intricately interwoven. The brief cases discussed in the previous section all point to the fact that simply solving the most salient adaptive problem does not ensure effective adjustment. For example, American Electronics attempted to create a new line of products which it hoped to sell to a different target market. However, the company did not make the required technological and administrative adjustments. The result was four years of largely wasted effort and heavy financial losses. In general terms, the model of adaptation highlights the various areas of an organization that might be affected by a particular strategic decision.

3   *Adaptation frequently occurs by moving sequentially through the entrepreneurial, engineering, and administrative phases, but the cycle can be triggered at any one of these points.* The process of adjustment at New Publishing Company was initiated by the development of a new technology for producing a college textbook, which in turn created an entrepreneurial opportunity. At Valley Community Hospital, the adaptive process began with an administrative change. In both cases, however, only a portion of the organization's adaptive problems was solved. (Although the point will be discussed fully in Chapter 7, we should note here that while adaptation can be triggered at any point in the adaptive cycle, the most rapid and effective adjustments appear to be those which are preceded by appropriate administrative changes.)

4   *Adaptive decisions made today tend to harden and become aspects of tomorrow's structure.* In the organizations we have observed, patterns of adjustment emerge which tend to constrain management's choices during the next cycle of adaptation. Four of these adjustment patterns are briefly described in the next section.

TYPES OF ORGANIZATIONAL ADAPTATION

It is our belief that in most successful organizations, management consciously develops and articulates (seeks consensus on) an internal organizational image just as it does a product-market image. That is, management attempts to demonstrate how and why the organization's structure and process reflect previous decisions about the market and, further, how these pave the way for future organizational development. Successful administrative solutions (General Motors' "federalism" of decentralized authority and centralized control, Sears' "flat" structure, etc.) may be as prized as product or technological innovations and often are genuinely marketable; executives are hired away to bring "their system" to other organizations. It is this combination of internal and external images that constitutes the strategy-structure relationship.

Since organizations enact their own environments, it is at least theoretically possible that no two organizational strategies will be the same. That is, every organization will choose its own target market and develop its own set of products or services, and these domain decisions will then be supported by appropriate decisions concerning the organization's technology, structure, and process. Because management is relatively free to choose among alternative forms of each of these major organizational features, the range of strategy-structure relationships is potentially vast. When competing organizations within a single industry are observed, however, patterns of behavior begin to emerge which suggest that these various organizational forms can be reduced to several archetypes. So far from our research and our interpretation of the literature, we have identified four such organization types. Each of these types has its own strategy for responding to the environment, and each has a particular configuration of technology, structure, and process that is consistent with its strategy. These organization types, which we have named the Defender, the Reactor, the Analyzer, and the Prospector, have the following general characteristics:

1 *Defenders* are organizations which have narrow product-market domains. Top managers in this type of organization are highly expert in their organization's limited area of operation but do not tend to search outside of their domains for new opportunities. As a result of this narrow focus, these organizations seldom need to make major adjustments in their technology, structure, or methods of operation. Instead, they devote primary attention to improving the efficiency of their existing operations.

2 *Prospectors* are organizations which almost continually search for market opportunities, and they regularly experiment with potential responses to emerging environmental trends. Thus, these organizations often are the creators of change and uncertainty to which their competitors must respond. However, because of their strong concern for product and market innovation, these organizations usually are not completely efficient.

3 *Analyzers* are organizations which operate in two types of product-market domains, one relatively stable, the other changing. In their stable areas, these organizations operate routinely and efficiently through use of formalized structures and processes. In their more turbulent areas, top managers watch their competitors closely for new ideas, and then they rapidly adopt those which appear to be the most promising.

4 *Reactors* are organizations in which top managers frequently perceive change and uncertainty occurring in their organizational environments but are unable to respond effectively. Because this type of organization lacks a consistent strategy-structure relationship, it seldom makes adjustment of any sort until forced to do so by environmental pressures.

Although similar typologies of various aspects of organizational behavior are available (e.g., Ansoff, 1965; Rogers, 1971; Segal, 1974;

Anderson and Paine, 1975), we believe that our formulation specifies relationships among strategy, structure, and process to the point where entire organizations can be portrayed as integrated wholes in dynamic interaction with their environments. Any typology, of course, is unlikely to encompass every form of organizational behavior—the world of organizations is much too changeable and complex to permit such a claim. Nevertheless, the behavior of organizations as total systems cannot be fully understood and predicted without concepts appropriate for this level of analysis. Typologies provide an excellent vehicle in this regard since their primary strengths are codification and prediction. Codification refers to the ordering of heterogeneous elements into distinct groupings; prediction is made possible when these groupings are composed of elements which do in reality "hang together" (Tiryakian, 1968). The typology described above appears, at least tentatively, to allow both codification and prediction. Each organization that we have observed appears to fit predominantly into one of the four categories, and its behavior also appears to be generally predictable given its typological classification. The "pure" form of each of these organization types is described in the next four chapters.

CONCLUSIONS

This chapter lays the basic foundation for the remainder of the book. We have shown by example and argument that the process of organizational adaptation is governed by the strategic choices of top managers. We have attempted to demonstrate that although these choices are numerous, complex, and more or less continuous, they can nevertheless be profitably analyzed by broadly categorizing them as entrepreneurial, engineering, or administrative decisions and by examining the consistency among them. Finally, we have noted that not all top-management groups approach these decisions in the same manner. We have suggested four types of organizations, each of which has its own unique adaptive strategy. In the next four chapters, each of these strategic types will be discussed in more detail.

Chapter 3

Defenders

The previous chapter concluded with a brief description of four types of organizational adaptation identified in our research. In this chapter, we discuss the characteristics and behavior of one of these organization types, the Defender, in more detail. The objectives of the chapter are to: (1) describe the three adaptive problems (entrepreneurial, engineering, administrative) as seen by the Defender; (2) discuss the organizational and managerial means used by the Defender to solve these problems; and (3) point out the costs and benefits of this particular mode of adaptation.

Below are four short descriptions of organizations encountered in our research which represent almost "pure" examples of the Defender strategy. As you read these examples, look for evidence of consistency in the way management has enacted the organization's environment and designed internal operations. In the first case, management has chosen a narrow product-market domain because of limited resources, and the organization has been carefully designed to serve this domain.

Trucker Farms is a partially integrated food-processing company located in northern California. "We began as a grower but then

moved into processing as competition stiffened in our market segment," says President Barbara Borst, a member of the family that
owns the business. "Today we grow and process a limited line of
specialty food items—mostly dried fruits and fruit juices—because we don't have enough land to grow other fruits or vegetables."

With approximately 100 employees, the company is a relatively small member of the food-processing industry. Trucker is
organized along functional lines; the heads of production, field
operations, sales and finance report directly to the president. Over
the years, manufacturing has become increasingly mechanized as
labor costs have risen. With mechanization has come strong pressure for efficiency in moving harvested goods through the various
stages of processing. "I work very closely with my production
manager and controller," says President Borst. "We're so small
that if we aren't extremely efficient, some large company will gob-
ble us up. But don't get me wrong, sales are still important, especially in the short run."

The firm has succeeded in routinizing most of its operations.
The only major factors which cannot be reliably predicted are
weather conditions, price competition, and labor relations. Obviously, nothing can be done about the weather, but management
has tried aggressively to reduce the impact of the other two variables. First, field operations has been told to keep costs at an absolute minimum while maintaining yield and quality. Second, as
indicated earlier, it is then up to production to hold the line in
processing costs. Third, a small product group continually attempts
to improve the quality of existing products so that the firm will not
compete exclusively on the basis of price. Finally, the company
pays wages slightly higher than average in order to prevent labor
strife and to keep a stable work force.

Trucker Farms is satisfied that it has solved its major adaptive
problems. Employee turnover is low, management has no desire to
grow rapidly or diversify, and products move smoothly from the
field to the grocer's shelf. Of course, the threat of intense price
competition is always present, and the company is an ideal acquisition target, but management believes that if Trucker Farms continues to become increasingly efficient in its field and processing
operations, it will always enjoy success in its segment of the
market.

The company in our second example, Willard Publishing, also has a
narrow and stable product-market domain, but it is the result of a deliberate choice by management. Furthermore, over the years this organization has developed a technological process that efficiently produces the
firm's limited range of products.

Willard Publishing Company is a successful and highly respected publisher of college-level textbooks in the social sciences and humanities and, to a somewhat lesser extent, in the natural sciences. In addition, the company publishes trade books (books of more general interest) that nevertheless are used often in college English, psychology, and sociology courses.

Founded in the early 1900s, the company was for years headed by its owner, Bill Willard. Primarily a publisher of novels, Mr. Willard entered into the publication of textbooks only after his company's novels began to be used regularly in college literature courses. Over the years, Willard has managed to gain a strong hold on certain segments of the social sciences textbook market where its books are respected because of the reputation of their authors, their content, and their readability.

Willard is a small company (less than 50 employees), and it has a very rigid definition of its product-market domain. Ronald Fox, the current president, says simply: "Why fool with a good thing? We'll consider publishing almost any book, but it must fit into our publishing program." As an example, Mr. Fox picked up a copy of a book that was currently on the best-sellers list. "We had an opportunity to bid for the rights to this manuscript. Two of my editors were extremely enthusiastic about the project, but I ended up rejecting it. We would have had to begin publishing all sorts of books in this area, and this just wouldn't have been consistent with our image."

The production process at Willard is quite stable. Manuscripts have been transformed into final form ready for printing and binding in basically the same way for years. Turnover in the production employee ranks is low, and each field editor knows from experience which artists, designers, and copy editors are best suited for reworking a particular type of manuscript. This stable pool of expertise, combined with the small size of the organization, allows editors to conduct informal "negotiations" with production employees in order to speed up a book's production or to switch emphasis to another project temporarily.

The top-management group at Willard has been stable and operates on a collegial basis. The president, college division director, national sales manager, and the senior editors have been with the company for years, and each individual's expertise and opinions are respected throughout the managerial hierarchy. Moreover, turnover in the organization as a whole is among the lowest in the industry.

Owing to its small size and success, Willard Publishing would appear to be a prime candidate for acquisition by a larger publishing house. However, according to Mr. Fox, this is not likely to occur. He points out that the firm has its particular market segment well covered. Further, management has no plans for dramatic growth, and all senior managers live comfortably due to the company's high salaries and private stock earnings. The company, therefore, sees little threat—either internal or external to the organization—to its present and future position within the industry.

As in the two previous cases, Federated Oil has a limited variety of products compared to other companies in its industry. Moreover, this organization has developed technological efficiency almost to its limits through a process called vertical integration. Finally, management is acutely aware of the company's strengths and is continually attempting to bolster them wherever possible.

Federated Oil (Fed-Oil) is a large, well-established oil company. Although the firm is fully vertically integrated with operations organized around five areas (exploration, recovery, transportation, refining, and marketing), Fed-Oil views itself as primarily a petroleum-refining organization. The firm has come to rely heavily on Middle Eastern sources of crude oil and has not been among the industry leaders in the marketing of gasoline and other end products. Fed-Oil's organization structure has shown great stability in comparison to other major oil companies which typically have undergone at least one major structural reorganization in efforts to improve rates of return on marketing and refining.

Fed-Oil began as a refinery and became vertically integrated through a deliberate evolutionary process. The company moved forward modestly into marketing in an effort to reduce the uncertainties associated with gasoline sales and extended backward to exploration and recovery to assure a steady supply of crude.

For more than two decades, Fed-Oil's president was Grayson Heffner, an engineer with an extensive background in refining. He personally supervised operations and singlehandedly made every major organizational decision. Mr. Heffner tended to regard developments in politics, international economics, and other areas as issues to be dealt with only when they became significant problems. Today, Fed-Oil's expertise in oil recovery and production is widely recognized in the industry.

Through the fifties and sixties, the oil industry's environment was stable and munificent: crude oil was in abundant supply, demand was expanding, and federal regulation was minimal, although growing. The Arab boycott shattered this tranquility in 1972, and it fueled the efforts of many companies that were already taking steps to broaden their earnings base. For example, one firm diversified through the acquisition of a major nationwide retailing organization. Others defined their businesses more broadly as "energy production" rather than just oil and integrated horizontally into related areas such as natural gas. Fed-Oil, in contrast, has engaged in more limited diversification. One vice-president states management's attitude toward diversification: "We think that any new business areas should directly complement our present strengths."

In the final example, Pioneer Community Hospital is operating as a true Defender: a limited range of services, an extremely efficient technology, and an administrative structure that is ideally suited to maintain stability and efficiency.

Pioneer Community Hospital is a voluntary hospital, a nonprofit organization that does not come under any governmental jurisdiction. Stephen Porter, the chief administrator, describes the hospital as "a high-quality community institution that provides excellent basic health care but refers out cases that are esoteric, highly complex, or require sophisticated medical machinery."

Over the last 5 years, the stability of the hospital's goals, structure, and performance has been striking. This period has been characterized by a lack of growth in either the number of patient beds or in the scope of medical services offered. The hospital maintained 140 beds in 1975 (22 fewer than in 1970), and changes in medical programs and services reflect consolidation and retrenchment rather than diversification. Low labor costs and efficient operations have generated an operating surplus during each of the last 5 years, allowing Pioneer to accumulate comfortable financial reserves.

Pioneer's controller describes the hospital as a "lean and hungry" organization. Above the department-head level, job responsibilities are substantial, and salaries are comparatively high. Below this level, wages are lower than at other hospitals in the area, and the ratio of employees to patients is also low. The principle that "everybody here does some bench work" applies to all supervisory and administrative positions. No administrator or department head has an assistant or a private secretary. The personnel department consists of one industrial psychologist who has complete responsibility for interviewing, testing, and statistical analysis. Each nursing supervisor at Pioneer is rotated periodically to direct patient care activities. The controller not only prepares but also types his own financial statements.

The low turnover of administrative personnel and infrequent changes in hospital policy allow departments to operate within largely autonomous spheres of activity. Few problems related to Pioneer's basic approach to the delivery of health care are unresolved; changes generally involve "fine tuning" for increased efficiency. Consequently, interdepartmental communication and coordination at Pioneer are informal and infrequent compared to similar hospitals. According to Mr. Porter, "about 60 percent of the 'work' done in other hospitals is nonessential," and he regards a high volume of memos, meetings, and reports as largely frivolous activity.

Organizational decisions normally are reached jointly by the chief administrator and the controller. Medical staff leaders are frequent and influential participants when their interests are affected, but members of the Board of Directors rarely become involved in hospital decisions. All administrative staff members maintain an open-door policy, and problems typically are handled in face-to-face discussions as they arise.

Pioneer's policy for responding to external change is to "wait until it's cast in concrete and then do as little as possible. We don't want to be first—it's a waste of time and money in many cases. We just respond as needed." The chief administrator estimates that he devotes about 90 percent of his time and energy to the hospital's internal operation and only about 10 percent to monitoring events and solving problems related to the external environment. He commented that Pioneer is nearly powerless with respect to many elements of the organization's environment. Being relatively small, the hospital has few political connections or other mechanisms of external influence. In sharp contrast to most other hospitals, it is Pioneer's policy to discourage members of the administrative and medical staffs from joining hospital and professional associations, attending conferences, or forging other external linkages.

Mr. Porter believes the regional health-planning agencies, required by the National Health Planning and Resources Development Act of 1974 are potentially threatening to community hospitals, and he believes there is "about a 20 percent probability that we will be forced out of business within 10 to 15 years." In the meantime, however, he intends to keep Pioneer Hospital's activities as simple and efficient as possible.

These four organizations are successful participants in industries which vary widely in terms of products, markets, and production and distribution techniques. All four of these organizations have been uniformly identified by managers of other organizations in the same industry as Defenders. What are their shared characteristics?

ENTREPRENEURIAL PROBLEMS AND SOLUTIONS

In each of these organizations, management has attempted to seal off a portion of the total market in order to create a stable set of products or services directed at a clearly defined market segment. As suggested by the statements of the chief executives of these four organizations, managers in Defenders typically perceive a great deal of stability in their organizational environments. To the casual observer, such perceptions may appear to be unwarranted, since industries such as health care are regularly described in both academic and popular publications as currently experiencing rapid and widespread change. At the industry level, Defenders deliberately create stability through a series of decisions and actions which lessen the organization's vulnerability to environmental change and uncertainty.

Domain Establishment and Surveillance

The most notable feature of the Defender's product-market domain is its *narrowness and stability.* Defenders typically direct their products or services only to a limited segment of the total potential market, and the segment chosen is frequently one of the healthiest of the entire market. Within its target market, the Defender often tries to offer clients or customers the full range of products or services they desire. By building a satisfied clientele, the Defender is able to stabilize relations with its portion of the market so that a continuous flow of output will be absorbed by this customer or client group. Trucker Farms, Willard Publishing, Federated Oil, and Pioneer Community Hospital all aim for a well-defined and restricted market that has changed little over the years.

A Defender's success in the industry hinges on its *ability to maintain aggressively its prominence within the chosen market segment.* This aggressiveness is most evident in the Defender's continuous and intensive efforts to become more efficient technologically. With stable products and markets, management can direct its attention toward reducing manufacturing and distribution costs while simultaneously maintaining or improving product quality. The result is seen in the Defender's ability always to be competitive either on a price or quality basis. For example, doctors frequently admit their patients to Pioneer Hospital for routine surgery because of the hospital's excellent overall patient care, efficiency in scheduling operations, experienced surgical nursing teams, and reasonable charges. However, they tend not to admit other patients with complicated illnesses that require intensive monitoring or therapy. Similarly, Trucker Farms has long been noted for its limited, but nevertheless high-quality and reasonably priced, product line. In both organizations, management is very aggressive in keeping costs down.

Perhaps as a result of the aggressive stance which the Defender takes toward its limited domain, management has a *tendency to ignore developments outside of this domain.* Managers in Defenders usually restrict their perceptions to a narrow range of external stimuli which are expected to influence the organization (mostly related to technological developments), and they allocate only a small amount of administrative time and personnel to monitoring other organizations, events, and trends. In addition, environmental scanning is performed only by a few top executives or their staffs. For example, Pioneer Hospital's tendency to ignore developments outside its domain is evidenced by the policy of discouraging membership in hospital and professional associations, and limited surveillance is suggested by the fact that the chief administrator invests only a small portion of his time in dealing with external affairs. Similarly, Fed-Oil's president regarded developments with only indirect impact on refining as a nuisance, and he refused to respond unless these developments created serious problems for the organization. Thus, the Defender's key executives tend to view the environment outside the organization's domain in a similar fashion, as a collection of relatively few important factors whose behavior can be predicted with considerable certainty and whose actions probably will not have a large impact on internal operations.

Growth

Defenders typically grow by *penetrating deeper into their current markets*. This type of growth is facilitated by a narrow and stable domain which allows the organization to become thoroughly familiar with client or customer needs. Product development in a Defender is usually a simple extension of the current product line or expansion into closely related areas. For example, Willard Publishing began as a publisher of novels which it sold to private bookstores and other trade dealers (as opposed to college and university bookstores). The popularity of these trade books in college literature classes first led the firm into the publication of English textbooks and then into the related disciplines of sociology, psychology, and other social sciences. However, despite predicted growth trends, Willard has chosen not to expand into less closely related areas such as law, business administration, and the vocational-technical fields.

Even within the Defender's established domain, *growth normally occurs cautiously and incrementally*. Expansion of production capacity is more often generated internally than achieved through acquisition. Consequently, Defenders are sometimes unable to keep pace with a rapid expansion of their own market segment. For example, the passage of Medicare legislation created for Pioneer Hospital a potentially large group of new patients among low-income and elderly members of the population. Pioneer responded to this opportunity by pulling staff members away from their normal activities and asking them to design a program to attract those Medicare patients falling within the hospital's area of expertise (routine checkups and surgery, etc.). However, due largely to Pioneer's past stability and lack of experience with rapid and substantial internal change, an effective program never materialized, and Pioneer still relies primarily on private patients who have been recommended by their personal doctors. In retrospect, Pioneer's chief administrator feels that the change attempt was expensive in both financial and behavioral terms: normal administrative duties were neglected, and relations between administrators and the medical staff were damaged.

Costs and Benefits of the Entrepreneurial Solution

To summarize, the Defender's entrepreneurial problem involves the creation of a narrow, stable domain, and this is accomplished through a limited mix of products and customers, aggressive efforts to "protect" the domain from competitors, a tendency to ignore developments outside of the domain, minimal product development, and growth through market penetration.

These solutions to the entrepreneurial problem contain both a major advantage and disadvantage. On one hand, because of the Defender's intimate familiarity with its domain, competitors often find it difficult to dislodge this type of organization from its position within the industry. On the other hand, the Defender runs the risk of fairly rapid extinction in the event of a major market shift, for it is gambling on the continued viability of its limited set of products and markets. Moreover, as evidenced by Pioneer Hospital's attempt to attract Medicare patients, Defenders are rarely adept in making rapid internal adjustments.

It appears that some Defenders may not be fully aware of the risks involved in maintaining a narrow product-market domain. For example, Fed-Oil's heavy reliance on Middle Eastern crude oil resulted in a severe interruption of refining operations when supplies were curtailed by the Arab boycott. According to Fed-Oil management, the organization's vulnerability had not been even remotely apparent until the boycott occurred. However, in each of the industries we have studied, some organizations clearly are willing to base their success on few products and markets. For example, college enrollments in the social sciences and humanities have been declining for several years and are not predicted to improve in the near or even intermediate future. Nevertheless, Willard Publishing, whose business is centered in these areas, does not intend to expand into currently healthier areas such as business administration and the vocational-technical fields. First, Willard management notes that the company has not suffered at all while several of its prime competitors are cutting back in these areas. Secondly, management realizes that the company would have trouble breaking into new fields, and its market image would be diluted by expansion. Clearly, Willard is not willing to alter its domain in any significant way, and this decision appears to have had no adverse impact on company sales and profits.

ENGINEERING PROBLEMS AND SOLUTIONS

As suggested by each of the examples at the beginning of the chapter, Defenders invest the majority of their financial and managerial resources in solving the engineering problem. The Defender's solution to its engineering problem, which is how to produce and distribute goods or services as efficiently as possible, relies heavily on a cost-efficient technology. Technological efficiency is, in turn, made possible by the organization's relatively stable product-market domain. In other words, a stable market that will absorb the organization's output on a continuous, high-volume basis frees the management of a Defender to develop the technology further without the fear of major losses due to unpredictable demand. Moreover, the Defender's general disregard for monitoring developments outside of its domain cuts down on expensive surveillance mechanisms, further reducing costs. Thus, the search for an overall solution to the Defender's engineering problem centers around improving such processes as quality and inventory control, materials handling, production scheduling, and methods of distribution. With standardized products and a stable market, improvements in these areas of production and distribution directly enhance overall organization performance. For example, by limiting its innovative activities to improving the organization's technology, Fed-Oil has become an industry leader in oil recovery and production, and it is these activities which are at the core of the organization's success.

In many cases, a Defender will establish only a *single core technology* which management attempts to buffer from external disturbances so that it can operate continuously and efficiently. In order to provide the technology with an uninterrupted stream of inputs, Defenders emphasize the importance of the purchasing function, and they employ quantitative inventory models to control costs. Buffering may also occur on the output end of the technology through the judicious management of product inventories and through an efficient distribution system.

Perhaps the ultimate buffering device available to the Defender, however, is *vertical integration.* By combining into a single technological system all or most of the stages of production (supplies of raw materials, manufacturing, distribution of final product), vertical integration offers two major technological characteristics sought by the Defender: (1) the ability to control the flow of materials through the production process, and (2) the ability to calculate accurately the costs of production. Although vertical integration requires a substantial long-term investment, it is a powerful device for increasing technical efficiency.

It should be reiterated, however, that technological development in a Defender has a very specific meaning. Unlike those organizations which actively search for new market opportunities and then attempt to develop the appropriate technologies for serving these markets, the Defender only concentrates on *updating its current technology to maintain efficiency*. For example, Trucker Farms has already integrated forward to some extent (to include processing as well as field operations), and the company is engaged in continuing efforts to mechanize its harvesting and processing operations further as better equipment becomes available.

Costs and Benefits of the Engineering Solution

The Defender designs its technological system to minimize variability and uncertainty. As much as possible, processes are routinized and machines substituted for human labor. Therefore, the Defender usually appears to be "lean and hungry" because few human, financial, or physical resources are underemployed. The resulting efficiency is the major determinant of successful organization performance since the Defender seeks few new product or market opportunities.

Although technological efficiency is the primary source of the Defender's success, the heavy investment in this area has a potential drawback. The payback period for technological investments may be lengthy, forcing the organization to remain on its present course for some time in order to obtain the desired economies. If, during this period, the technology must be reworked to deal with unfamiliar or unpredictable problems, then these economies are reduced or lost entirely.

ADMINISTRATIVE PROBLEMS AND SOLUTIONS

In order to promote maximum efficiency, the Defender's solution to the administrative problem should flow logically from its solution to the entrepreneurial and engineering problems. That is, the Defender's use of administrative mechanisms such as planning, structure, and control should be consistent with the way the organization has defined its domain and developed its technology. In the Defender's case, the solution to the administrative problem must provide management with the ability to control all organizational operations centrally.

Dominant Coalition and Managerial Succession

As pointed out in Chapter 2, the dominant coalition is simply that group of individuals whose influence on the organization is greatest. Members of the dominant coalition make crucial strategic decisions, and they determine how resources will be allocated in the organization. In the majority of Defenders, this group is composed of the chief executive officer (or general manager in the case of a division), the controller, and the heads of production and sales. In nearly every case that we have observed, the controller or production manager is a very influential member of this group. Marketing, which in a Defender normally does not include activities such as research and promotion, ranks well below the controller and production manager in terms of influence, as does research and development. This finding, of course, is entirely consistent with the Defender's solutions to the entrepreneurial and engineering problems already discussed. That is, because of its stable market and heavy emphasis on technological efficiency, *financial and production experts wield considerable power in the Defender.* For example, at Trucker Farms, the president's key subordinates are the controller and the head of production. The president of Fed-Oil during most of its existence was an engineer and the former head of refining operations. Excluding purely medical issues, the dominant coalition at Pioneer Hospital is composed solely of the chief administrator and the hospital's controller.

In these and other Defenders we have observed, the *tenure of the dominant coalition has been lengthy, and its members usually have been promoted from certain functional areas within the organization.* Because most of the Defender's adaptive problems are of an engineering or administrative nature, the dominant coalition does not need to possess a great deal of expertise in externally oriented areas such as marketing or research and development. Instead, coalition members are drawn from those functions which are most critical to organizational success, namely production, finance, or engineering. Generally speaking, in a Defender it is more advantageous for the dominant coalition to know the strengths and capacities of "our company" than it is for them to know the trends and developments in "our industry."

Planning

Because of its stable domain and technology, planning in the Defender tends to be *intensive rather than extensive, oriented toward problem solving rather than problem finding, and undertaken prior to organizational action.* The Defender's inclination to perceive a relatively simple and stable environment permits an intensive approach to planning that takes only a narrow spectrum of factors into consideration. In the absence of a major threat to the organization's current domain and operations, the planning sequence proceeds through a series of steps which allows the organization to exploit current and foreseeable environmental conditions fully. These steps mainly involve the setting of output and cost objectives which are then translated into specific operating goals and budgets.

The key line executives in the Defender's planning group are the chief executive officer, the controller, and the head of production, in fact, the dominant administrative coalition. In the typical case, their role might be to offer some initial broad guidelines to the entire planning group (e.g., calculate the optimal time to refurbish the plant within the next 5 years), after which the more routine chores of preparing sales and production forecasts, calculating appropriate inventory levels, etc., are left to staff specialists. Later, after the action programs developed by staff planners have been costed out, line executives reenter the process to compare the financial figures to overall resources and to select those programs which promise to be the most profitable.

As the organization moves forward, actual results can be compared to projected figures and any necessary adjustments made. Thus, planning in the Defender follows the classical planning sequence:

$$\text{Plan} \rightarrow \text{Act} \rightarrow \text{Evaluate*}$$

In this mode, planning is finalized before action is taken. At Trucker Farms, for example, production schedules and staffing requirements are developed well in advance of harvesting. Trucker's profits are tied closely to the company's ability to estimate crop yield and to tailor processing operations accordingly. Barring unforeseen weather problems, Trucker's operations usually run according to plan.

Structure

The specialization seen in a Defender's products, markets, and technology extends into the organization structure (the set of subunits which comprise the organization and the relationships among these subunits). Defenders tend to rely on *functional organization structures* which group specialists with similar skills into separate units. A functional structure is well suited to organizations which have a single or dominant core technology because each subunit becomes extremely adept at performing its particular portion of the production and distribution process.

---

*Our description of alternative planning approaches used by different types of organizations is based largely on concepts developed by Robert Biller.

Furthermore, within each of the functional subunits, there is an *extensive division of labor.* The development of highly specialized work roles enhances the interchangeability of employees who operate the technology (thus reducing the importance of any single employee group), and it permits the organization to hire and train individuals and then insert them into the technological process with a minimum of interruption. Thus, by employing individuals who possess only limited and specialized skills, the Defender keeps its wage bill, training costs, and turnover costs to a minimum.

Finally, Defenders develop a relatively *high degree of formalization,* the codification of job descriptions and operating procedures which specify appropriate behaviors for organization members. Given its emphasis on stability and efficiency, the Defender cannot afford deviations from prescribed behaviors.

Control

The prevention and correction of deviations from plans is, of course, the responsibility of the organization's control system. The Defender not only wants to spot performance deviations early in order to maintain efficiency but is also able to spot them because of the stability inherent in its operations.

The characteristics of a functional organization structure, most notably specialized expertise, require the Defender's control system to be *centralized.* Only top-level executives have the necessary information and the proper vantage point to control operations that span several organizational subunits. Decision-making prerogatives may be centralized at the executive level, as in the case of Fed-Oil where the president is able to make nearly every major organizational decision singlehandedly, or alternatively control may be polycentralized, as in the case of Pioneer Hospital where department heads act in a relatively independent fashion within their own areas of responsibility and engage in limited lateral communication.

However, whether decision making is centralized or polycentralized, Defenders normally restrict information flows to vertical channels: directives and instructions flow down the hierarchy, and progress reports and explanations flow up. Under stable conditions, deviation in operating performance is infrequent, and the proper corrective response usually is known in advance. Therefore, Defenders control the performance of their operating units through the use of *"long-looped" vertical information systems* where information concerning lower-level units is cycled all the way to top management. Generally, such critical functions as quality control and production scheduling report not to the production unit but directly to top management. Although control might also be accomplished with short feedback loops which allow operating units to appraise and adjust their own performance immediately, Defenders seldom choose this option, perhaps because of the fear of costly mistakes.

Coordination and Conflict Resolution

A functional structure creates great interdependence among organizational subunits because each is engaged in only a portion of the entire technological process. Defenders are able to manage subunit interdependence with *uncomplicated and inexpensive forms of coordination* such as standardization and scheduling. These types of coordination can only be used in situations which are stable and repetitive, hence they are well suited to the Defender whose interdependence tends to be largely sequential (the output of one subunit is the input for another). Sequential interdependence is seen readily at Fed-Oil where the major subunits are exploration, transportation, refining, production, and marketing; but it is also evident at Pioneer Hospital.

It is frequently said that the modern general hospital is a complex "professionalized" organization requiring constant and intensive coordination. In theory, the admission of each patient leads to the formation of a new task force of health professionals who cooperate closely in meeting the patient's unique medical needs. At Pioneer, however, such complicated interdependence exists only in the operating room. Most patients at Pioneer have routine ailments; patient care is therefore fairly simple and highly formalized, and the medical and nonprofessional staffs are kept to a minimum. Thus, the typical new patient at Pioneer is not met by a task force of health professionals but rather by his personal doctor and the hospital staff who then proceed to guide the patient through a familiar set of hospital routines, ranging from an efficiently administered battery of presurgical tests to a smooth but tightly scheduled trip through the operating and recovery rooms. Pioneer thus avoids the complicated and expensive coordination mechanisms required by hospitals which admit individuals with rare diseases requiring a variety of diagnostic tests, medical specialists, and equipment.

Coordination by standardization and scheduling also reduces the amount of communications flowing between subunits and the frequency with which nonroutine decisions must be made. As a result, lateral relations are limited, and any *conflicts that arise between subunits usually can be handled through normal hierarchical channels.* For example, at Willard Publishing, the publishing process involves moving the manuscript through the separate editorial, production, and sales departments. If, in the somewhat unlikely event that a serious disagreement arose over a particular manuscript, it would be resolved by an executive well up in the organizational hierarchy (e.g., the College Division Director). Major interunit conflicts occur so seldom at Willard that no permanent (or even temporary) coordinators have been installed as liaisons between the organization's subunits.

Performance Appraisal and Maintenance

As indicated throughout this chapter, the Defender's fundamental emphasis is on efficiency (doing things right) rather than on effectiveness (doing the right things). When the basic strategy of the organization is to hold goals, markets, and products constant as long as possible, the question, "Are we doing the right things?" may seldom be raised, and the appraisal of performance comes to be determined by meticulously counting the quantities and costs of standardized inputs required per unit of output. As a result, the Defender's usual method of appraising performance involves *comparing present indices of efficiency with those achieved by the organization during previous time periods.* That is, the Defender generally will not evaluate its performance by comparing it to other similar organizations because of the belief that "we can do what we do better than anybody."

This emphasis on efficiency has clear implications for the Defender's personnel planning and for the allocation of rewards to organization members. The most crucial new employees or replacements are those hired in manufacturing or cost-control areas, and the importance attached to these functional areas is reflected in both the reward system and in opportunities for mobility. If, due to a crisis of some sort, the Defender is forced to engage in budgetary cutbacks, production and finance are among the last areas to be affected. In fact, a more typical response may be to increase their influence in an attempt to contain costs elsewhere in the organization.

Costs and Benefits of the Administrative Solution

The structural and process characteristics which a Defender adopts in solving the administrative problem heavily emphasize the lagging, or rationalizing, aspect of the administrative role. That is, specialized subunits, centralized decision making and control, intensive planning and scheduling, etc., combine to reduce uncertainty within the organization. These characteristics, which in combination provide top management with the ability to control operations closely, flow logically from the previous solutions to the entrepreneurial and engineering problems. The result, as stated on many occasions, is increased stability throughout the organization and its chosen environment.

The risk which the Defender faces is, of course, ineffectiveness.

That is, the Defender's leading or innovative activities are primarily focused internally, with high salaries and advancement opportunities accorded technical and operating personnel. With few resources devoted to scanning the environment, the Defender possesses little capability for locating new product or market opportunities. Moreover, because of its specialized and finely tuned expertise, the Defender probably could not adjust rapidly to a new opportunity even if it became apparent.

CONCLUSIONS

In this chapter, we have described the characteristics and behavior of the Defender, demonstrated the manner in which these qualities are linked together to form a consistent pattern, and discussed the costs and benefits of the Defender strategy. We have illustrated the process by which the Defender aligns itself with a particular portion of the overall environment and manages the internal interdependencies created by its form of alignment. This adjustment process produces a unique configuration of domain, technology, structure, and process (a limited range of products and customers, a cost-efficient technology, and a highly specialized and formalized organization structure).

Furthermore, we have described how the Defender maintains its relationship with its chosen environment. By presenting examples drawn from our research, we have suggested that Defenders enact an environment of greater stability than do their counterparts within the same industry. Even in industries widely noted for their rapidly changing conditions, there are potential pockets of stability within which a Defender can thrive. Thus, following the strategic-choice approach, we have argued that the Defender deliberately creates and maintains an environment for which a stable form of organization is appropriate.

Finally, we have pointed out the major risks associated with the Defender strategy. We have shown that the Defender relies on the continued viability of a single narrow domain; that the organization receives a return on its heavy technological investment only if the major problems facing the organization continue to be of an engineering or technological nature; and that this type of organization is optimally designed to serve its present domain but has little capacity for locating and exploiting new areas of opportunity. In short, the Defender is perfectly capable of responding to today's world. To the extent that the world of tomorrow is similar to that of today, the Defender is ideally suited for its environment.

Table 3-1 summarizes the Defender's salient characteristics and the major strengths and weaknesses inherent in this pattern of adaptation.

Table 3-1   Characteristics of the Defender

Entrepreneurial problem	Engineering problem	Administrative problem
Problem: How to "seal off" a portion of the total market to create a stable set of products and customers	*Problem:* How to produce and distribute goods or services as efficiently as possible	*Problem:* How to maintain strict control of the organization in order to ensure efficiency
Solutions: 1. Narrow and stable domain 2. Aggressive maintenance of domain (e.g., competitive pricing and excellent customer service) 3. Tendency to ignore developments outside of domain 4. Cautious and incremental growth primarily through market penetration 5. Some product development, but closely related to current goods or services	*Solutions:* 1. Cost-efficient technology 2. Single core technology 3. Tendency toward vertical integration 4. Continuous improvements in technology to maintain efficiency	*Solutions:* 1. Financial and production experts most powerful members of the dominant coalition; limited environmental scanning 2. Tenure of dominant coalition is lengthy; promotions from within 3. Planning is intensive, cost-oriented, and completed before action is taken 4. Tendency toward functional structure with extensive division of labor and high degree of formalization 5. Centralized control and long-looped vertical information systems 6. Simple coordination mechanisms and conflicts resolved through hierarchical channels 7. Organizational performance measured against previous years; reward system favors production and finance
Costs and benefits: It is difficult for competitors to dislodge the organization from its small niche in the industry, but a major shift in the market could threaten survival	*Costs and benefits:* Technological efficiency is central to organizational performance, but heavy investment in this area requires technological problems to remain familiar and predictable for lengthy periods of time	*Costs and benefits:* Administrative system is ideally suited to maintain stability and efficiency but is not well suited to locating and responding to new product or market opportunities

Chapter 4

Prospectors

In the previous chapter, we discussed how Defender organizations enact and respond to their environments. Prospectors, the subject of this chapter, respond to their chosen environments in a manner that is almost the opposite of the Defender. This chapter describes the Prospector's perceptions of and solutions to the three problems of adaptation and points out the costs and benefits of this particular adjustment strategy.

As before, we present four short descriptions of organizations which are almost pure examples of Prospectors. Then we draw comparisons across all four organizations, identifying shared characteristics and demonstrating internal consistency among them. In the first case, note the rapidity with which the company enlarged its domain, continually redefining its products and markets. Note also the technological and administrative problems arising from these prospecting activities.

Computer Services is a young, rapidly growing company that provides computerized processing of various kinds of information. The company was one of many information-processing firms

49

formed in the middle to late sixties, and it survived the large shake-out that occurred in the industry at the end of that decade. Today its growth has continued unabated, and the organization has passed through several stages of development.

At its inception, Computer Services offered only raw computer power on a time-sharing basis, as did its competitors. Early customers were scientists at universities and research laboratories who developed their own computer programs and simply used Computer Services' facilities. Unlike most of its competitors, however, Computer Services recognized that its customers would someday be able to meet their own needs internally; if the company continued to offer only computer power, it would eventually become obsolete. Meanwhile, as time-sharing firms continued to enter the industry, product differentiation between competitors would become increasingly difficult to achieve.

Therefore, Computer Services began early to develop software packages, providing customers with "canned" programs which were compatible only with Computer Services' equipment. At first, these packages were mainly scientific, since the company continued to focus on the heaviest users of time-sharing computers. But soon the firm expanded its customer base to include commercial users, and packages were developed to handle nonscientific business problems. Within a few years, the mix of customers had undergone a sharp change, and scientific users had become a small part of the company's business. Because business applications potentially involve many areas of an organization, software packages became more complex and produced more revenue than their narrow-scope scientific brethren.

At about the same time that Computer Services extended its services beyond raw computer power, management perceived an emerging trend in the industry. It foresaw the on-line, remote user remaining connected to the computer via telephone for several hours a day. And it realized that unless the user was located in the same local areas as the computer his telephone bills would soon outstrip his computer savings. Therefore, Computer Services pioneered a global communications network which currently offers local dial-up service in over 60 U.S. cities as well as a few major European cities. This network, called "Current," proved highly attractive, since it provided corporate customers, whose offices were spread throughout the country, with access to the same computer system. Computer Services' next step was to offer the communications network itself as a product by tying In other companies' private computers.

Computer Services' product-market domain has continued to grow along several different lines. The company now offers computer-maintenance service to customers who have their own computers, specialized medical information service, cable television billing, and computerized tax preparation. Because of its desire to enter these markets rapidly and to minimize uncertainty over technical and financial success, Computer Services' method of entry has been to acquire small companies already in these fields.

Computer Services is a marketing-oriented firm that not only reacts quickly to market change but also anticipates change and responds accordingly. For example, in the case of commercial applications, management first perceived a market opportunity and then developed the product offering. In the case of computer maintenance and network services, it developed the resources for internal use and then searched for a market in which to sell them.

Computer Services' founder and current board chairman was a former marketing manager in a large conglomerate. He has promoted consistently the idea that marketing is the basis of the organization's ability to compete. The other two major company divisions, Programming and Operations, clearly have less overall influence in the organization than marketing. Indeed, as the firm continues to buy more of its software from independent software houses rather than creating its own programs, the influence of the Programming division declines steadily. The company has only small departments for finance and administrative services (personnel and legal).

Computer Services' organization structure appears to be in a constant state of flux. After the development of the nationwide communications network, Computer Services organized according to geographic area, with the unit in each area completely responsible for all computer operations. However, after a few years, marketing began to complain about the nonmarketing demands being placed on it by this organizational arrangement. Consequently, the company switched to its present functional structure: marketing, programming, and operations are separate entities. However, this structure also has been inadequate in that the different areas cannot work together smoothly, and numerous informal communications channels have developed. Status reports are regularly copied and distributed by the originator to colleagues in other areas. The organization now appears to be on the verge of another major change in organization structure.

While much larger and more mature than Computer Services, Star Electronics is also a Prospector seeking always to be first among the developers of new products. Note the emphasis which Star places on research and development and the way in which marketing interacts with production.

Star Electronics is a large manufacturer of precision electronics equipment which it sells in both consumer and industrial markets.

This equipment includes small computers, electronic calculators, digital volt meters, electrical testing equipment, etc. The firm has approximately 30,000 employees organized into 20 divisions.

The company is noted for its research and development capabilities. Top management has fostered within each of the divisions an atmosphere conducive to product and market innovation. "We go for the new products first and then organize around them; that's why we have so many divisions," says one general manager. Star's practice is to create a new division whenever any of its present divisions reaches approximately 2,500 employees.

Prices generally have been falling in electronics, and price competition is very keen in most of the market segments served by Star. However, though the firm has many formidable competitors, it typically does not attempt to compete actively on a price basis. Instead, Star tries to be the first to bring out a new product and then relies on its marketing departments to sell prospective buyers on the high quality built into each model. "We are a first-to-market company, and we take the price declines as they come," says President David Ortman. "By the time prices have declined substantially, our production departments will have begun making the product cheaper, and, more often than not, we'll have a new product ready to replace the old one." At any one time, the company is engaged in two to three hundred research and development projects which result, on the average, in new products every 2 to 3 years.

New general managers at Star Electronics must possess at least one college degree in electrical engineering, and they should have both marketing and research and development experience. The company believes that this particular blend of education and managerial experience is what gives Star its solid R&D marketing punch, one that allows the firm to cash in on its new products even though they are introduced to the market at higher prices. Moreover, the general manager has the technical background to understand problems of production, which follow R&D and marketing in terms of strategic importance. Each of the major divisions reflects the company's basic orientation, and other functions such as accounting, finance, and personnel are considered to be ancillary services.

The technological process at Star operates on a 2- to 3-year cycle. Teams of six to eight engineers and scientists work on an R&D project for approximately 2 years before the product is ready to be manufactured. However, marketing also enters at this point, and an aggressive campaign is developed to sell the new product when it comes out of production. Timing is crucial here, since profits adequate to cover R&D costs must be obtained before competition forces prices down. This cycle is then repeated for each new generation of products.

Recently, Star electronics has been looking for possible acquisitions, but the stated corporate policy is not to move into areas so diverse that the firm cannot make a substantial technical contribution.

In the third example, an organization is just beginning to push into new market areas. Notice the awareness of Cooperative Canners' top management concerning the administrative adjustments which will be necessary to accomplish the organization's emerging strategy.

Cooperative Canners is a young, medium-sized food-processing company that is seeking to catch up with the giants in the industry. "At the moment we are mostly a private-label supplier of canned vegetables and fruits," says President Thomas Bolt, "but eventually we want to offer a full product line under our own brand names." With 2,000 employees, Cooperative is clearly larger than the small firms in the industry; however, it is not nearly as large as the industry giants, whose employees may total 30,000.

The company is composed of a group of growers who have contracted to turn over their harvest of fruits and vegetables to the cooperative. Traditionally, the bulk of the harvest went into private brands, but this is no longer the case as the company increasingly has offered products under its own brand names.

The president of Cooperative Canners came from one of the largest firms in the industry where his experience was in marketing, finance, and manufacturing. "Marketing is the main problem facing this company," says Mr. Bolt. "We are attempting to market products under our own label that have been offered by the competition for years. That's our main battle—along with financing any new products we decide to offer." Accordingly, Cooperative is hiring a number of managers in the areas of marketing and finance.

The firm has been functionally organized to this point, with vice-presidents of planning, finance, marketing, and manufacturing reporting to the president. Recently, however, management has begun to reconsider the adequacy of this structural arrangement. Cooperative's product line has expanded considerably in the past few years, and management believes that the company may have to be reorganized into product divisions soon.

A final, longer-range problem facing Cooperative Canners concerns management's interest in entering the frozen foods market. Cooperative presently does not possess the capability to produce and distribute frozen foods, so a considerable research and development effort would have to be mounted before the company could compete successfully in this area. A small task force has been appointed to investigate the problems associated with entering the frozen-food market.

In the final example, Riverside Hospital further demonstrates the vigor with which Prospectors pursue expanding domains. Notice, however, that the Riverside case also illustrates a common administrative dilemma faced by many Prospectors: how to maintain effective control over changing services, markets, and technologies.

Riverside Hospital is a 110-bed community hospital that serves four new suburban communities which are located in a central-California valley. Following 3 decades of rapid growth, population levels in the valley appear to be stabilizing. Riverside is primarily a provider of basic surgery and medical care for patients with short-term, curable ailments. Richard Silverman, Riverside's chief administrator, describes the mission and role of the hospital as "promoting the health and well-being of the people of the valley by providing community-oriented primary medicine, either directly or by acting as a catalyst for the development of independently-based health services."

Riverside Hospital was built in 1966. In addition to a normal complement of medical-surgical services, it currently provides maternity and pediatric care and operates a 24-hour emergency room. In 1973, to serve the needs of the far end of the valley, Riverside developed an experimental Family Medical Center located 15 miles from the main hospital. This facility is an attempt to combine a walk-in clinic and a suite of doctors' offices to provide both treatment for minor emergencies and scheduled physical examinations and consultations. Recently, Riverside has set up a 24-hour crisis-intervention service in cooperation with community groups. The hospital has also assumed responsibility for managing the ambulance service in all four valley communities.

Mr. Silverman says that, "In 1971, we faced the question of whether the hospital should continue to define its mission in its own terms or in terms of the community's needs. We could have maintained our traditional operations, avoided risk, and realized a good return on our investment. Alternatively, we could redefine the hospital's mission in community terms as an organization that would extend itself beyond familiar bounds to answer requests and demands from people whether or not they were among our current group of patients. We chose the latter and have developed a comprehensive master plan for extending our mission to meet the health needs of the entire valley. It calls for a flexible and expandable central hospital, fully supported by decentralized family-care centers in each community. In the future, the adequacy of community health care will not be determined by counting beds but by the extent of problem-specific health care programs, ranging from preventive treatment through testing, ambulatory care, acute care, rehabilitation, and follow-up."

Mr. Silverman is able to devote about 70 percent of his time to managing the hospital's expanding arena of external relationships because virtually all responsibilities for day-to-day operations have been delegated to the department-head level. However, Riverside's strong emphasis on identifying new needs and developing innovative delivery systems has led to problems in controlling costs and has sometimes sparked counterproductive conflict among the board of directors, the administration, the medical staff, and the community. Efficiency in staffing has been difficult to achieve, and although productivity in some areas is felt to be unsatisfactory, the problems associated with developing and updating productivity standards in the face of ongoing organizational change have hampered productivity measurement and control. Several doctors have commented that beyond a review of the physicians' record-keeping practices, the hospital exerts only minimal control over the quality of care provided.

Riverside is experienced in the use of contingency planning. This competence was perhaps best illustrated in 1975 by the hospital's response to a month-long strike by physicians who were protesting skyrocketing malpractice insurance premiums. Although Riverside's average daily occupancy fell to 40 percent of capacity, and the number of operations performed during the strike dropped from a projected 350 to only 15, the hospital adapted so effectively that it netted $10,000 during the strike. This favorable outcome resulted primarily from the chief administrator's ability to anticipate the timing and severity of the strike. He directed each department head to develop a set of projections concerning the strike's probable impact on levels of departmental utilization, and he required detailed plans for cutting departmental costs without eliminating essential services. Mr. Silverman describes the strike as a valuable learning experience: "We learned that given sufficient warning, we can adapt to almost anything—including a drastic drop in our patient load."

When the four organizations described above were discussed with managers in each of their various industries, they were uniformly identified as Prospectors. In the following sections, we will discuss the characteristics and behavior of this type of organization.

ENTREPRENEURIAL PROBLEMS AND SOLUTIONS

Unlike the Defender, whose success comes primarily from efficiently serving a stable domain, the Prospector's prime capability is that of finding and exploiting new product and market opportunities. One of the purest expressions of the Prospector strategy came from the president of Star

Electronics when he said, "We are a first-to-market company. . . ." For a Prospector, maintaining a reputation as an innovator in product and market development may be as important, perhaps even more important, than high profitability. In fact, because of the inevitable failure rate associated with sustained product and market development activity, Prospectors may find it difficult to attain consistently the profitability levels of the more efficient Defenders.

Domain Establishment and Surveillance

The Prospector's domain is usually *broad and in a continuous state of development,* as opposed to the Defender, whose product-market domain is narrow and stable. The systematic addition of new products or markets, frequently combined with retrenchment in other parts of the domain, gives the Prospector's products and markets an aura of fluidity uncharacteristic of the Defender. The dynamic nature of the Prospector's domain is perhaps best exemplified in the case of Computer Services. The company's initial service was the sale of raw computer power to scientists, but the firm expanded rapidly into a variety of other services which are now sold to many different industrial and consumer markets (e.g., computerized processing of medical and income-tax information). Moreover, given its past experience, there is little reason to assume that Computer Services' current domain will retain its present form for very long. However, an organization does not necessarily have to be growing rapidly to be a Prospector. Star Electronics has not grown dramatically in recent years, yet its mix of products and markets has undergone continuous transformation during this period. Approximately every 3 years, a significant portion of the company's products is replaced by new or improved models.

In order to locate new areas of opportunity, the Prospector must develop and maintain the *capacity to monitor a wide range of environmental conditions, trends, and events.* The Prospector, therefore, invests heavily in individuals and groups who scan the environment for potential opportunities. One means of spotting and exploiting opportunities is to develop an elaborate surveillance capability by decentralizing scanning activities to appropriate subunits within the organization. For example, each of the 20 divisions at Star Electronics is relatively free to explore any product, market, or technological development which might lead to an improved version of its present product line or to new markets. Another means of moving quickly into new areas of opportunity is to buy previously developed expertise. Computer Services has entered several new markets by acquiring small companies already operating in these areas.

Because their scanning activities are not limited to the organization's current domain, Prospectors are frequently the *creators of change in their industries.* In fact, change is one of the major tools used by the Prospector to gain an edge over competitors. As Prospectors develop new products and open new markets, competitors are faced with increased change and uncertainty in their own environments, and they must develop their own responses to these contingencies. The Defender, as shown in the previous chapter, has probably already taken steps to insulate itself from these changes and will respond only if the organization's own domain is affected adversely. Thus, within a given industry, the Prospector actively seeks out areas of opportunity and therefore perceives much more environmental change and uncertainty than the Defender or the other two organization types.

Growth

The growth pattern of the Prospector has two distinguishing characteristics. First, *growth primarily results from the location of new markets and the development of new products.* In expanding horizontally into related products and markets, the Prospector behaves just as aggressively as the Defender does in penetrating deeper into its current markets. Computer Services, for example, attempts to stay at the leading edge of computerized information processing both by entering established markets (e.g., commercial applications) and by creating new markets (e.g., network services).

A second characteristic of the Prospector's growth pattern concerns the rate of growth. Whereas the Defender tends to grow in steady increments, the Prospector may grow in spurts. Prospecting is an uncertain activity, but when the organization "strikes gold," the results may be spectacular. Within the space of 10 years, Computer Services grew from a "one-man show" to a multimillion dollar company, but since that time growth has leveled off considerably.

Costs and Benefits of the Entrepreneurial Solution

To reiterate, the Prospector's success is based on finding and exploiting new product and market opportunities. Therefore, the Prospector's entrepreneurial problem is how to perform the elaborate environmental surveillance continually required to improve its choice of domain. This type of organization is, if you will, a domain "definer" as opposed to a domain "defender." A true Prospector is almost immune from the pressures of a changing environment since this type of organization is continually keeping pace with change and, as indicated, frequently creating change itself. Thus, in direct contrast to the Defender, which insulates itself from environmental change, the Prospector enthusiastically searches for new entrepreneurial ventures in an effort to manipulate the competitive arena in its favor.

There are two potential costs of the Prospector's effectiveness orientation. First, because of the need for flexibility in all of its operations, the Prospector seldom attains the efficiency necessary to reap maximum economic benefits from any of its chosen markets. Because of its changing domain, the Prospector is usually not in a position to establish the stable technologies and organization structures which Defenders use to extract maximum advantage from their domain. Secondly, the constant shuffling of products and markets may cause a Prospector to overextend itself. That is, if anticipated demand does not materialize in a significant number of new ventures, the phrase "first to market" begins to develop a hollow ring.

ENGINEERING PROBLEMS AND SOLUTIONS

Unlike the Defender, the Prospector's choice of products and markets is not limited to those which fall within the range of the organization's present technological capability. The Prospector's technology is contingent upon both the organization's current and future product mix: entrepreneurial activities always have primacy, and appropriate technologies are not selected or developed until late in the process of product development. Therefore, the Prospector's overall engineering problem is how to avoid long-term commitments to a single type of technological process, and the solution to this problem is guided by the question, "What products *should* we make?" not by the question "What products *can* we make?"

Because of the generally dynamic nature of the Prospector's domain, the life-expectancy of any particular product is comparatively short. Consequently, technological processes must be flexible, and Prospectors seldom try to attain high levels of stability and efficiency in their production and distribution systems. In order to maintain flexibility, Prospectors minimize long-term capital investment in production processes, and they postpone the commitment of resources until the market viability of a new product has been demonstrated. Therefore, in a Prospector, *a considerable portion of the technological core is frequently engaged in the production of prototype products.*

The Prospector is also less likely than the Defender to integrate all of its production processes into a single core technology and, instead, develops *multiple technologies* for its different products. A series of relatively self-contained technologies can be added to or discontinued with only minor disruption, and all can operate with only limited interdependence. The presence of multiple technologies, some of which are only rudimentary processes for creating prototype products, requires the Prospector to use different mechanisms for buffering its technological system from those used by the Defender. As described previously, the Defender protects technological stability with structural buffers such as standardization, mechanization, and perhaps vertical integration. In contrast, the Prospector protects technological flexibility by employing individuals who have a variety of skills and who can exercise judgment in selecting which skills to apply in a given situation. To the Prospector, any given technological process is disposable; however, the people who operate it are indispensable. Thus, to the fullest possible extent, the Prospector's *technologies are embedded in people, not in routine or mechanical operations.*

Costs and Benefits of the Engineering Solution

As indicated, the Prospector designs its technological system to maximize flexibility in order to facilitate new product development. Extensive human discretion is required to operate a nonstandardized technology, leading to a work force that is largely capable of directing and controlling its own technological operations. This people-intensive approach maximizes flexibility while minimizing standardization.

Although a flexible technology allows facile reallocation of productive resources, flexibility has its costs. Because valuable technological capability is lodged in human operatives, personnel replacement is a lengthy and expensive process. Coordinating multiple and semiautonomous technologies is also costly. In general, the Prospector's reluctance to invest heavily in any given technology may result in inefficiencies compared to its competitors who develop more standardized and efficient approaches.

ADMINISTRATIVE PROBLEMS AND SOLUTIONS

Unlike the Defender, the Prospector's domain is allowed—indeed encouraged—to change. This variability in the Prospector's product-market mix is reflected in the organization's technology which must be flexible enough to accommodate a changing domain. Therefore, generally speaking, the Prospector's administrative problem is how to facilitate rather than control organizational operations. That is, the Prospector's administrative system must be able to deploy and coordinate resources among many decentralized units and projects rather than to plan and control the operations of the entire organization centrally.

Dominant Coalition and Managerial Succession

As is true of the Defender, the Prospector's dominant coalition both reflects and reinforces those functions which are most critical to the organization's success. Thus, the Prospector's *dominant coalition centers around the marketing and research and development functions.* Moreover, the Prospector's dominant coalition is also *larger, more diverse, and more transitory* than the Defender's. As suggested in the examples at the beginning of this chapter, Prospectors tend to be organized into product divisions which are responsible for nearly all phases of the development, production, and marketing of the goods or services within their area. Because of their knowledge about the specific environmental conditions facing their own units, division general managers and their key staff members are also potential members of the dominant coalition along with the organization's top executives.

An apparent paradox seems to be developing here. The reader may recall that Star Electronics has 20 operating divisions. If each general manager and his key staff specialists were members of the dominant coalition, then the entire coalition might include upwards of 30 individuals. Very few organizations can operate with a policy-making body this large, especially the Prospector which cannot afford to be unwieldy. However, in situations of this sort, where power is widely distributed, some smaller group of senior executives frequently emerges to conduct coalition business. This core group may be defined formally, by the election or appointment of representatives, or informally as a result of day-to-day operations. At Star Electronics, for example, a core group composed of several senior division managers is contacted informally for their opinions about a particular strategic issue when top management must take swift action affecting the entire organization. Management's belief is that the opinions of these senior division managers would reflect those of their counterparts were it possible for the entire group to convene.

The Prospector's dominant coalition is also, as noted, more transitory than the Defender's. This is another way of saying that the influence of a particular segment of the dominant coalition may rise or fall depending on the organization's current areas of prospecting. For example, when several community groups requested Riverside Hospital's cooperation in establishing a 24-hour crisis-intervention service, members of the medical staff who specialized in psychiatry were the first to be consulted by the chief administrator. Subsequently, these individuals served, along with the chief administrator, as the primary liaison between the hospital and the community groups. However, after the service had been established, the psychiatric specialists performed no further liaison or administrative duties.

The Prospector draws its top managers mostly from the ranks of marketing or product development, the two areas of primary strategic importance. However, there are other aspects of the Prospector's managerial succession process which are different from the Defender's. First, a key executive in a Prospector organization is *as apt to be hired from the outside as promoted from within.* To return to a distinction made in the previous chapter, the Prospector attempts to develop a "cosmopolitan" managerial team that is linked to important areas of the industry, whereas the Defender tries to develop a "local" executive group that is familiar primarily with the organization and its particular domain. For this very reason, a second difference in the Prospector's succession process is that the *tenure of members of the dominant coalition is seldom as long as the Defender's.*

Planning

Because the Prospector continuously monitors an eclectic array of external organizations and events, it must process a diverse and sometimes contradictory flow of information about conditions in current and potential domains of operation. Therefore, the Prospector's planning process is usually *broad rather than intensive, oriented toward problem finding, and contingent upon feedback from experimental action.*

Management's inclination to perceive a complex and changing environment necessitates a comprehensive planning approach that takes a broad spectrum of factors into consideration. Exploration of uncharted areas precludes intensive planning and requires the Prospector to prepare tentative organizational responses to a series of potential opportunities.

The Prospector's planning orientation also stresses problem finding over problem solving. Organizational objectives are allowed to coalesce around current areas of prospecting and thus seldom achieve a stable equilibrium. The Prospector frequently must act on the basis of incomplete information and await feedback from the market and other relevant environmental elements before large-scale commitments are made and detailed plans developed. For example, in planning the development of a series of four community-based Family Medical Centers, Riverside Hospital found itself unable to predict the amount and kind of care that would be demanded. Therefore, rather than completing detailed plans and then contracting for construction of all four facilities, the hospital set up a prototype center. By converting a commercial location in a shopping center into temporary facilities, Riverside was able to postpone commitment and more detailed planning until adequate information was obtained about the community's medical needs.

This example is characteristic of the Prospector's typical planning sequence. Unlike the Defender, whose planning process is usually finalized before implementation begins, the Prospector must often directly engage a new problem or opportunity before detailed planning can be completed. Experimental action of this sort requires the Prospector to employ a fundamentally different planning sequence from that of the Defender, one that does not lock the organization into a particular direction until the shape of events comes into clearer focus. An initial evaluation of a number of potential opportunities is followed by limited exploratory action in the most promising area. Only after this brief foray into the problem or opportunity area will the Prospector attempt to develop a more detailed operating plan. Thus, the Prospector's planning sequence can be summarized as follows:

$$\text{Evaluate} \rightarrow \text{Act} \rightarrow \text{Plan}$$

Structure

The Prospector must be willing to alter its organization structure in order to facilitate rapid responses to environmental change. Prospectors localize their resources to the point of most effective utilization by assigning a high proportion of their members to task forces, project teams, and other relatively nonpermanent groups whose function is to develop a particular product or explore a particular market. The logical extension of this approach to structure is the *product organization,* in which all of the resources required to research, develop, produce, and market a related group of products are placed in a single, self-contained organizational subunit. This decentralization of entrepreneurial and engineering activities enables the Prospector to apply its expertise in many areas without being unduly constrained by management control.

Because organization members are seldom permanently assigned to a given project, the Prospector must maintain a substantial pool of employees whose skills can be transferred easily to other projects. For example, the task force appointed to investigate Cooperative Canners' possible entry into the frozen foods market was composed of a marketing, financial, and manufacturing specialist. Upon completion of this feasibility study, these individuals then joined the vice-president of planning in formulating a proposal to restructure the organization around the company's emerging product lines. In order to maintain the ability to shift individuals from one project team to another frequently, the Prospector has a *less extensive division of labor* than the Defender. As noted earlier, the Prospector utilizes professional employees who possess general skills and whose jobs are broadly defined in order to permit maximum autonomy. In addition, Prospectors develop only a *low degree of structural formalization,* since it would not be economically feasible to codify job descriptions and operating procedures in an organization whose tasks change frequently. Indeed, formalization is a means of reducing the probability that deviant behavior will occur, but, in many instances, this is exactly the type of behavior the Prospector is attempting to encourage.

Control

In order to foster behavior which will lead to effectiveness, the Prospector's control system is *results-oriented*. That is, it emphasizes outcome measures such as a product's acceptance by the market rather than input measures such as the efficiency with which resources were utilized (as would be the case in a Defender organization).

This effectiveness orientation requires the Prospector's control system to be decentralized. In part, control is decentralized because the information needed to assess current performance and to take appropriate corrective action is located in the operating units themselves, not in the upper echelons of management. Furthermore, the professionalized nature of the Prospector's work force permits individuals to exercise a considerable amount of self-control, largely enabling operating units to control their own performance. For example, when several customers of Star Electronics complained about a cooling-system malfunction in the firm's desk-top computer, the product division sales manager took the problem directly to the project coordinator, who in turn contacted a specialist in engineering and asked for his recommendations. The engineer isolated the responsible component and developed a modification which corrected the problem. The project coordinator then met with the production managers who redesigned several assembly procedures to incorporate the change. In this instance, corrective action was taken without recourse to higher management, and such behavior is considered to be legitimate in a Prospector organization.

This example from Star Electronics also illustrates the Prospector's preference for *short, horizontal feedback loops*. If the members of operating units are to exercise discretion effectively, they must have timely access to performance information. Therefore, when a deviation in unit performance is detected, this information is not channeled to higher management for action but rather is fed directly back to the unit for immediate correction.

Coordination and Conflict Resolution

Because of its many decentralized activities subject only to general top-management control, the Prospector must employ *complex and expensive forms of coordination* in order to manage subunit interdependence. Many of the Prospector's operations are highly interrelated, and simple coordination mechanisms such as standardization and scheduling will not suffice. For example, at any given time, Star Electronics is engaged in 200–300 research and development projects, many of which employ overlapping project teams. The work of these project groups could not be coordinated with standardized procedures or even a very detailed plan. Instead, individuals intimately familiar with the nature of these research and development efforts, called "project coordinators," are used to bring together the information and other resources necessary to perform the work on a set of related projects.

Compared to the Defender, the Prospector has a greater potential for diffused and varied forms of conflict and must therefore develop a different set of conflict-resolution mechanisms. In the Prospector organization, with numerous individuals and groups scanning the environment for opportunities, there is the likelihood of widespread disagreement over the direction which the organization should be taking. These disagreements cannot be resolved through normal hierarchical channels because higher executives do not have the time or the expertise to monitor the organization's diverse operations closely. Therefore, *conflict must be directly confronted by the affected units and resolved through use of coordinators or integrators* who act as liaisons between interdependent project groups. In a Prospector organization, top management provides only overall coordination and a forum for resolving major organizational conflicts.

Performance Appraisal and Maintenance

As discussed in the previous chapter, the Defender views organizational performance primarily in terms of efficiency (doing things right) while the Prospector evaluates performance in effectiveness terms (doing the right things). While an organization system is undergoing relatively continuous change, the comparison of levels of efficiency over time becomes difficult and only partially meaningful. Consequently, Prospectors usually define organizational performance in terms of outputs or results, and they appraise effectiveness by *comparing past and recent performance with that of similar organizations.* Although somewhat of an oversimplification, Computer Services evaluates its performance primarily in terms of maintaining industry leadership in product-market innovation; it has not always been among the most profitable firms in the industry.

This emphasis on effectiveness has direct implications for the Prospector's managerial succession process and for the allocation of rewards to organization members. Boundary-spanning positions such as marketing and product development are regarded as most crucial, and the importance attached to these areas is reflected in both the reward system and in opportunities for promotion. During hard times, the Prospector behaves much like the Defender: it cuts back in areas not directly related to its distinctive competence. Thus, whereas the Defender protects the production and finance functions, the Prospector protects research and development and marketing.

Costs and Benefits of the Administrative Solution

The structural and process characteristics which the Prospector adopts in solving the administrative problem heavily emphasize the innovative or leading aspect of the administrative role. That is, temporary project teams, decentralized decision making and control, few standard operating procedures, etc., serve to enhance the organization's ability to respond rapidly to environmental change and even to create such change. These administrative solutions flow logically from previous choices regarding the entrepreneurial and engineering problems, and flexibility is the common theme running through the Prospector's mode of adaptation. To the extent that the Prospector deals with the lagging aspect of administration—rationalizing organizational activities—it is mainly to facilitate and coordinate a system in which major strategic decisions are being made at middle-management levels.

In striving toward effectiveness, the major risk encountered by the Prospector is the inefficient use of resources. At any given time, a Prospector may be both underutilizing and misutilizing a significant proportion of its resources. Because of the complex and uncertain nature of many of the tasks engaged in by the Prospector, the "learning curve" associated with a particular project may be lengthy. During this period, high-priced professional employees are required to break the task down into manageable proportions. At the same time, projects with different time horizons from idea to end product are difficult to coordinate, and there may be periods when a particular individual is not being optimally used across the various projects to which he has been assigned.

Worse than underutilization is the misutilization of resources. By its very nature, prospecting is risky, and many projects simply will not be successful. Of course, it is difficult to draw the line between an acceptable and an unacceptable rate of failure when it comes to product and market innovation, but the Prospector clearly misutilizes more resources than the Defender.

CONCLUSIONS

In this chapter, we have described the process by which Prospectors enact and respond to their environments and the costs and benefits associated with this particular mode of adaptation. Specifically, we have shown that the Prospector enacts an environment that is more dynamic than those of other types of organizations within the same industry. The Prospector does so by continually modifying its product-market domain to take advantage of perceived opportunities and by emphasizing flexi-

Table 4-1   Characteristics of the Prospector

Entrepreneurial problem	Engineering problem	Administrative problem
Problem: How to locate and exploit new product and market opportunities	*Problem:* How to avoid long-term commitments to a single technological process	*Problem:* How to facilitate and coordinate numerous and diverse operations
Solutions: 1. Broad and continuously developing domain 2. Monitors wide range of environmental conditions and events 3. Creates change in the industry 4. Growth through product and market development 5. Growth may occur in spurts	*Solutions:* 1. Flexible, prototypical technologies 2. Multiple technologies 3. Low degree of routinization and mechanization; technology embedded in people	*Solutions:* 1. Marketing and research and development experts most powerful members of the dominant coalition 2. Dominant coalition is large, diverse, and transitory; may include an inner circle 3. Tenure of dominant coalition not always lengthy; key managers may be hired from outside as well as promoted from within 4. Planning is broad rather than intensive, problem oriented, and cannot be finalized before action is taken 5. Tendency toward product structure with low division of labor and low degree of formalization 6. Decentralized control and short-looped horizontal information systems 7. Complex coordination mechanisms and conflict resolved through integrators 8. Organizational performance measured against important competitors; reward system favors marketing and research and development
Costs and benefits: Product and market innovation protects the organization from a changing environment, but the organization runs the risk of low profitability and overextension of its resources	*Costs and benefits:* Technological flexibility permits a rapid response to a changing domain, but the organization cannot develop maximum efficiency in its production and distribution system because of multiple technologies	*Costs and benefits:* Administrative system is ideally suited to maintain flexibility and effectiveness but may underutilize and misutilize resources

bility in its technology and administrative system in order to facilitate rapid adjustment.

Several risks, however, are associated with the Prospector strategy: the organization may overextend itself in terms of products and markets; it may be technologically inefficient; and its administrative system may, at least temporarily, underutilize and misutilize resources. In short, the Prospector is effective—it can respond to the demands of tomorrow's world. However, to the extent that the world of tomorrow is similar to that of today, the Prospector cannot maximize profitability because of its inherent inefficiency.

Table 4-1 summarizes the Prospector's salient characteristics and the major strengths and weaknesses associated with this pattern of adaptation.

Chapter 5

Analyzers

Based on our research, we believe that the Defender and the Prospector reside at opposite ends of a continuum of adjustment strategies. Between these two extremes, we have observed a third type of organization called the Analyzer. The Analyzer is a unique combination of the Prospector and Defender types, and it represents a viable alternative to these other strategies. In this chapter, we discuss the Analyzer, noting its unique characteristics and how these compare to and contrast with the features of the Defender and the Prospector.

A true Analyzer is an organization that minimizes risk while maximizing the opportunity for profits, that is, an experienced Analyzer combines the strengths of both the Prospector and the Defender into a single system. Thus, the word that best describes the Analyzer's adaptive approach is balance. In the following example, look for the characteristics that Silicon Systems shares with the Prospector and the Defender. Note particularly how the company defines its product-market domain.

Silicon Systems is a medium-sized and very profitable company in the electronics industry. Founded in the mid-sixties, Silicon has approximately a thousand employees who make calculators and related products for the consumer market and a variety of electronic components for industrial customers.

"Outsiders are usually surprised at how little long-range planning we do," says President John Doig, Jr. "But why should we? We need to be able to act quickly when a new product design appears on the market, not develop elaborate plans that might have to be junked later on. We do some careful planning but only for our industrial business." Instead, Silicon invests heavily in both marketing and applied engineering so that it can rapidly manufacture and sell any new product it chooses.

Silicon is a matrix organization that includes both product and functional divisions. There are three major functional units (manufacturing, marketing, and engineering) and a few smaller ones. In addition, there are four product divisions, each of which is composed of a product manager and small staffs in marketing and research and development. Three of these divisions serve industrial markets while the fourth (and most recent) division serves the consumer market. Product managers have more power than their functional counterparts who must adjust their production or marketing schedules to fit the needs of the four product divisions.

As indicated above, Silicon attempts to achieve a balance between its investments in marketing and in engineering. This practice came about as a result of the company's entry into the consumer market a few years ago. Silicon had been known as a product innovator for the first several years of its existence, but management decided that the firm could operate strongly from a stable industrial-products base while experimenting with the more lucrative consumer market. Therefore, management cut overall research and development activities drastically, leaving only small R&D groups in each of the four product divisions. These groups now simply monitor product innovations engendered by Silicon's major competitors and select those designs which appear to be the most successful. At the same time, management rapidly built up the engineering group so that Silicon could quickly follow the introduction of a new product into the market with its own version of that product. This capability is particularly important in the consumer market where product life cycles are shorter.

Turnover in the position of product manager tends to be high, for Silicon does not like its new products to fail, even in the short run. "We're walking a narrow line here," says President Doig. "We're no longer the innovator we used to be, and we've never been as efficient as some of the other firms. But so far, no one has been able to move as fast as we do when it comes to getting a new design through engineering and production and onto the market."

Silicon Systems, like most Analyzers, defines its entrepreneurial problem in terms similar to both the Prospector and the Defender: how to locate and exploit new product and market opportunities while simultaneously maintaining a firm core of traditional products and customers. The Analyzer's solution to the entrepreneurial problem is also a blend of the solutions preferred by the Prospector and the Defender. That is, the Analyzer moves toward new products or new markets, but only after their viability has been demonstrated. This periodic transformation of the Analyzer's domain is accomplished through imitation—only the most successful product or market innovations developed by prominent Prospectors are adopted. At the same time, the major part of the Analyzer's revenues is generated by a fairly stable set of products and customer or client groups—a Defender characteristic. Thus, the Analyzer must be able to respond quickly when following the lead of key Prospectors while at the same time maintaining operating efficiency in its stable product and market areas.

In the second case, Arlington Community Hospital has defined its domain along the lines of the Analyzer. Note here, however, how this hospital has been organized internally to meet the characteristics of its dual domain.

Arlington Community Hospital is a voluntary general hospital founded in the early 1900s. It currently maintains 320 patient beds and has a reputation as a venerable and stable institution catering to the high-income groups in its geographic area. During the last decade, however, Arlington has undergone a series of rather dramatic internal changes.

In 1968, after serving as a source of strong central authority for nearly 20 years, Joel Rogers, Arlington's chief administrator, became convinced that changes in the hospital's basic approach to providing health care were overdue. His primary objectives were to expand Arlington's role in the community through increased service to low-income groups covered by Medicare and to halt the erosion of Arlington's traditional patient base caused by competing hospitals with better reputations for innovative medical techniques and programs. Mr. Rogers felt that Arlington could duplicate the more successful of these new programs and services without harming its existing system. In order to provide sufficient time to formulate policy consistent with these objectives and to facilitate the necessary internal changes, Mr. Rogers began withdrawing from personal involvement in the hospital's daily operations, delegating increased responsibility to the incumbents of three newly created administrative positions.

By 1975, this process had led to the subdivision of the hospital into three semiautonomous components. The three administrative heads of these divisions manage through a team approach and hold frequent informal meetings to coordinate their various activities. Bernard Karlstrom (Patient Care and Supportive Services) oversees most of the hospital's traditional day-to-day operations. In describing his division, Mr. Karlstrom says: "My chief concern is containing costs to meet the demands for increased public accountability coming from the hospital's various constituents."

Stephen Ross (Clinics and Diagnostic Services) is responsible for the hospital's rapidly growing outpatient clinic as well as a series of other new programs. Mr. Ross is also involved in upgrading and expanding the hospital's diagnostic machinery and facilities. He comments: "Right now, my biggest problems are recruiting primary physicians into our outpatient clinic and training new employees fast enough to keep pace with the patient load. Campaigning for the capital investment we need to improve our diagnostic services is another one of my concerns."

Lance Cannon (Resources and Planning) manages the bulk of the hospital's external relations, is in charge of all planning activity, and is currently coordinating a major construction program to replace Arlington's antiquated patient care and surgical facilities. Mr. Cannon, an MBA marketing specialist, describes his job as follows: "I'm more of a liaison than an administrator—I deal with a wide variety of people and problems. Lately I've been putting a lot of time into acting as an intermediary between our outpatient clinic and the medical chiefs of staff to develop joint plans for expanding clinic operations."

Today, Arlington has increased the Medicare component of its patient population to over 40 percent. Although little emphasis has been given to sponsoring basic medical research, the hospital has enjoyed considerable success in adopting new patient-oriented programs while holding the line in its traditional areas both in terms of patient charges and occupancy rates.

As evident at Arlington Hospital, the Analyzer's solutions to the engineering and administrative problems must reflect its entrepreneurial orientation. The Analyzer's engineering problem has two facets: the organization must develop an efficient technology for producing and distributing its traditional products or services, and it must create prototypical technologies for producing new products or services. The Analyzer's solution to this dichotomous engineering problem is essentially achieved through separation. For a considerable portion of its products, the Analyzer uses a standardized technological process which is buffered to protect technological stability. For its newly emerging products, the organization develops separate, nonstandardized technologies, which are employed until production techniques are sufficiently understood to move the product to standardized production. Arlington Hospital's health care delivery system reflects both these technological processes.

The duality evident in the Analyzer's domain and technology is reflected in its administrative system. The Analyzer's administrative problem—how to differentiate the organization's structure and processes to accommodate both stable and dynamic areas of operation—is solved by some form of matrix structure where managerial responsibilities are roughly divided according to stability or flexibility. In the case of Arlington Hospital, these managerial responsibilities have been allocated among three key individuals.

In the following sections, we discuss in more detail the Analyzer's solutions to the three main adaptive problems and the costs and benefits of this particular adjustment strategy.

ENTREPRENEURIAL PROBLEMS AND SOLUTIONS

As indicated above, the Analyzer's entrepreneurial problem is how to locate and exploit new product and market opportunities while simultaneously maintaining a stable core of products and customers. The Analyzer's domain, therefore, is a *mixture of products and markets, some of which are stable, others changing.* Two routes to becoming an Analyzer are exemplified by the cases of Silicon Systems and Arlington Community Hospital. In the past, Silicon was noted for its product innovation, particularly in the area of electronic components for industrial usage. Due to its success in this field, the company is now using its industrial product line to support its entrance into the larger and more lucrative consumer market. Arlington Hospital, on the other hand, had been a stable institution that had undergone only a few changes in its traditional hospital services and programs. However, because of the chief administrator's belief that the hospital was foregoing too many potential opportunities, Arlington is currently maintaining its traditional service base while expanding its offerings to a wider range of clients.

With the stable portion of its domain reasonably well protected, the Analyzer is free to imitate the best of the products and markets developed by Prospectors. Successful imitation is accomplished through *extensive marketing surveillance mechanisms.* The ideal Analyzer is always poised, ready to move quickly toward a new product or market that has recently gained a degree of acceptance. For example, Silicon Systems uses product managers and staff marketing specialists to monitor developments in the market and to observe the behavior of its major competitors in an effort to locate opportunities. Once a new product is spotted, these groups are responsible for its rapid movement through the necessary stages of engineering and production so that the Analyzer's version of the product arrives on the market shortly after it was introduced by a Prospector. Thus, whereas the Prospector is a *creator* of change in the industry, the Analyzer is an *avid follower* of change. Its goal is to adopt the most promising innovations developed by Prospectors without engaging in extensive research and development.

The Analyzer's growth pattern is a mixture of that of the Prospector and the Defender. Much of the Analyzer's *growth occurs through market penetration* since the organization's basic strength comes from its traditional product-market base. However, to the extent that the Analyzer is successful in pursuing its strategy, a substantial amount of *growth may also occur through product and market development.*

ENGINEERING PROBLEMS AND SOLUTIONS

As indicated earlier, the Analyzer must achieve and protect an equilibrium between conflicting demands for technological flexibility and for technological stability. This equilibrium is accomplished by the partitioning of production activities to form a *dual technological core.* The stable component of the Analyzer's technology bears a strong resemblance to the Defender's technology. It is functionally organized and exhibits high levels of routinization, formalization, and mechanization in an attempt to approach cost efficiency. The Analyzer's flexible technological component, on the other hand, resembles the Prospector's technological orientation. In manufacturing organizations, it frequently includes a large group of applications engineers (or their equivalent) who are rotated among teams charged with the task of rapidly adapting new product designs to fit the Analyzer's existing stable technology.

The Analyzer's dual technological core is thus a marriage of the engineering solutions of the Prospector and the Defender, with the *stable and flexible components welded together by an influential applied research group.* To the extent that this group is able to develop solutions that match the organization's technological capabilities with the new products desired by product managers, the Analyzer can update its product line without incurring the Prospector's extensive research and development expenses.

Furthermore, the Analyzer's capability for updating portions of its domain eliminates the desirability of some of the more constraining structural mechanisms used by the Defender to protect technological stability. That is, the Analyzer will buffer its technology to some extent through standardization and routinization, but it will not reduce the technology to a limited-purpose mechanism by moving toward complete vertical integration and its attendant requirements for homogeneous inputs. Thus, the Analyzer's technological system is characterized by a *moderate degree of technical efficiency.*

ADMINISTRATIVE PROBLEMS AND SOLUTIONS

The Analyzer's administrative problem, as well as its entrepreneurial and engineering problems, reflects its intermediate position between the Defender and the Prospector. Generally speaking, the administrative problem of the Analyzer is how to differentiate the organization's structure and processes to accommodate both stable and dynamic areas of operation.

Dominant Coalition and Managerial Succession

The Analyzer's dominant coalition *focuses upon the functions of marketing, applied research, and production.* This particular composition of critical functions reflects portions of both the Prospector's and the Defender's dominant coalition. Like the Prospector, for example, the Analyzer's dominant coalition includes the marketing function. Marketing's preeminence results from the Analyzer's penchant for imitating successful Prospectors: marketing specialists are best suited for identifying those newly developed products and markets which are likely to be profitable. Similarly, the Analyzer's dominant coalition tends to be large (i.e., includes product managers) and somewhat transitory (i.e., product managers' influence rises and falls depending upon the areas that the organization is currently emphasizing), and the tenure of coalition members may not be particularly lengthy.

Beyond these characteristics, however, the similarity between the Analyzer's and the Prospector's dominant coalition ends. In particular, the Analyzer substitutes an applied engineering group, or some other employee group that performs a similar function, for the Prospector's research and development group. The reason for engineering's influence, as explained in the previous section, is that this group is charged with moving new products selected by the Analyzer quickly into standardized production. In many of the manufacturing organizations identified as Analyzers in our research, the chief executive was an engineer. Succession through the applied research group to the top executive position is clearly consistent with engineering's pivotal role in adapting new product designs for efficient production. Engineering, along with marketing, thus provides the main source of top-executive talent.

Finally, like the Defender, the Analyzer includes the production function in its dominant coalition. Production often does not wield as much power as marketing and the individual product managers, but it is nevertheless present because much of the organization's profitability is based on the ability of the production unit to operate efficiently.

Planning

Because the Analyzer must plan for both stability and change, it does not have a unified planning process. Rather, planning in the Analyzer is *both intensive and comprehensive.*

Intensive planning occurs primarily between the functional divisions of marketing and production and concerns the stable portion of the Analyzer's business. Together these units explore the projected sales picture for the organization's traditional products or services and then develop a detailed plan for matching targeted sales with production capacity. In this regard, the Analyzer obtains benefits from planning similar to those obtained by the Defender, namely, a series of well-defined steps pointed toward a specific set of output and cost goals and supported with operating budgets. Thus, the planning sequence used by the Analyzer for its traditional business parallels that used by the Defender:

$$Plan \rightarrow Act \rightarrow Evaluate$$

Broad market planning for the development of new products occurs through the close interaction of applied research and marketing's product managers. This group's planning task is to evaluate the product and market areas currently being investigated by Prospectors and those areas likely to be investigated in the foreseeable future. Although the new product portion of the Analyzer's planning process is similar to the Prospector's, it should be noted that the Analyzer is able to avoid the Prospector's experimental engagement of a new problem area. That is, once the Analyzer accepts a new product, it aggressively moves the design through engineering and into production. Concurrently, a marketing campaign is readied that will be closely coordinated with the product's introduction to the market. Thus, for the Analyzer's new products, the planning sequence may be characterized as follows:

$$Evaluate \rightarrow Plan \rightarrow Act$$

Structure

The Analyzer must differentiate its organization structure to reflect the hybrid nature of its domain and technology. The appropriate structure for accommodating both stability and change is the *matrix structure.* A major characteristic of the matrix structure is the combined presence of functional divisions, where similar specialists are grouped together, and self-contained groups with specific product responsibilities. These product groups can be added, modified, or disbanded with relative ease since they do not contain difficult-to-decompose production capabilities, and their personnel may be reassigned to functional divisions or to emerging product groups.

A form of matrix structure is readily observable at Silicon Systems. The company has three major functional divisions (production, marketing, engineering) and four product divisions (three for industrial products and one for consumer products). The functional divisions are large, contain an extensive division of labor, and are highly formalized, while the product divisions are small and operate with a minimum of standard procedures. The operations of these functional and product divisions are largely independent of each other. Only when new product designs are being modified for standardized production do the functional and product groups become highly interdependent.

A version of the matrix organization is also evident at Arlington Community Hospital. The hospital's traditional and stable areas of operation have all been grouped together under an administrator for patient care and supportive services. Conversely, the hospital's innovative programs and services are the responsibility of another administrator (clinics and diagnostic services). The two areas are brought together by the administrator for resources and planning who is in charge of all planning and coordinating activity at Arlington. Thus, the hospital has differentiated its structure to achieve both stability and flexibility while simultaneously providing a mechanism for integrating the two types of operations when and where it becomes necessary.

Control

Generally speaking, achieving adequate control of organizational performance is both more critical and more problematical for an Analyzer than for the other organization types. The Analyzer's success is contingent upon maintaining a delicate equilibrium among subunits that have disparate structures and processes resulting in higher levels of differentiation and complexity than are present in the more internally homogeneous Defender or Prospector.

An assortment of control techniques may be employed to maintain the performance of the Analyzer's differentiated subunits. In functional units, control systems are centralized and budget-oriented to encourage cost-efficient production of standard products. Because decisions that concern production scheduling or the insertion of new products into the ongoing technology are best made near the top of the functional hierarchy, these units normally employ long-looped vertical information systems. Conversely, in product and project groups, control systems are decentralized and results-oriented so as to enhance the effectiveness with which new products can be adapted to the existing technology. Because only the product groups possess the information required to assess and correct performance, these units usually employ short-looped horizontal information systems.

In order to ensure satisfactory levels of both efficiency and effectiveness, the Analyzer's dominant coalition must *manage fundamentally different control mechanisms.* Efficiency must be continuously traded off against effectiveness, for disproportionate emphasis on either one can interfere with the attainment of the other and thus impair performance.

Coordination and Conflict Resolution

The Analyzer uses *both simple and complex forms of coordination.* In stable operating areas, reliance on functional structures allows coordination to be achieved in a straightforward and inexpensive fashion, primarily through the use of standardization and planning. Conversely, product and project groups that operate in areas of greater uncertainty require more elaborate and costly forms of coordination such as product managers or project coordinators. Both types of coordinating mechanisms operate relatively independently of each other.

As a result, the conflict experienced by the Analyzer is usually predictable and containable. Most conflict occurs within the product groups and between these groups and applied research, and it is resolved by product managers and others who are close to the problem. Predictable conflict and extensive coordination occur just before and during the process of inserting a new product into the standardized technology. In these situations, the project manager usually serves as a liaison between production personnel and applied engineering personnel, and he or she plays an active role in formulating procedures for a new product's timely introduction by minimizing costs and by handling any adverse consequences that may arise as a result of incorporating the new product into the system.

Performance Appraisal and Maintenance

In order to prosper, the Analyzer must preserve its firm base of efficient operation while pursuing effectiveness through the well-conceived addition of new products and markets. This dual objective leads to internal differences in the definition and appraisal of organizational performance. In stable subunits, performance tends to be defined in terms of efficiency and measured against cost budgets. In adaptive subunits, performance is defined in terms of effectiveness and measured against projections of market penetration and profit. Those Analyzer organizations that are able to accomplish these twin performance-appraisal objectives frequently are among the most successful organizations in their respective industries.

CONCLUSIONS

We have argued that balance is the common characteristic of the Analyzer's solutions to the three problems of organizational adaptation. If it is successful in developing and maintaining this balance, the Analyzer exhibits a different configuration of domain, technology, structure, and process from that of the Defender or the Prospector. Although this particular configuration is a combination of Prospector and Defender characteristics, the Analyzer strategy has its own unique strengths and weaknesses.

The Analyzer defines its entrepreneurial problem as how to locate and exploit new product and market opportunities while simultaneously maintaining a firm base of traditional products and customers. The organization solves this problem with a hybrid domain of stable and emerging products, the former used as a base to support the latter. Marketing is regarded as a particularly crucial function that must not only locate new product or market opportunities but also promote the sale of the organization's traditional products or services. The Analyzer avoids the expense of research and development, choosing instead to imitate the successful actions of Prospectors. The result is the ability to grow through market penetration as well as product and market development.

The Analyzer is able to serve its mixed domain by creating a dual technological core. The stable component of the technology is a near-efficient production system that is able to create products or services on a standardized basis. The flexible component exists in the form of a large and influential applied research group whose function is to adapt new product designs to fit existing technological capabilities. The dual nature of the Analyzer's technology allows the organization to produce familiar products or services efficiently while keeping pace with developments engendered by Prospectors.

The administrative system needed to differentiate and integrate the stable and dynamic areas of operation is built around some version of a matrix organization. Heads of key functional units, most notably engineering and production, unite with product managers to form a balanced dominant coalition similar to that of both the Defender and the Prospector. Other characteristics of the Analyzer's managerial processes such as planning, control, and coordination also reflect an intermediate posi-

Table 5-1   Characteristics of the Analyzer

Entrepreneurial problem	Engineering problem	Administrative problem
Problem: How to locate and exploit new product and market opportunities while simultaneously maintaining a firm base of traditional products and customers	*Problem:* How to be efficient in stable portions of the domain and flexible in changing portions	*Problem:* How to differentiate the organization's structure and processes to accommodate both stable and dynamic areas of operation
Solutions: 1. Hybrid domain that is both stable and changing 2. Surveillance mechanisms mostly limited to marketing; some research and development 3. Steady growth through market penetration and product-market development	*Solutions:* 1. Dual technological core (stable and flexible component) 2. Large and influential applied research group 3. Moderate degree of technical efficiency	*Solutions:* 1. Marketing and applied research most influential members of dominant coalition, followed closely by production 2. Intensive planning between marketing and production concerning stable portion of domain; comprehensive planning among marketing, applied research, and product managers concerning new products and markets 3. Matrix structure combining both functional divisions and product groups 4. Moderately centralized control system with vertical and horizontal feedback loops 5. Extremely complex and expensive coordination mechanisms; some conflict resolution through product managers, some through normal hierarchical channels 6. Performance appraisal based on both effectiveness and efficiency measures, most rewards to marketing and applied research
Costs and benefits: Low investment in research and development, combined with imitation of demonstrably successful products, minimizes risk, but domain must be optimally balanced at all times between stability and flexibility	*Costs and benefits:* Dual technological core is able to serve a hybrid stable-changing domain, but the technology can never be completely effective or efficient	*Costs and benefits:* Administrative system is ideally suited to balance stability and flexibility, but if this balance is lost, it may be difficult to restore equilibrium

tion between that of the Prospector and the Defender. Thus, The Analyzer's administrative system is ideally suited to balance stability and flexibility.

Of course, the Analyzer strategy is not without its costs. The duality in the Analyzer's domain forces the organization to pursue a middle course in its other adaptive solutions, and it requires management to be continually vigilant in maintaining the delicate balance among the organization's domain, technology, and structure. The Analyzer's dual technological core means that the organization can never be completely efficient nor completely effective. The matrix organization structure, with its twin characteristics of stability and flexibility, limits the organization's ability to move fully in either direction should the domain shift dramatically.

Table 5-1 summarizes the Analyzer's salient characteristics and the major strengths and weaknesses inherent in this pattern of adaptation.

Chapter 6

Reactors

In the previous three chapters, we described three types of organizations, each of which has its own pattern of response to environmental conditions. We argued that each of these response patterns is both consistent and stable. In other words, when presented with a change in its environment, the Defender, the Analyzer, and the Prospector all set into motion a series of characteristic actions aimed at incorporating the change into the organization's ongoing behavior. Generally speaking, these actions may range from the Defender's attempt to develop greater efficiency in existing operations to the Prospector's exploration of change in an effort to open up a new area of opportunity. Over time, these action modes stabilize to form a typical pattern of response to environmental conditions.

However, in Chapter 2, we also mentioned a fourth type of organization, the Reactor, whose pattern of adjustment to the environment was both inconsistent and unstable. In our view, the Reactor is an unstable organization type because it lacks a set of consistent response mechanisms that it can put into effect when faced with a changing environment. This inconsistency potentially may stem from at least three sources: (1) management fails to articulate a viable organizational strategy; (2) a strategy is articulated but technology, structure, and process are not linked to it in an appropriate manner; or (3) management adheres to a particular strategy-structure relationship even though it is no longer relevant to environmental conditions.

In this chapter, we present a general discussion of Reactor organizations. Each of the three cases emphasizes a major route through which organizations become Reactors. In the first case, Daro Development's president, a "one-man" Prospector, dies, leaving the remainder of his management team unable to articulate the organization's strategy. In the second case, Cohen Publishing Company is struggling to pursue an Analyzer strategy, but its current structure is not well suited to this task. Finally, Exotic Foods, a Defender, is being forced out of its domain but is reluctant to give up its present strategy and structure.

A WEAKLY ARTICULATED STRATEGY

Daro Developments, Inc., is a medium-sized Midwestern firm built almost single-handedly by its founder, Dan Rogers. Daro's principal areas of business are the development and operation of shopping centers and medium-priced apartment complexes. Around this core, Daro has moved outward into construction, management of non-Daro developments, and most recently into the provision of consulting services in the area of urban planning.

The growth of Daro, while rapid and multidirectional, was not without its logic. It began in 1960 when young Dan Rogers, a fresh honors graduate of a first-rate architecture program, was presented by his uncle with the opportunity to design and develop a small shopping center on a portion of family-owned property. Although a number of costly mistakes were made, the center ultimately achieved not only critical acclaim for its design but also substantial financial success. With financial backing from his family, Dan designed and developed a second small shopping center in a neighboring community and then a medium-sized center in a nearby metropolitan area. These centers also received recognition for their design features, and the third was brought in at budget, despite rising costs, largely because of Dan's coordination skills and boundless energy.

Dan's managerial efforts on the medium-sized project convinced him that control over construction activities was essential to successful shopping center development. Thus, Daro Developments, Inc. (incorporation was necessary prior to the second venture) drew together its own construction capability to handle key building assignments. A construction supervisor and foremen were placed on the permanent personnel roster, and work crews were contracted and equipment leased for each operation.

The three early developments opened up many additional individual and joint-venture opportunities across a two-state area, and further successes in the shopping center arena led Dan to look for other design and development opportunities. Apartment complexes appeared to be a natural complement to shopping centers, and an integrated apartment-shopping center development soon won nationwide recognition. However, Dan's pleasure over his critical recognition and expanded operations was blighted by the near failure of one of his shopping centers built 18 months earlier. In Dan's view, the center had been poorly managed from the beginning. He convinced the mortgage holders to allow him to participate in the selection of a new management group and in the creation of sound maintenance and accounting systems. The new management group and their methods were highly successful—so effective, in fact, that they were granted managerial contracts in an apartment complex and shopping center in an adjacent community. Shortly thereafter, that group became the building block for the Property Management Division of Daro Developments, Inc.

The most recent addition to the firm, the Urban Planning Division, was begun in 1971. It grew out of Dan Rogers' growing recognition as a developer whose integrated designs were esthetically pleasing and environmentally sound. Dan's regular appearances before planning groups, and his numerous articles in both trade and academic journals, made his advice highly sought after. The demands on Dan's time were enormous, however, and beginning in the late sixties, he started to bring environmental and urban planning specialists into the firm. Initially, these specialists were used to meet the needs of Daro's own developments, but later their services were offered to other developers and to urban-planning groups. The division now includes 25 professional employees and a sizable clerical staff.

Throughout the sixties and early seventies, Rogers remained on top of each segment of his growing firm, scouting for new locations, arranging financing, appearing on site to make changes, and playing a principal role in the consulting services division. In each area, a hand-picked officer was in constant contact with Rogers. In a sense, each unit was simply an extension of Rogers' creative abilities.

Daro Developments was shaken to its foundation in 1975 when Dan Rogers' personal plane crashed in a thunderstorm en route to the opening of a new shopping center, killing Rogers, his pilot, and his personal secretary. Rogers' nephew, Art Thomas, a 33-year-old lawyer, moved into the CEO position, working closely with Cal Edwards, a former bank president who had served Rogers for years as chief financial officer.

Since Rogers' death, work already under way and planned has moved ahead efficiently, but the flow of new developments has been slowed. Opportunities abound, but dissension has developed among the top executive group concerning which areas should be emphasized. Art Thomas, for example, feels the consulting division should be expanded, while Cal Edwards has argued for enlarging the property management area (the major source of cash flow). Key decisions have been difficult to make, Art feels, because day-to-day issues from all areas constantly demand his attention and because the divisions, while listed as separate operating units, have not been operated as true profit centers, making it quite difficult to determine accurately what contribution each is making to overall profit.

At the moment, Art is attempting to get each area to move ahead slowly while an overall plan of action is developed. He has asked the heads of each division to submit 1-, 3-, and 5-year plans detailing growth opportunities and capital needs. He is beginning to doubt, however, that these projections will be of much value. "The problem is," he complains, "everyone here is damned good at carrying out orders, but no one is used to thinking on his own. The next ten years are going to bring major changes in every area we are now into, and I'm not at all sure we have the capabilities to respond."

The experience of Daro Developments typifies one common way that an organization may become a Reactor: managerial failure to articulate an organizational strategy. With Dan Rogers at the helm, Daro was evolving logically and successfully. The extension of Rogers' personal skills (later bolstered by the expanding organizational resources of Daro Developments, Inc.) into the shopping center, construction, apartment complex, and urban planning arenas represented a natural growth pattern characteristic of numerous organizations. However, unlike many successful organizations which have followed this "prospecting" mode, Daro has not clearly articulated a Prospector strategy. The best evidence in this regard comes from the remaining members of top management; currently there is wide disagreement among them concerning Daro's future domain and, to a lesser extent, its organizational structure. Perhaps if Dan Rogers were still alive, he could have described the type of organization he envisioned. Without his guidance, however, top management does not seem able to set a clear course for Daro. Presently, the organization is a loose collection of semiautonomous units each of which is justifiably able to argue strongly for more emphasis on its particular domain and operations.

At the moment, Daro Developments probably could become either an Analyzer or a Prospector. Daro's currently decentralized structure would facilitate a return to active prospecting, but several substantial process changes would be required before this strategy could be effectively pursued. For example, Art Thomas, the chief executive officer, spends most of his time enmeshed in routine operating details. One reason, of course, is that Thomas is new to the job; a more important reason is that Daro's division managers are not used to operating independently as heads of full-fledged profit centers, the type of behavior which would be required in a Prospector system.

In addition to sorting out the roles and relationships of Art Thomas and the other members of his management team, the organization's planning, communication, and control systems would have to be carefully defined. Dan Rogers was the key element in each of these systems, and it appears that the company cannot continue to operate effectively in this personalized manner. Currently, planning and control are being performed in a haphazard fashion, with only the company's momentum propelling those projects already underway toward completion. Once these projects have been completed, however, management's disagreement over future business emphases will probably throw the planning and control mechanisms into disarray. To be a true Prospector, as noted in Chapter 4, Daro's planning system would have to be general and oriented towards results rather than methods. Further, it would have to guide as well as sanction some experimental actions before specific plans were finalized. Similarly, the control system would need to be decentralized to the extent that division managers themselves could take whatever actions were necessary to keep their operations under control. Unfortunately, because of past experience, none of the division managers at Daro could immediately function effectively within planning and control systems such as these. Therefore, if Daro Developments chose to become a Prospector, a prolonged developmental period would be required during which Thomas and his division heads would formulate acceptable planning and control processes.

Alternatively, Daro management could choose to articulate an Analyzer strategy. Such a strategy might be warranted given the fact that the company no longer enjoys the immense skills of Dan Rogers. Without Rogers' ability to intervene personally in any of Daro's projects with useful guidance and expertise, management might reasonably conclude that the active prospecting mode of the past is no longer feasible, at least in the short to intermediate future. However, in order to pursue an Analyzer strategy, Daro would have to alter its organizational structure considerably to reflect the requirements of this strategy. The first step would be to separate the company's business into those areas which are relatively stable and consistently profitable and those which are more speculative. In Daro's case, the shopping center and apartment management division represent the company's most stable areas of operation and its primary source of cash flow. This division would most likely emerge as Daro's "core" business and would be used to support the firm's ventures into other areas such as consulting.

The second step in implementing an Analyzer strategy would be to create appropriate processes for facilitating the simultaneous operations of these stable and fluctuating business groupings. In the property management division, for example, more intensive planning would be required so that the addition of new shopping centers and apartments would proceed logically and smoothly. Also, more stringent financial controls would be necessary in this division in order to ensure that it remains a healthy base to support the rest of the company's ventures. In other divisions such as consulting, however, division managers would be allowed much more discretion to pursue their activities. Here, only broad planning objectives and control mechanisms would be used. This would allow managers in these areas to respond rapidly to opportunities by diverging from plan when it appeared to be profitable to do so. Thus, if Daro Developments chooses to become a "pure" Analyzer, it will evolve a much different organizational form from the one that would result if it decides to return to its former prospecting mode.

In sum, because it lacks a clear strategy, Daro Developments can be characterized at the moment as a Reactor. Management is unable to articulate a strategy for the organization because the only individual who had a vision of the company's future is gone, and the current strategic vacuum is being filled with conflicting demands from division heads, each of whom has legitimate reasons for expanding his own domain. Note that Daro's environment does not appear to have changed in any appreciable way. However, stymied by its present lack of strategy, the organization is reluctant to act in a manner that will achieve an acceptable equilibrium with this environment.

STRUCTURE IMPROPERLY LINKED TO STRATEGY

Although many organizations have experienced an evolutionary process similar to that of Daro Developments, one might nevertheless argue that adaptive problems of this sort are less likely to occur in a more established organization. In this regard, consider the following, perhaps more typical, example.

Cohen Publishing Company is a medium-sized book publishing firm that has been known for many years as a publisher of high-quality textbooks and trade books. However, Cohen is also known throughout the industry for its large and rapid fluctuations in profitability. "Some outsiders believe that every few years we topple from the pinnacle of success to the brink of bankruptcy and then work our way back up," says President Allen J. Schwartz. "This isn't true, but we do experience a lot of instability in this company."

Cohen Publishing began as a trade publisher with only a very small college operation. However, early in its history, Cohen acquired a textbook publishing firm of approximately equal size in order to round out its publishing program. Since that time, the company has made three major acquisitions, two trade publishers and one textbook publisher, all of which were noted for high-quality books in their respective areas. Although the actual operations of each of the acquired firms have been blended into those of the original organization for some time now, there remains within this larger structure a number of competing views about the proper direction and emphases of Cohen Publishing. To accommodate these differing viewpoints, Cohen has traditionally allowed each of its major editorial groups a substantial amount of freedom to develop its own publishing programs. When each group is successful in the same year, overall company results are often spectacular. Of course, the opposite is also true, but in most years performance is somewhere in between, hence the evaluation by many that Cohen is a highly volatile company.

Cohen Publishing has many capabilities spread throughout its structure. It publishes children's books; trade books; textbooks for elementary, high school, and college students; and it has several specialized units such as an audiovisual department and special projects groups. Therefore, given a potential opportunity of almost any sort, Cohen can usually respond because the needed expertise is already contained somewhere within the organization. Moreover, as indicated, editors are allowed a great deal of freedom, and they are continually alert for innovative ideas concerning their particular domain.

However, many individuals in the organization believe that the structure of Cohen Publishing does not facilitate continuous innovation. Below the corporate level, which includes such major divisions as elementary-high school texts, higher education, trade, international, etc., much of the company is organized along functional lines. For example, the College Department (part of the Higher Education Group) is composed of four major units: editorial, sales, production, and marketing. Each of these units is formally separated, so that an editor who is developing a particular project must cross unit boundaries in order to produce, market, and sell his or her product. Since the College Department deals with most of the fields and disciplines in the college market, this work flow process can, and often does, become cumbersome.

Several years ago, a series of meetings was held with corporate management. The main conclusion emerging from these meetings was that editors in the Higher Education Group all had different perceptions of their publishing needs and various methods for pursuing their activities. Therefore, despite the individual success of numerous editors, higher management was not able to provide overall coordination and control of their efforts. President Schwartz remarked at that time, "We still want to locate the most exciting authors and projects, but somehow we have to get our operations under control."

Thus, corporate management decided that each editor in the College Department would be asked to develop a 5-year publishing plan for his particular field; a summary report of all editorial plans would be presented at a corporate-level meeting approximately 9 months later. Each editor's individual plan was to be reviewed and summarized by the three editors-in-chief (in the humanities, social sciences, and natural sciences). Corporate management believed that such a process would not only result in more relevant and specific plans, but also that the "educational" benefits from participating in the process would help to stabilize the organization's operations in the future. Few higher executives are willing to attribute the changed nature of Cohen Publishing entirely to this new planning process, but President Schwartz reported several years later that "things have calmed down considerably." There was at the same time, however, a feeling by many that management's heavy emphasis on planning had produced a new cautiousness in the company that might ultimately injure the innovative activities which Cohen had been known for in the past.

Unlike Daro Developments, Cohen Publishing's management was, at least until recently, certain that the company should be a Prospector. The typical top executive at Cohen believed that the organization should be at the forefront of new product and market development in both the trade and text areas. Over the years, Cohen Publishing had successfully pursued this strategy, particularly in its trade division. However, because of the general tightening of the industry during the late sixties and early seventies, Cohen management felt that it was time to stabilize the organization somewhat so that it could cope with the more stringent conditions which industry observers were predicting for the future.

By "stabilization" Cohen management meant its desire to reduce the fluctuations in profitability which were so characteristic of the company. The answer to this problem, management believed, lay in long-range planning: objectives would become clearer and fewer mistakes would be made during the process of reaching these objectives. At the same time, however, management did not want to lose the company's prospecting capabilities. Thus, in the language of our model, Cohen Publishing wished to become an Analyzer.

A close examination of Cohen's present structure-process arrangement, however, suggests that a pure Analyzer strategy probably cannot be pursued by this organization in its present form. First, as mentioned in the example, substantial portions of the company's major operating units (such as the trade and textbook divisions) are organized along functional lines. It does not appear that these functional structures have been developed especially for product-market domains that are inherently stable. Rather, they seem to have evolved solely to achieve the benefits of specialization and efficiency. As a result, trade and text editors—who have been instructed to prospect and rewarded for doing so—frequently have to overcome these "benefits" of specialization and efficiency in order to produce and market their projects in a timely fashion.

To be a true Analyzer, Cohen management would have to decide which of the domains covered by the company's various divisions could indeed be "stabilized." For example, in fields that change little from year to year, editors might be instructed to develop only solid textbooks which could be revised from time to time. Prospecting in these areas would be left to other companies, and new developments would be monitored rather than actively pursued. If proper groupings of this sort could be made, the functional structures that presently exist might need little modification in order to produce quality books on a continuous, efficient basis. These operations would also be centrally planned, coordinated, and controlled. Most importantly, however, editors in these areas would have to be rewarded differently than in the past, for successfully imitating the best products and services of their competitors rather than for the direct development of innovative educational materials.

In domains identified as more turbulent, on the other hand, Cohen Publishing would require major structure-process modifications. Here the current prospecting behavior of editors is already appropriate; it is the context in which they operate that needs changing. With respect to structure, for example, the strict separation of key units such as production and marketing slows down the process of rapid response to perceived product or market opportunities. This functional arrangement would have to be modified to form relatively autonomous groupings that permit editors to work closely with production and marketing people. With respect to changes in process, the most important change concerns planning. Top management's current desire to implement a long-range planning system throughout the organization might adversely affect the adaptive units because their operations could not be planned entirely in advance. To require a strong commitment to plans geared for 3 to 5 years in the future would be self-defeating since these units need to be responsive to perceived opportunities, not to predetermined plans.

In sum, to be a true Analyzer, Cohen Publishing must separate its stable and turbulent product-market domains and then structure the organization differently in each area. Further, such processes as planning, control, and the allocation of rewards must be linked appropriately to each of these different structures. Cohen's present structure-process arrangement is preventing the organization from vigorously pursuing an Analyzer strategy.

ADHERENCE TO AN OUTMODED STRATEGY AND STRUCTURE

Both Daro Developments and Cohen Publishing exhibit a weak link in the strategy-structure relationship. In the final case, Exotic Foods, the organization enjoys a relatively strong strategy-structure alignment. However, the company's environment has changed to such an extent that its present strategy and structure are no longer feasible.

Exotic Foods is a partially integrated food-processing company that produces a fairly broad line of dried fruit, nut, and fish products. During the past 30 years, the company has grown to moderate size in an industry dominated by several large firms.

For many years, Exotic was an industry pioneer in both the processing and marketing of dried fruits and nuts. However, in the face of rising labor costs and increased competition, the company's early dominance in these markets has declined. "Our current markets are almost saturated," says President Jack Milks, "so we're considering moving into several lines of canned vegetables. But before we introduce a new product, we have to be absolutely certain we're not taking on a loser."

The president's concern with profitability may result from Exotic's tenuous cash flow position. Low profit margins in fish products and fruits, coupled with the high overhead costs of maintaining large harvesting and processing operations, have created almost continuous cash flow problems for Exotic Foods in recent years, despite the fact that the company's extreme cost consciousness has led to the appointment of a controller in each of its four major divisions. "Somehow we've got to expand into more profitable markets," Mr. Milks continues, "but we can't sacrifice efficiency to do it."

In an attempt to broaden the firm's base in 1972, Exotic bought a chain of "quick-stop" retail grocery stores. This decision was taken following nearly 18 months of agonizing analysis that frequently led to sharp dissension among members of the top executive group. Last year, due to the chain's increasingly lackluster performance, Exotic seriously began to consider selling the stores, though it seemed certain that divestment would result in a sizable loss.

Avram Goldman, vice-president for marketing and the primary proponent of the acquisition, commented sardonically: "Our timing was terrible. When I first suggested buying those stores, all of the important indicators were good. But by the time people who had almost no grasp of the factors involved in retail sales had aired every one of their apprehensions, the situation was completely different. This company's so phobic about losses that we plan and argue and replan until we're unable to take decisive action."

Exotic Foods is divided into four functionally organized units: field operations, grocery products, manufacturing and merchandising (nonfood lines), and administration. Each of these divisions is highly specialized with responsibility for coordination and control resting at the corporate level. However, in recent years, top management has found it necessary to rely heavily on ad hoc committees to provide coordination across the four divisions. These committees are "expediting" groups rather than permanent departments, and their composition changes periodically. "Our product lines, production processes, and organization structure have been established for years," says Mr. Milks, "But we're making much greater use of our committee system now to resolve disagreements that arise between the divisions. Frankly, these committees have not increased efficiency very much, and, if we add more product lines, I don't think we'll be able to continue operating this way."

Like Daro Developments and Cohen Publishing, Exotic Foods is experiencing difficulty in coping with its environment. However, Exotic's problem is of a much different sort. Up to the present time, management has had a reasonably clear conception of the organization's strategy. Exotic Foods is a Defender within the food-processing industry, one whose product-market domain has remained fairly narrow and stable for years. Moreover, during this time management has taken a series of steps designed to bring the organization's structure and processes consistently into line with the requirements of the Defender model. For example, the organization's structure has not varied to any significant extent from the functional groupings which were established at the company's inception. This structure was further reinforced through vertical integration—harvesting, processing, and some retail sales now occur under the same corporate roof. Finally, in order to ensure production efficiency, each of the four divisions was assigned a controller whose duty was to develop procedures for keeping costs down.

Now it appears that Exotic's environment is changing. The company has experienced rapid saturation of its primary markets, yet its current structure and efficiency orientation seem to be preventing the organization from moving in a more effective direction. This problem is compounded by Exotic's experience with the retail grocery chain. Not only was this venture undertaken awkwardly, but its likely aftermath (sales of the stores at a tremendous loss) has also left several members of top management leery about making any major changes to solve the company's problems. Thus, Exotic Foods illustrates a Reactor characteristic that is probably more widespread than the characteristics exhibited by either Daro Developments or Cohen Publishing, a tendency for management to cling to a particular strategy-structure relationship in the face of a major shift in the organization's environment.

As was pointed out in Chapter 3, the primary risk faced by a Defender is ineffectiveness, the inability to locate new product or market opportunities. Indeed, in times of crisis, the typical Defender is probably both unable and unwilling to search for solutions to its adaptive problems by scanning the environment for potential opportunities. Instead, it is more likely to rely on its distinctive competences to produce adaptive solutions. This appears to be the case at Exotic. As profit margins have slipped in recent years, Exotic management has not actively investigated new product and/or market areas (except canned vegetables) but instead has established an ad hoc committee system that cuts across division boundaries. The mandate for these various committees has been to find ways of improving operating efficiency and thereby reducing costs, a distinctly Defender-like tactic. However, by management's own admission, these committees have not been very successful, and they are destined to become even less so if Exotic adds more products to its line in the future.

What can Exotic Foods do at this point? It is clear that the organization cannot return to being a pure Defender in its current market. It is also very unlikely that Exotic can become a Prospector; its vertically integrated, functional structure does not permit rapid movement toward new product or market opportunities. Most likely, Exotic will be forced to become an Analyzer, keeping a firm base of healthy products while moving into carefully selected new market or product areas. To do so, management will need to develop the ability to scan the environment for potential opportunities opened up by Prospectors, and it will have to learn how to incorporate these opportunities into its own organizational system on a cost-efficient basis. Exotic's current structure-process arrangements clearly will not suffice in this regard; an Analyzer strategy cannot be pursued with a patched-up Defender structure. In fact, to escape its predicament, Exotic Foods will most likely require a thorough diagnosis of its present operations, a topic to which we turn in the next chapter.

CONCLUSIONS

This chapter concludes our discussion of the four organization types. As noted in Chapter 2, these four types encompass most of the organizational behaviors which we have observed in several widely differing industries. Reactors represent a "residual" type of behavior in that organizations are forced into this response mode when they are unable to pursue one of the three stable strategies of Defender, Analyzer, or Prospector.

As illustrated by the examples of Daro Developments, Cohen Publishing, and Exotic Foods, Reactors are unstable organizations because they do not possess a set of mechanisms which allows them to respond consistently to their environments over time. Frequently, such organizations fall into an unpleasant cycle of responding inappropriately to environmental change and uncertainty, performing poorly as a result, and then being reluctant to act aggressively in the future.

Although there are undoubtedly numerous reasons why organizations become Reactors, we have identified three. First, top management may not have clearly articulated the organization's strategy. Such appears to be the case at Daro Developments where the chief executive's absence has left a strategic void. Without a unified, cohesive statement of the organization's direction, consistent and aggressive behavior is precluded.

A second and perhaps more common cause of organizational instability is that management does not fully shape the organization's structure and processes to fit a chosen strategy. Unless all of the domain, engineering, and administrative decisions required to have an operational strategy are properly aligned, strategy is a mere statement, not an effective guide for behavior. Cohen Publishing wishes to become an Analyzer, but its present structure-process arrangement is inconsistent with its desired strategy.

A third reason for instability and perhaps ultimate failure, exemplified by Exotic Foods, is a tendency for management to maintain the organization's strategy-structure relationship despite overwhelming changes in environmental conditions. Here is where a Reactor must come squarely to grips with its behavior. Will management be able to tolerate its own indecisiveness further, or will it move the organization toward one of the three viable strategies?

In the next chapter, we address this question and related issues by using our model of organizational adaptation (the adaptive cycle) and the four organization types to diagnose patterns of organizational behavior and to indicate where and how organizations can make adjustments in order to achieve a more effective relationship with their environments.

Chapter 7

Applications of the Model

In the preceding six chapters, we described and illustrated a general model of organizational adaptation—an adaptive cycle that encompasses the key decisions and actions that occur as an organization perceives, enacts, and responds to conditions in and around its domain. The adaptive cycle defines the linkages among these decisions and actions, emphasizes the need for consistency, and acknowledges the constraints which one managerial action or decision imposes on subsequent organizational behaviors. We also provided four "overlays" for the adaptive cycle, each describing a particular pattern of movement through the adaptive process. Our research indicates that organizations can be typed according to their response pattern and that the actions of a given type of organization are internally consistent and self-sustaining.

The question before us now is the inevitable "So what?" Can this theoretical framework aid managers in diagnosing the current adaptive posture of their organization? Can it provide guidance in maintaining a desired strategy? Does it suggest the actions necessary to move from one strategy to another? The answer to each of these questions is, we believe, a guarded "yes." The answer is guarded for two reasons: first, because the framework has not yet been completely tested and, second, because it is difficult for managers to suspend their past perceptions and behaviors and view their organization's condition and needs objectively, even with the help of a new theory.

The purpose of this chapter is to illustrate how the model (the adaptive cycle and the four strategic types) can be used for diagnostic purposes under ideal conditions of managerial objectivity and information availability, and then to discuss applications under normal or less than ideal circumstances. In the first example, Alpha Electronics, a consultant confirms the organization's current Prospector strategy as essentially sound. Because top management was willing to become actively involved in a relatively thorough diagnosis of the company's condition, the few modifications recommended by the consultant were readily accepted. In the second and third cases, the diagnostic and change process is hampered by strong, but understandable, resistance by management. At Fortress Insurance, consultants have recommended that this Defender become an Analyzer, but top management is not ready to make the necessary changes in organizational structure and process to pursue this strategy. At Dalton Chemicals, a move from Defender to Prospector is being considered, but a consultant's recommendation against this move is not accepted by a key member of the top-management group.

AN APPLICATION OF THE MODEL UNDER IDEAL CONDITIONS

The following example (a composite of behaviors in several real organizations) illustrates the application of the adaptive model as a diagnostic and prescriptive device under ideal circumstances.

Alpha Electronics is a relatively small (1,200 employees) but rapidly growing manufacturer of complex test equipment used by the computer industry and other firms involved in the design and construction of sophisticated electronic devices. Bill Cobb, Alpha's president (and one-third owner) is a brilliant applied physicist who has been directly involved in developing and patenting most of the key components of his firm's products. However, because he is so active in research and development, he has bowed to the wishes of his two absentee partners and brought in a marketing specialist (hired from a computer manufacturer) and a controller (hired from a nonelectronics manufacturing firm of which one of the partners is a director) to help manage the business. Over the past year, Bill has left most day-to-day operations to the marketing manager and controller while he spent his time in the lab and on a well-deserved vacation.

During his vacation, Bill had time to think seriously about the long-term future of his firm. He recalled with growing unease a number of events of the past year, particularly the sudden departure of Tom Diller, who had done an outstanding job of operating one of the manufacturing units and who had been in line for a large raise and stock bonus. Tom had gone to work for a large electronics firm and, Bill felt, if given the opportunity, he could bring that organization into serious competition with Alpha.

Upon his return, Bill sought out an acquaintance in the business school at the university where Bill frequently lectured. The acquaintance in turn directed Bill to a consultant who was also a part-time lecturer at the university. Bill invited the consultant for a tour of the plant and shared with him some of the concerns that had been building in his mind.

"The main thing is," Bill concluded, "I'm simply not sure that we are headed where I want us to go. I have the feeling that some of the things we were doing right are beginning to go sour."

The consultant suggested an overall appraisal of Alpha's external environment and internal operations, starting with Cobb himself; Karen Watson, the marketing vice-president; and Curtis Van Ortman, the controller. These initial discussions produced some interesting insights into areas of goal agreement and dissent among the three top executives. Bill felt the firm must continue to pioneer new components to meet the testing needs of increasingly sophisticated equipment. Karen agreed, but also wanted to broaden Alpha's market by adapting some of its exotic components for sale to smaller firms with less complicated needs. "Alpha's cash flow has to be improved," she said. "We need to increase our sales volume while holding down costs."

"That's exactly what I explained to Tom Diller," Curtis said. "He came in demanding to know why I had not okayed a $12,000 contract to expand that little lab of his in unit one. I explained that each unit demanding its own research facilities when we had a damn good lab on the main floor was precisely the sort of thing that was keeping us at a return rate I considered unhealthy—in fact, embarrassing."

"Now I see why Tom left," Bill responded. "I half promised Tom and the other unit heads that we would move toward decentralizing the main lab—sort of give each group its own area of operation complete with R&D.

At the conclusion of the meeting, Bill and Karen agreed to begin a systematic survey, with the aid of a long-time industry observer, of market opportunities in both the traditional product areas served by Alpha and the new, less expensive arena suggested by Karen. In the meantime, Curtis agreed to update his figures on the returns generated by each of the products, cost out all the capital requests presently in hand (before denying any more), and list all the cost-saving moves he thought were warranted.

While the top group was busy on its tasks, the consultant asked Bill to introduce him to the unit heads and their subordinates and to arrange a series of meetings which would take him down to a sample of first-line production teams. The consultant discovered in these interviews that Bill had succeeded in hiring an enormously bright and enthusiastic group of young engineers and scientists. The unit heads were excited about describing their product lines, particularly the latest innovations they had devised. "We like to say," one of them explained, "that no big piece of test equipment comes off the line exactly as it was designed—we make improvements while it's going out the door."

At the shop floor, the consultant found a much less enthusiastic group of supervisors. "We're caught in the middle," one said. "Bill (the president) and Charlie (the unit head) run down every 5 minutes with a change order, and then we get called on the carpet by the accountants when costs exceed our estimates."

The consultant discovered that while each unit had considerable autonomy with regard to production schedules and design modifications, unit heads were only marginally involved in pricing and cost accounting. The units were not set up as true profit centers, and only recently had unit cost data been accumulated.

By the time the consultant had worked his way down the hierarchy to the production units, Bill and Karen had completed the first phase of their market survey. The preliminary findings indicated that Alpha still had a sizable (though shrinking) lead in the market for high-priced, complex test equipment, and that there was indeed a broad market for less expensive test units using some of the key (patented) components of the more complex equipment.

As the consultant discussed these data with the top team, he explained his own diagnosis. Bill, Karen, and most of the unit heads, the consultant believed, wanted Alpha to behave in a "prospecting" mode, and the company appeared to have the capability to do so. Alpha had been first in the market with much of its equipment, and only now were some of its competitors beginning to move into several of the areas pioneered by Alpha. If the firm's success was to continue, however, the organization would have to do more, not less, research across the full range of its product line. Thus, the consultant explained, Bill's inclination to decentralize many aspects of R&D was probably sound.

Decentralizing research and development activities, however, would probably not be enough. The unit heads felt little responsibility for cost control or long-term customer service. In addition to R&D, they needed to have the responsibility for producing, pricing, servicing, and making a profit on their output. In other words, the unit should be a complete profit center.

The move into lower-priced test equipment seemed like a good idea, the consultant noted, but one that would probably detract from Alpha's main efforts unless carefully controlled. He recommended that a wholly owned subsidiary be formed, possibly around the acquisition of a small existing manufacturer of simple equipment. Such an organization would probably already have developed expertise in cost control and could gradually introduce the higher quality components available at Alpha. Moreover, as some of the larger equipment reached the point where designs were reasonably set and a continuing market appeared to exist, these lines could perhaps also be shifted to the subsidiary.

The meeting continued on through dinner and late into the evening as the group tested out the conditions necessary for growth along the proposed lines. The consultant pointed out that if Alpha made the recommended changes, it would probably operate for some time as a collection of self-contained divisions or units with a partially decentralized sales force. In addition, Bill could continue working on product innovations in his small central lab. Of course, limits would have to be placed on capital expenditures, but eventually the profits from the subsidiary should be such as to allow even broader prospecting.

Analysis

Without moving precisely point by point, the consultant whom Bill Cobb called in at Alpha Electronics applied a diagnostic checklist quite similar to our theoretical model. The consultant examined Alpha's profile with respect to the three elements of the adaptive cycle, typed the organization as a Prospector, noted inconsistencies in its adjustment pattern, and made recommendations designed to solidify Alpha's strategy as a Prospector. However, this diagnostic process can be seen more clearly by examining it step by step.

Domain Decisions   The consultant first tested the degree of consistency that existed among Alpha's *perceived* domain, its *enacted* domain, its *desired* domain, and its *objective* domain. In this particular company, there was a fairly high degree of consistency.

Bill Cobb had perceived the need for test equipment that was as sophisticated as the elaborate circuitry on computers and other devices with which he worked. His creative genius had led to the development of immediately marketable components that could be utilized in such test equipment. Almost overnight Cobb had been "in business," with partners eager to buy into his firm. Bill had designed and led production of a wide range of equipment which, to this point, had been far enough ahead of the field virtually to sell itself. Thus, enactment had closely followed perception: Alpha was pushing out in the complex test equipment area as fast as the genius of Cobb and his young scientists would allow, with each unit serving to advance the state of the art within its particular specialty. Furthermore, there was little question that Bill and many of his managers desired to continue to be pioneers in the development and manufacture of sophisticated test equipment. Finally, it appeared that market conditions, when viewed as objectively as possible, were such that Alpha could pursue this course for some time to come, providing that management kept a closer eye on profits and generated enough operating funds to finance the continuing research needed to stay at the edge of the art.

Engineering Decisions   At this point in the diagnosis, the question before Alpha and the consultant was, "Could Alpha deliver?" That is, did Alpha possess the technical resources necessary to remain a Prospector? The answer appeared to be "yes"—if these resources could be appropriately allocated and developed. The scientific know-how was clearly present, but Alpha's technological processes were at that time dispersed among the central lab and the production units with little clear notion of the role of each.

Administrative Decisions   It was evident to the consultant that Alpha was a Prospector both by chance and design but that its structure and control processes were not yet completely consistent with that market orientation. If Alpha were to continue producing advanced equipment only, it would need to focus unit managers' attention on a clear product area and turn these units into self-contained divisions capable of researching, designing, building, and servicing a limited line of equipment at the edge of the art. Concurrently, only a small set of corporate offices would be needed to provide basic research support, market analysis and follow-up, and overall financial control. The existing admixture of centralized control and decentralized responsibility was distinctly troublesome.

Thus, in the language of our model, administration had not been brought fully into line with existing domain and engineering decisions. Particularly apparent to the consultant was the fact that Alpha's structure and process were not geared toward facilitating upcoming moves. The idea of expanding the company's product line to include cheaper, smaller, but still high-quality, test equipment seemed sound, both from the market survey and from Alpha's need for a steady flow of funds.

However, to attempt to move into this market with a structure solely designed for prospecting might well prove disastrous. High-volume production of standardized units, however innovative, was not in keeping with Alpha's prime technological competence. Rather, it seemed to be much more reasonable to buy into that market, purchasing in the process the needed production and administrative expertise. In this fashion, Alpha's R&D skills could be fully exploited without overwhelming the management of an innovative operation.

Insurance Against Primary Risk   In this instance, the consultant presented a ready-made "insurance policy" in the form of a subsidiary which could operate in a more stable market segment than that of Alpha and in a more cost-efficient manner than was possible in the parent firm. The long-run task now facing Alpha and the consultant was that of developing management's ability to determine when a particular product design was well enough developed to allow it to be shifted to the subsidiary while the experimental designs were retained within the several divisions of the parent organization. Solving this problem would, of course, be a continuous process that would require a carefully constructed reward system in order to maintain equity between the parent company and the subsidiary.

At the moment, the consultant, the top-management group, and representatives from each of Alpha's operating units are designing a licensing arrangement which will make it profitable to the various divisions to "sell" designs to the subsidiary as soon as they are perfected. The "price" the subsidiary is willing to pay for new products will in turn provide a market test of their value. A portion of the royalties paid by the subsidiary will go directly to the parent division that developed the product. The division can use these funds in any way it chooses, the expectation being that most of the royalties would be plowed back into research and development. Similarly, additional subsidiary operations are being considered as offshoots for Alpha-designed components in nontest equipment areas. With these actions, Alpha is designing a system which will allow it to move into new areas continuously (ahead of its competition) while still reaping maximum benefits from its R&D investments.

It is not always the case, however, that management's perceived, desired, enacted, and objective domains are as consistent as those at Alpha or that the organization's needs for internal consistency and insurance against risk are as readily apparent. The next two examples illustrate these more complex and realistic circumstances.

APPLICATIONS OF THE MODEL
UNDER NORMAL CONDITIONS

Fortress Insurance, at least until the early seventies, was one of the largest Midwestern-based underwriters of individual and group life insurance. The company was founded in the early part of this century and grew rapidly through the teens and twenties. It did not become a truly national organization, however, until the late forties, and it was not until the early sixties that sales outside the Midwestern region outstripped those in the company's original area of operation. While still strong in the Midwest (approximately one-third of all sales are in that region), major inroads in both sales and investments have been made in all areas of the continental United States. (Group insurance offerings had begun in the early fifties.)

In the late sixties, Fortress's rate of growth in life insurance began to slow. Reluctantly, top management began to consider the possibility of broadening Fortress's activities in the direction of becoming a full-line insurance company (adding auto, home, and casualty insurance plans), a move which several of Fortress's competitors were already making. Three separate consulting contracts were let between 1968 and 1970 to analyze Fortress's present and future market position, and all three studies, in one form or another, recommended movement into full-line operation.

In 1971, with the advice and assistance of the consulting firm that carried out the 1970 study, Fortress acquired controlling interest in three Midwestern firms, which among them offered a full line of auto, casualty, and homeowners insurance. Following the consultant's advice, Fortress has left the top managers of the acquired firms in control and has moved cautiously toward the ultimate goal of integrating these operations into the Fortress structure. At this point, while reasonably satisfied with the dollar flow from these operations, Fortress officials are concerned because they do not feel they are capitalizing on the complementary market and cost-efficiency effects they had anticipated. Only in the Midwest have substantial moves been made to integrate sales and claims forces, and even there integration is far from complete. In many areas, at least three distinct sales forces are still in the field, and life salesmen are making little apparent effort to push the new lines.

Concurrent with the move to the full-line offering, Fortress has made a reluctant and belated (compared to their competitors) move toward regionalizing their operations. Starr Insurance, a company whose sales were half those of Fortress in 1950 and virtually equal in 1970, announced the move to full regionalization 4 years ago.

The advertising campaign accompanying the move stressed Starr's effort to bring the entire organization closer to the customer in order to provide more rapid response to information and claims requests and to provide, overall, "small company service with big company safety."

To this point, Fortress has established Northwest, Southwest, and Northeast regional offices; the head office serves as the Midwestern regional office. None of these offices, however, is full-service. Life salesmen throughout the country report to regional managers, but only in the Southwestern office (located nearest to corporate headquarters) is there a complete underwriting and claims staff. All group sales and claims are still routed to the home office, as are all nonlife policies and claims. Only in the Northwestern region has an attempt been made to collect all sales personnel under the regional manager. A cynical observer of Fortress's regionalization efforts to this point refers to them as a move toward "dispersed centralization."

Analysis

Top management at Fortress is frustrated and uncertain about the proper direction for the organization. In some instances, management has made moves which it feels have created rather than solved problems. Consequently, management is hesitant to push forward aggressively in any direction and yet it believes that some action is necessary.

Could the same diagnostic approach illustrated in the Alpha Electronics case be applied here? We believe it could, and quite profitably, but it is highly unlikely that Fortress Insurance will follow the approach used at Alpha. Quite the contrary, top management at Fortress is in no mood to subject itself to a probing analysis of the organization's perceived, enacted, desired, and objective domains nor to explore the requisite engineering and administrative actions each might require.

Assuming such analysis were sought, however, what would it reveal? Many of the needed answers are contained (sometimes implicitly) in the reports of the three consultants mentioned earlier.

Domain Decisions   At Fortress, the dominant coalition's perceptions concerning the appropriate domain for their organization appear to be belatedly coming into agreement with objective conditions in the environment. The three studies commissioned by Fortress unanimously concluded that firms offering full lines of insurance would have a general competitive advantage over those providing a single type of insurance. Fortress's declining market share and the earlier moves by competitors toward full-line offerings seemed to confirm these conclusions. Nevertheless, the behavior of Fortress's top managers suggests that their desired domain was still that of a single-line life insurance offering, that is, continuing to do what they knew best how to do. Thus, it is not surprising that Fortress's enacted domain is not consistent with objective market conditions. Instead, top management is moving slowly, grudgingly, and frequently ineffectually away from what it wants to do toward what it feels is probably necessary.

Engineering Decisions The hesitancy with which Fortress is enacting its new domain is clearly reflected in its failure to solve the organization's engineering problem, the need to develop a cost-efficient approach to the sales and service of its expanded product line. No formal, organizationwide effort has been made to retrain sales representatives to handle the complete product line, and virtually all underwriting and claims activities for each line are still handled by separate staffs (which have differing methods and philosophies).

Administrative Decisions Fortress's inability to realize potential cost savings from combined full-line operations is understandable when its current administrative dilemma is examined. Top management has hesitated to combine clerical and administrative staffs along functional lines until agreement is reached on the extent to which regionalization will be pursued. Management groups in the acquired companies have abetted this hesitancy with assertions concerning the uniqueness of their operations which appear to be self-serving, but which Fortress's management has been fearful of discounting. Moreover, two of the three subsidiary managers have argued that regionalization should occur within, not across, product lines, an argument supported by several of Fortress's most senior and successful life-insurance salesmen. Such arguments have prolonged a debate which several members of Fortress's dominant coalition were reluctant to end simply because regionalization will most likely diminish the degree of control exercised by home-office personnel.

The Starting Point for Change Fortress is clearly reacting reluctantly at all points in the adaptive cycle. This reluctance should not be surprising, however, since Fortress appears to be, in the language of our model, a Defender that has been forced out of its niche by changes in the environment. Fortress is being pushed toward an Analyzer market orientation without the technological processes and administrative structure required to support this strategy.

As is most often the case when major changes in response patterns are required (or desired), a new administrative solution is the key to successful change. Entrepreneurial and engineering decisions flowing out of the existing administrative group are likely to reflect variations on traditional themes—solutions which serve to protect the present power balance within the organization.

In Fortress's case, a rapid move to full regionalization appears to provide a viable starting point for overall administrative reform. Combining the resources of Fortress and its three subsidiaries, there is sufficient managerial and technical talent to staff five full-service regions. Task forces can be formed to assist in creating regional centers, training clerical and sales personnel in full-line operation, and setting up efficient underwriting and claims procedures. Capital investments will need to be made, of course, especially for building and data-processing facilities. (But note that an early decision toward regionalization might have resulted in the acquisition of nonlife subsidiaries whose existing facilities would have met the needs of geographic dispersion.) Ultimately, decisions will need to be made that arrange home-office resources along product or functional lines, but it would probably be easier to restructure at the regional level where most changes will result in enhanced rather than diminished managerial status and responsibility. Overall reductions in sales personnel can be handled through attrition (the lowest turnover rate among the four organizations is 12 percent), and the initial redundancy will protect current markets while the entire sales force is undergoing retraining. A similar approach to home-office staff reductions can be followed, thus lessening the resistance to necessary changes there.

To make the required administrative changes, Fortress will most likely need outside assistance of two kinds. First, Fortress should probably hire a manager with extensive experience in regional operations. Second, Fortress needs to bring in experts in organizational change processes, persons skilled in anticipating and helping to resolve the conflicts that inevitably arise from any large-scale change effort.

At Fortress, the first of these moves is far more likely to occur than the second, but neither appears imminent. Instead, Fortress's situation (primarily with respect to earnings and growth) will probably have to get much worse before the dominant coalition takes decisive action.

We suggested earlier that, wherever possible, adjustments to administrative structure and process should be made prior to, rather than following, extensive shifts in domain or technology. This prescription is, of course, far easier to offer than to document. Nevertheless, we have come to believe, along with others (e.g., Ansoff and Stewart, 1967), that lack of administrative knowledge and skill may pose a more significant barrier to organizational growth and development than either financial or technological constraints. Unless the existing dominant coalition has a clear conception of how increased environmental uncertainties can be absorbed and new internal interdependencies managed, numerous routes to profitable growth may be ignored, avoided, or pursued so cautiously that possible levels of return are unrealized. This point is further emphasized in the next case.

Dalton Chemicals was founded in the late thirties as a bulk processor and supplier of two compounds widely used by major chemical companies in the production of commercial and consumer products. The company had well-established sources of supply for raw materials, and Bill Dalton, along with two of his chemical engineering classmates, created soundly engineered production processes which have proved so cost-efficient that Dalton has survived competition from the major chemical companies themselves and other bulk producers. To date, competitors have been successful only where their locations have proved advantageous in terms of transportation costs.

In 1963, Morris Dalton, the son of the founder, completed his doctorate in chemistry and joined the firm as assistant director of research and development, a six-person group which over the years had served primarily a process engineering and quality assurance advisory function. By 1968, Morris was R&D director, and the department had grown to 20 people, including six chemists with doctorates. Bill Dalton, now chairman of the board, and Harvey Thompson, a chemical engineer who had succeeded Bill Dalton as president, had somewhat grudgingly acceded to the growth of the R&D unit mainly because young Morris had led the way in the development of a third compound, which could utilize existing raw material sources and production processes and which was slowly making a significant contribution to sales and profits.

In 1970, Morris Dalton announced the development of a consumer product that utilized two of the Dalton compounds and appeared to have features unavailable in competitors' lines. After considerable debate, centered around Bill Dalton's and Harvey Thompson's argument that the firm had been profitable precisely because it had avoided competing in the consumer market, it was decided that ample funds were available to attempt a limited venture with the new product. Careful engineering, including rebuilding some equipment taken off the main production line, held capital expenditures to slightly under $300,000 for the product. The major new expense was for a two-person addition to Dalton's historically small sales group and a modest advertising campaign aimed at major distributors.

The new product, sold under the trade name Dalmor, moved into production in early 1971. During its first 3 years, Dalmore had steady sales growth, and by mid-1974 the entire project was neatly in the black. However, it was also clear early in 1974 that competitive products from the major firms would be on the shelves by 1975, after which Dalmor would be lucky to hold the market share it had achieved. Nevertheless, Morris was excited about the product's success and the movement into the consumer market, and he and his group were ready with two new products and had a third in the last stages of testing.

The set of decisions that Dalton management now faced was the most important that had come before it since the firm was founded. Bill Dalton wanted to retire, and Harvey Thompson was hoping to conclude his service within 3 years after succeeding Bill as chairman. Morris was the logical successor to Harvey Thompson, but both Harvey and Bill were worried about the direction in which Morris would take the company, particularly if Morris became the sole executive officer following Harvey's retirement. In discussions with the law firm that handled Dalton Chemicals' legal affairs, Bill and Harvey were advised to contact a consultant for help in these decisions. The head of the law firm suggested a consulting partnership which had been of major help to another of the firm's clients, and a contact was made.

Although the consulting firm specialized in acquisitions and mergers, two of the partners had become increasingly interested in the administrative problems associated with new ventures by mature firms. Their interests had led them to consider much the same set of variables suggested in our diagnostic model, and thus their approach with Dalton followed essentially the same procedure used by the consultant in the first case in this chapter, Alpha Electronics.

After extensive discussions with Bill, Harvey, and Morris, the consultants met with the heads of production, sales, and engineering, and spent the better part of a day hearing about new products and ideas from Morris and his group. In addition, the consultants assigned two of the junior members of their firm to make an appraisal of the long-term soundness of Dalton's main bulk markets and of the prospects for the new products being considered for marketing under the Dalmor brand. Following further private conversations with Bill, Harvey, and Morris, the consultants scheduled a weekend meeting for the top team and key members of the board.

At the meeting, the consultants led the group through an analysis of Dalton's current situation and its future prospects. The bulk compound market which Dalton had staked out over the years was apparently quite sound for the next 10 to 15 years at least. No major growth in new bulk markets was likely, but a steady 3 to 5 percent increase in sales seemed safe to predict. Moreover, the third compound which Morris and his group had developed had growth potential outside its present uses, as did a fourth bulk compound under test. Thus, if Dalton chose to remain essentially a Defender, that strategy appeared sound and profitable, and no substantial administrative or technological adjustments would be necessary.

Next, the major risks facing a Defender, new product development or substantial domain shifts, were acknowledged by the consultants, and the costs and benefits of using the Dalmor development as a hedge against these risks were examined. On the positive side, it seemed likely that Morris and his group were quite capable of developing additional commercial and consumer products to broaden the Dalmor line; this group had already gained widespread recognition within the industry for their basic and applied knowledge in the areas related to Dalton's raw materials and compounds. On the negative side, it appeared that moving toward a broad Dalmor line would require both major capital investments in processing and packaging machinery and a significant increase in sales and marketing personnel. Moreover, the consultants were concerned that an expansion of the Dalmor line would draw serious competition from the major chemical companies (their information was that the major companies' soon-to-be-released products would be priced to compete with the successful Dalmor consumer product and would be supported by a large advertising effort).

Discussions on these points continued for several hours with a consensus emerging that the administrative shift required to expand the Dalmor line was perhaps larger than anyone within the firm had imagined. Dalton Chemicals had no real marketing capability, and its sales group was small and highly specialized. Four of the five representatives were graduate chemists or chemical engineers, and all regarded themselves as professional consultants, not bulk-compound salesmen. All of the key managerial personnel at Dalton were geared, both by training and experience, for the cost-efficient operation of bulk processes, and no one but Morris had an interest in new product development. Moreover, in the discussions, it became increasingly clear that neither Morris nor any of the members of his group had long-term interests in producing and marketing consumer products. Their real interest lay in the development of new product and process ideas.

Early in the second day of the meeting, the consultants unveiled what appeared to be an ideal strategy for Dalton. Dalton Chemicals would remain essentially unchanged. Harvey Thompson would move to chairman and Carl Russell, Harvey's top assistant, would move into the presidency. Morris would become vicechairman of the board of Dalton and president of Dalmor Laboratories, a wholly owned but independently managed subsidiary with two main purposes: (1) developing new bulk compounds for production by Dalton, and (2) developing commercial and consumer products to be sold to or licensed for production by other chemical companies. Dalmor Laboratories would receive royalties on compounds developed for production by Dalton, and the soundness of Dalmor for the first several years would be assured by payments of royalties on the two compounds already developed by Morris and his group. No major administrative changes would be required under this strategy, and the equipment already used by Dalmor in the production of its one consumer product would be used throughout the life of that product (if it could not be licensed to another producer) and then maintained for prototype processing of new developments.

Analysis

In Dalton's case, the consultants' analyses and advice appeared to make maximum use of the organization's existing resources and also provided insurance against Dalton's primary risk: the development of new compounds or processes that might make its main products obsolete. Moreover, the consultants' recommendations, in effect, "purchased" this insurance at minimum cost.

Despite the apparent soundness of the consultants' advice, however, it seems unlikely to be accepted. Morris Dalton is still enamored with the idea of "running the business" and is in no sense convinced that he cannot "challenge the big boys on their own turf." Now, more than a year following the weekend meeting, no real resolution to Dalton Chemicals' dilemma has been achieved. Bill Dalton and Harvey Thompson are still in their posts and hopeful that in time Morris will agree to the consultants' recommendations.

A DIAGNOSTIC CHECKLIST

These three case examples have provided vehicles for examining a diagnostic approach that goes beyond many, if not most, approaches typically employed by organization and management theorists today. The prime value of this approach, we believe, lies in (1) its view of the organization as a total system and (2) its emphasis on administrative (structure-process) decisions as crucial elements in successful organizational adaptation.

The most important features of this diagnostic approach can be summarized in a list of questions that need to be asked by management, arranged in the order in which they should be posed. This checklist is shown in Figure 7-1.

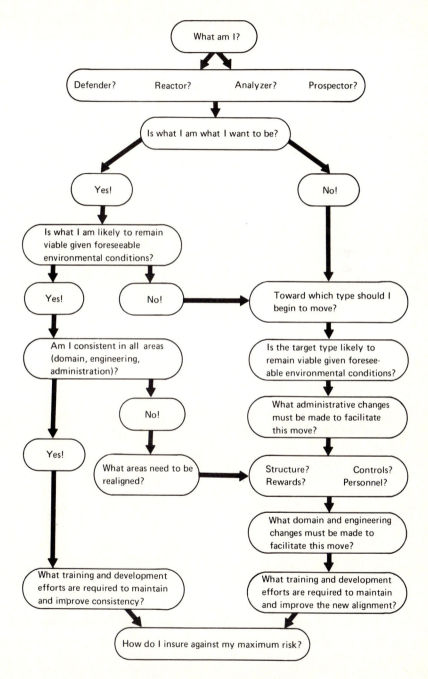

Figure 7-1 Diagnostic checklist.

The checklist suggests that diagnosis should begin with an examination of the organization's current shape—its enacted product-market domain and its technology, structure, and processes. Of course, determining an organization's type may be difficult. The dominant coalition's image of the organization may not correspond at all with the view of others or with the organization's actual behavior. Moreover, what type an organization is can really only be answered in comparative terms; it is either more or less diversified, aggressive, or innovative than its peers within its industry group. Comparison of organization types across industries is only of minimal value (unless the focus is specifically on, for example, conglomerates).

The second question asks whether management is satisfied with its basic strategic orientation. For many, if not most, organizations the internally generated answer to this question is likely to be "yes," simply because the existing strategy has been developed by those answering the question. Thus, unless the dominant coalition is quite new, with few links to the existing organizational strategy, a "no" answer is likely to occur only when (1) the strategy is not what was intended, or (2) environmental events have been adverse and dramatic enough to force rethinking.

If the first two questions are answered as objectively as possible, then the stage is set to either:

1 Verify the soundness of the existing strategy over the foreseeable future; make certain that technological and structure-process decisions are in line with this strategy; and move to develop or bolster the organization's insurance against the primary risk associated with its strategy; or

2 Identify the desired (perhaps necessary) new strategy and verify its soundness; move to make the necessary structure-process changes which will allow movement to that strategy; utilize this new administrative setup to generate the specific market and engineering moves required to implement the new strategy; and, again, develop means of insuring against the primary risk associated with the new strategy.

Need for Outside Consultants

Note that the checklist (and the discussion of it) once more emphasizes the importance of making key administrative changes before engineering or market changes. Such changes usually include bringing into the dominant coalition new skills and perspectives and supporting these additions with appropriate structure-process modifications.

In addition, the cases explored in this chapter and the discussion of the use of the diagnostic checklist shown in Figure 7-1 both point to the value of bringing outside opinions and expertise into the process of organizational change. As suggested earlier, members of an organization's current dominant coalition are almost certain to be myopic concerning the flaws of strategies and structures which they have had a major part in building. However, even when organizations have clear indications that both their alignment with their environment and their mechanisms for handling internal interdependencies are in need of thorough evaluation, members of the dominant coalition may be unable to envision the model toward which they should move or the process of getting there. Both theory and research indicate that organizations tend to search for new approaches in the narrow terrain around known solutions. Limited search occurs not only because it is cheaper and provides security but also because many, more divergent alternatives are simply not in the conceptual repertoire of the top decision makers. Thus, outside consultants with various specialized skills may be necessary to help top management conceive and explore alternative strategies and structures.

Once new strategy and structure goals have been identified, the process of moving toward them may also benefit from outside help in the form of both consultants and new management personnel. For example, the transition from the functionally structured, centrally controlled system of the Defender toward the mixed system of the Analyzer or the product-structured, decentralized system of the Prospector requires rethinking not only roles and relationships but also approaches to communications, control, and rewards. Although some new skills can be acquired by bringing in outside managerial talent, many work groups (managers and their subordinates) at all levels of the organization may need to be trained to accept new roles and responsibilities. Experts in organization change and development may be of major assistance in preparing for and carrying out such transitions.

Though the need for outside consultants may be clear in a specific case, the type of consultant to bring in may not be readily apparent. While external specialists may offer fresher and more objective advice to a particular management, they too are limited in the conceptual models that they possess. For example, consultants whose expertise revolves around the relationship between strategy and structure may not possess the knowledge of interpersonal relations needed to implement large-scale changes in organizational behavior. Conversely, behavioral experts, such as Organization Development (OD) theorists and practitioners, may not be completely familiar with the concept of strategy and its implications for organizational structure and process. Therefore, the former group of advisors may aid in the development of alternative market strategies and the structural arrangements needed to implement them, but these specialists may not be fully aware of the attitudinal and behavioral obstacles that lie in the way of a successful transition to a new form of organization. Behavioral experts, on the other hand, may be skilled at facilitating the process of change throughout the organization, but they may tend to ignore the target of change (an improved alignment with the environment) and its potential ramifications for structure, work flow processes, control systems, and so on. Thus, despite their relevance, neither group of outside advisors may be prepared to offer the organization the full array of knowledge and expertise required to employ the diagnostic checklist illustrated in Figure 7-1. In our view, managers must possess an operational model of organizational adaptation so that they will be intelligent consumers of the advice which they are offered about diagnosing and changing their organizational systems.

Differences in Consulting Approaches   It is worth mentioning here that consultants and consulting firms differ not only in their areas of prime expertise but also in the manner in which they interact with the organization. Major differences in consulting style are illustrated in the three examples in this chapter, particularly in the cases of Alpha Electronics and Fortress Insurance.

At Fortress, three separate consulting organizations were hired, in sequence, to examine Fortress's market position. Each of the consulting firms assigned persons with market and data-analysis skills to the Fortress contract. In each instance, interviews were held with and data collected from various Fortress executives and staff specialists. Data were collected in a similar manner from industry associations and governmental sources. Further, two of the consulting firms conducted interviews with small, but carefully selected, samples of Fortress's current policyholders and with potential customers in several market areas. Finally, and perhaps most important, knowledgeable industry observers were interviewed concerning market and service trends.

From each of these firms, Fortress received a lengthy written report, supplemented by an oral presentation to top management, specifying what the consultants believed would develop within Fortress's market environment. Although the reports varied in terms of some sales-projection figures, their basic forecasts were quite similar, most likely due to the influence of the industry observers. More important, the recommendations in all the reports were also highly similar. Fortress was advised to diversify through acquisition and to regionalize its operations. None of the reports, however, discussed the processes by which these changes were to occur. No insights were provided as to how the dominant coalition was to remold its own role, build consensus for the organizational changes among middle-level executives, handle the conflicting demands of new and existing units, and so on. Top management had been provided a clear-cut goal with only limited information about how to achieve it. Moreover, top management now had a solution to a problem which only they and the consultants owned; most members of the organization had little or no evidence that anything was wrong with Fortress's existing strategy.

In contrast, the consultant's approach at Alpha was far less formal and involved more members of the Alpha hierarchy at several levels. Recall that the consultant relied heavily on the top-management group to conduct its own appraisal of market opportunities and their feasibility for Alpha. Moreover, key members of the several operating divisions were brought into the analysis and planning process at each major phase of development. The consultant did not "report" to the group his solutions to their problem; instead both the consultant and the group were joint participants in the diagnostic process. Most important, the consultant constantly focused the attention of Alpha's management on the interaction of market and administrative requirements.

Falling between the two extremes illustrated by the Alpha and Fortress cases, consultancy at Dalton Chemicals was characterized by broad discussions with key personnel but little involvement on their part in the development of the final solution. It may well be that a good part of Morris Dalton's reluctance to accept the consultants' plan stemmed from the fact that it was handed to him in complete and final form.

Of course, in each of these examples, the consultants were not in sole charge of their relationship with the organization. Fortress asked for and got a complete "market study." Alpha's top executive came to the consultant with a much less clear-cut request and much greater openness to an analysis of the entire organizational system. Moreover, involvement of key personnel at Alpha was greatly facilitated by its small size. At Dalton, two members of the dominant coalition were much more certain that a problem of crisis proportions existed than was the third (Morris Dalton) even though the third member's future was certainly to be most strongly influenced by any solution. Despite these differences, however, consultants and consulting firms usually differ in the extent to which they involve members of the client organization in problem definition and analysis and in the formulation of solutions. Therefore, it is wise for management not to delegate to consultants the responsibility for defining the appropriate approach to be employed. Managers must be informed consumers not only of the advice they receive from consultants but also of the means by which the advice is generated.

The Problem of Risk Management

The final step in the diagnostic checklist illustrated in Figure 7-1 is that of protecting against the primary risk associated with the organization's existing or proposed strategy and structure. Recall that for the Prospector, the primary risk is that of cost inefficiency, the problem of realizing the potential returns on many of its numerous ventures. Conversely, the cost-efficient Defender faces the primary risk of ineffectiveness, of having environmental conditions change dramatically enough to damage its narrow domain. In two of the cases above, consultants proposed (or helped the organization develop) rather elaborate mechanisms as hedges against these threats. The Prospector, Alpha Electronics, focused attention on the acquisition of a cost-efficient subsidiary to manufacture low-priced spinoffs of the custom-engineered test equipment produced by the parent firm. In the other case, Dalton Chemicals was urged to continue in its Defender mode while setting up an essentially independent laboratory to develop new products and processes.

In both of these cases, the rationale for separating the organization's stable operations from its risky ventures seems understandable. Neither the skills nor the interest to manage the risk-hedging operations were present in the parent organization, and close operational integration seemed more likely to be conflicting rather than complementary. Are these conditions always present, however? Could not a Defender simply bring in the scanning capacity (e.g., research and development experts or marketing specialists) necessary to protect the organization against unanticipated market developments? Could not a Prospector simply expand the office of the controller in order to force divisions to adopt more cost-efficient procedures?

The answer is "perhaps"—but only if the dominant coalition is unusually flexible and competent at managing continuous tension. When it is not, the "insurance" unit, department, or individual may well take on the role of professional devil's advocate, someone (or some unit) who is ceremoniously listened to before the opposite course of action is taken.

To some extent, the successful Analyzer builds in its own risk hedge by emphasizing both cost-efficient operation in stable areas and rapid movement into successful areas opened up by Prospectors. Certain industries lend themselves more easily to this role than others, however. That is, where scanning activities can be accomplished simply by watching and then quickly following the lead of Prospectors (a practice that usually can occur only in low-technology industries), the Analyzer's dual posture requires less skill to manage than when scanning activities require highly specialized scanning competence (e.g., highly trained scientists or marketing personnel). The latter situation is becoming increasingly apparent in many (usually high-technology) industries, placing extremely heavy demands on Analyzer-type organizations. In fact, it seems likely that a new organizational form may well be emerging as a means of managing the interdependencies between stable and turbulent areas of organization activity. We will have more to say on this point in Chapters 9 and 10.

CONCLUSIONS

In this chapter we have portrayed our theoretical model in action, examining its usefulness in the process of organizational diagnosis and change. The three cases described in this chapter were, in the main, simple; the organizations involved were neither as large nor as complex as many of those with which the reader may be familiar. Nevertheless, these examples accurately reflect existing patterns of organizational behavior in the industries we have observed. It is our belief that most of the larger, more complex organizations which are part of these and other industries are essentially elaborate versions of the types that we have found in our studies. Despite the difficulties which these expanded organizations pose for diagnosis, we nonetheless believe that our framework can be useful in this regard. In a large, multidivisional organization, for example, the model might first be applied at the overall corporate level and then to the various operating regions. Only in some of the extremely complex organizations to be discussed in Chapter 9 does the theoretical framework, in its present form, fail to offer a useful guide for managerial decisions and actions.

However, whether or not managers find the adaptive model (or some improved version) beneficial for testing the health of their organizations on a regular basis depends not only on the model's descriptive adequacy but also on its perceived prescriptions for managerial behavior. It seems likely that a manager will not seriously consider moving his organization toward a new or different organizational form unless he or she is confident that people and processes can be properly managed within the new system. Therefore, in the next chapter, we examine the relationship between our theoretical framework and past and current theories of management.

Chapter 8

Management Theory Linkages to Organizational Strategy and Structure

In the previous chapter, two organizations were struggling to make appropriate strategy-structure-process alignments with their environments. In one of the organizations, Dalton Chemicals, a key member of the dominant coalition, young Morris Dalton, was blocking the path to effective and efficient alignment. His pursuit of his own personal goals was preventing, at least temporarily, the moves that other top Dalton executives (and their consultants) believed were needed.

In the other organization, Fortress Insurance, a reluctant dominant coalition was making halfhearted, and thus frequently self-defeating, moves toward a weakly articulated new strategy-structure relationship. Much of the reluctance at Fortress was also self-serving; the structure-process changes needed to implement the new strategy would be almost certain to disrupt many of the existing bases of departmental and personal power.

Given that resistance to new strategy-structure alignment was, in both cases, at least partially linked to real or potential threats to personal achievement and status, the cases can be viewed as quite similar. Examined from a different perspective, however, that of management theory, there are important differences in the two examples. In fact, they are only marginally related.

In retrospect, Morris Dalton's behavior can be seen and explained rather clearly. The nature and degree of his resistance, however, would have been difficult to predict in advance. His educational background, his recent role and experience in the organization, and even his own statements concerning his lack of interest in the long-term management of "business" problems might well have led one to predict his quick acceptance of the consultants' proposal. Instead, for a variety of difficult-to-foresee but certainly understandable reasons, he is balking—reluctant to give up a set of unfocused goals which he is probably unable, even perhaps unwilling, to pursue. Moreover, Morris's ability to block the proposed adaptive moves is an artifact of the particular makeup of Dalton's dominant coalition.

Conversely, the resistance to new strategy-structure requirements at Fortress was highly predictable, and deliberate steps could have been taken to minimize its impact (as, in fact, was the case at Starr Insurance, Fortress's more successful competitor). The resistance at Fortress was more predictable than that at Dalton because it derived not only from the particular personal needs of members of top management but because it flowed out of their role experience, their "knowledge" of how organizations could and should be managed. Fortress's long and mainly successful experience with a limited product line and a centralized, functional organization structure had taught members of the dominant coalition a set of principles of management, supported by underlying assumptions about human behavior, which were difficult to unlearn.

In the following pages, we will examine some of the linkages between an organization's strategy and structure and the dominant coalition's management theory (assumptions about people and prescriptions concerning how they should be directed and controlled). Our general thesis is that developments in organizational form and theories of management have evolved in a logical and complementary manner. Moreover, we will argue that the evolutionary process in both areas is continuing and that it is possible to forecast, at least in part, the shape of its coming stage.

EVOLUTION IN ORGANIZATIONAL STRATEGY AND STRUCTURE

One of the major socioeconomic inventions of the twentieth century is the federally decentralized form of organization pioneered in the twenties and thirties by several prominent firms (e.g., General Motors and Sears) and widely emulated in the forties, fifties, and sixties by numerous organizations. We referred in Chapter 1 to the landmark study by Chandler (1962) which documented the emergence of this organizational form. It is appropriate now that we explicitly tie Chandler's historical discussion of organizational strategy and structure to our discussion of organizational types (the strategic typology).

Chandler described four phases of development in organizational strategy and structure, which Fouraker and Stopford (1968) refined into three distinct, evolutionary types.* Type I organizations emerged early in the history of the large American industrial corporation. These organizations tended to be owner-managed, limited to a single product line, and characterized by a structure in which all major decisions flowed directly from the entrepreneur-administrator. The chief executive attempted to monitor all activities, and his staff served merely as an extension of his will. Such organizations could move quickly and forcefully in limited areas, constrained only by the adeptness and energy of their unitary director. Size and complexity were, of course, the natural enemies of organizations built around a single problem solver, particularly one whose entrepreneurial instincts might push him away from ongoing operating problems.

Organizations that moved beyond Type I usually did so by attracting professional managers who saw challenge in attempting to rationalize the use of resources accumulated by owner-managers. Rationalization took the form of dividing the organization's tasks so that they could be managed by career administrators with specialized skills. The end point of such rationalization efforts was the Type II organization, a structure molded along functional lines (with divisions of manufacturing, sales, engineering, finance, etc.) and controlled centrally through a master operating plan and budget. The Type II organization, which appeared around the turn of the century, usually produced a limited line of related products with a common core technology. Growth occurred chiefly through vertical integration (backward to incorporate suppliers and forward to the establishment of its own market outlets). Type II organizations proved to be a cost-efficient and profitable means of providing standardized products and services on a high-volume basis to relatively stable but growing markets. However, as Chandler pointed out, the rigid vertically integrated form of the Type II organization did not allow easy movement into new market or product areas. By dividing activities along functional lines, Type II organizations fostered specialists rather than generalists. Only at the top of the organization hierarchy was there reason to examine the system as a whole or the information and expertise to

---

*Others who have used the same terminology are Salter (1970), Scott (1970), and Thain (1969).

coordinate its parts. Moreover, members of the dominant coalition tended to approach problems from the viewpoint of their previous area of functional specialization.

Thus, even successful Type II organizations eventually found their growth constrained as their traditional markets became saturated. They had the resources to expand their product lines, but each succeeding product or market innovation became increasingly difficult to administer. As Fouraker and Stopford (1968, pp. 49–50) described the dilemma:

> The functional approach of the Type II firm required that the senior marketing executive coordinate the marketing activities for all the organizations, even though they might utilize different forms of distribution, advertising, and sales effort. The senior production officer was confronted with similar complexity. These functional responsibilities could be delegated to subordinates, most appropriately on the basis of product assignments, but profit contribution of functional specialists could not be measured against performance, so control and comparison became even more difficult. The unavoidable problems of conflict and coordination at the lowest levels of the organization would frequently have to be passed up to the highest functional levels for adjudication. And some operating issues could not be settled there, but would have to reach the office of the chief executive.

It was against this backdrop, the desire to diversify thwarted by administrative complexity, that the search for a new organizational form began. Chandler described the almost simultaneous evolution of Type III structures in four pioneering firms during the twenties and thirties: Du Pont, General Motors, Sears, and Standard Oil. In each of these firms, a financial or operating crisis served to speed up tentative plans for reorganization already under way. That is, diversification efforts had led each firm into situations in which overburdened top management had lost control over funds, inventories, key entrepreneurial decisions, and so on. The move to place a series of general managers in charge of largely self-contained product or regional divisions which could then be evaluated on the basis of profit performance was viewed as essential if control were to be maintained and expansion continued. Each division could be directed toward a particular market, could design and produce its own product or service, and could make the operating decisions necessary to coordinate its own functionally structured components. In a sense, each division faced the same set of problems that the larger parent organization had failed to solve, but now the magnitude of these problems was reduced to more manageable proportions. At the top, corporate officers could devote their time to decisions about capital expenditures, relationships with other organizations and regulatory bodies, the potential for movement into new markets, and so forth. In addition, top management could use the profits of the operating divisions to maintain corporate staff specialists who, unencumbered by day-to-day demands, could aid the firm in extending the state of the art in its product or service area. Thus, research and development would occur both at the division level (focused on specific products and markets) and at the corporate level (focused on more basic, industry-advancing problems).

Most important, by the 1950s it was clear that the development of the decentralized, divisionalized structure not only provided a means of managing the organization's current diversification, but it also provided a clearly understandable mechanism for further growth. New product or service divisions could be plugged into the corporate socket with ease, subject only to the availability of current (capital), and limited in number only by the then-distant danger of overloading the corporate circuit.

Linking the Strategic Typology to Chandler's Framework

Chandler's research chronicled the evolution of organizational strategy and structure across a wide variety of industries over a considerable period of time. Our research indicates the *simultaneous* presence of Defenders, Prospectors, Analyzers, and Reactors *within* the same industry. Therefore, it seems appropriate to ask, Are there identifiable linkages between our strategic typology and Chandler's framework?

The Defenders we have observed have many characteristics similar to Chandler's (as labeled by Fouraker and Stopford) Type II organization prior to diversification efforts. Note that "pure" Defenders have limited product or service lines, functional structures, and centralized control systems focused on cost efficiency, the common strategy-structure form exhibited by large, mature organizations in the U.S. prior to the 1920s. Similarly, the Prospector corresponds, in several key areas, to the Type III strategy-structure form which Chandler describes as emerging in leading U.S. firms during the twenties and thirties. Recall that Prospectors seek to develop broad, diversified product lines and tend to manage these through decentralized operating departments or divisions. Many of the Prospectors in our studies do not have the elaborate corporate and staff structures that emerged to support product and service divisions in giant firms such as Du Pont, General Motors, and Sears, but their basic mechanism for growth—diversification through the creation of semiautonomous operating units—corresponds to Chandler's Type III form.

The remaining two types, Reactors and Analyzers, fit somewhat less neatly into Chandler's framework. Many of the Reactors we have studied appear to be in somewhat the same position as were the firms Chandler described during their transition stage, their diversification efforts running afoul of administrative (structure-process) constraints. Unlike the leading firms in Chandler's study, however, Reactors tend to be moving toward diversification less certainly and with less enthusiasm. They are more likely to have been pushed out of their domains. Thus, the Reactor's search for a structure-process form appropriate to its "imposed" strategy is seldom an aggressive one.

Analyzers, on the other hand, appear from our research to have more or less consciously adopted a strategy-structure form combining elements of both Type II and Type III structures as described by Chandler. Small Analyzers are alert to diversification opportunities but seek to limit and pace their expansion activities to meet the constraints of their established core technology. That is, they seek to emulate only the most profitable lines developed by Prospectors, thus limiting the stress placed on their internal coordination mechanisms. Larger Analyzers create semiautonomous divisions to handle major diversification efforts but tend to do so only when those products and markets are viewed as relatively stable and manageable. Typically, larger Analyzers set up program or project structures to handle market and product innovations until these can be incorporated into their stable and efficient core technology.

In sum, the four types of organizations observed in our studies exhibit characteristics which, as Chandler described, took many years to develop. However, although there are many similarities between the Defender and the Type II organization and the Prospector and the Type III organization, the two categorization schemes are not equivalent. All of our categorizations are relative to an industry or some other appropriate grouping. A firm classified as a Defender in one industry may have many Type III strategy-structure characteristics, while a Prospector firm in another industry may have many Type II characteristics. In addition, the fact that we describe a transitional or unstable type (the Reactor) and a hybrid type (the Analyzer) is the result of efforts to describe current intraindustry differences in organizational form and behavior which are likely to be more subtle than the major historical trends uncovered by Chandler. Nevertheless, Chandler's research provides the necessary historical context for understanding today's organizational forms.

EVOLUTION IN MANAGEMENT THEORY

We stated at the beginning of this chapter that the evolution of organizational strategy and structure (from Type I to Type III) has been paralleled and complemented by a similar evolutionary process in the area of management theory.* A theory of management has three basic components: (1) a set of assumptions about human attitudes and behavior, (2) managerial policies and actions consistent with these assumptions, and (3) expectations about employee performance if these policies and actions are implemented. (See Table 8-1).

During the latter part of the nineteenth century and the early decades of the twentieth century, mainstream management theory, as voiced by managers and by management scholars, conformed to what has been termed the *Traditional* model. Essentially, the Traditional model maintained that the capability for effective decision making was narrowly distributed in organizations, and this approach thus legitimized unilateral control of organizational systems by top management. Accorcording to this model, a select group of owner-managers was able to direct large numbers of employees by carefully standardizing and routinizing their work and by placing the planning function solely in the hands of top managers.

Beginning in the twenties, the Traditional model gradually began to give way to the *Human Relations* model. The Human Relations model accepted the traditional notion that superior decision-making competence was narrowly distributed among the employee population but emphasized the universality of social needs for belonging and recognition. This model argued that impersonal treatment was the source of subordinate resistance to managerial directives, and adherents of this approach urged managers to employ devices to enhance organization members' feelings of involvement and importance. Suggestion systems, employee counseling, and even company unions had common parentage in this philosophy. The Depression and World War II both acted to delay the development and spread of the Human Relations model, and it was not until the late forties and early fifties that it became the prime message put forth by managers and management scholars.

However, beginning in the mid-fifties, a third phase in the evolution of management theory began with the emergence of the *Human Resources* model. This model argued that the capacity for effective decision making in the pursuit of organizational objectives was, in fact, widely dispersed and that most organization members represented untapped resources which, if properly managed, could considerably enhance

*The discussion in this section is based on Raymond E. Miles, *Theories of Management,* McGraw-Hill, New York, 1975.

Table 8-1   Theories of Management

Traditional model	Human Relations model	Human Resources model
Assumptions:	*Assumptions:*	*Assumptions:*
1. Work is inherently distasteful to most people	1. People want to feel useful and important	1. Work is not inherently distasteful. People want to contribute to meaningful goals which they have helped establish
2. What workers do is less important than what they earn for doing it	2. People desire to belong and to be recognized as individuals	
3. Few want or can handle work which requires creativity, self-direction, or self-control	3. These needs are more important than money in motivating people to work	2. Most people can exercise far more creative, responsible self-direction and self-control than their present jobs demand
Policies:	*Policies:*	*Policies:*
1. The manager's basic task is to closely supervise and control his subordinates	1. The manager's basic task is to make each worker feel useful and important	1. The manager's basic task is to make use of his "untapped" human resources
2. He must break tasks down into simple, repetitive, easily learned operations	2. He should keep his subordinates informed and listen to their objections to his plans	2. He must create an environment in which all members may contribute to the limits of their ability
3. He must establish detailed work routines and procedures and enforce these firmly but fairly	3. The manager should allow his subordinates to exercise some self-control on routine matters	3. He must encourage full participation on important matters, continually broadening subordinate self-direction and control
Expectations:	*Expectations:*	*Expectations:*
1. People can tolerate work if the pay is decent and the boss is fair	1. Sharing information with subordinates and involving them in routine decisions will satisfy their basic needs to belong and to feel important	1. Expanding subordinate influence, self-direction, and self-control will lead to direct improvements in operating efficiency
2. If tasks are simple enough and people are closely controlled, they will produce up to standard	2. Satisfying these needs will improve morale and reduce resistance to formal authority—subordinates will "willingly cooperate"	2. Work satisfaction may improve as a "by-product" of subordinates making full use of their resources

Source: Raymond E. Miles, *Theories of Management,* McGraw-Hill, New York 1975, Figure 3-1. Reprinted with permission.

organizational performance. The Human Resources approach viewed management's role not as that of a controller (however benevolent) but as that of a facilitator removing the constraints that block organization members' search for ways to contribute meaningfully in their work roles. In recent years, some writers have questioned the extent to which the Human Resources model is applicable, arguing for a more "contingent" theory emphasizing variations in member capacity and motivation to contribute and the technological constraints associated with broadened self-direction and self-control. Nevertheless, the Human Resources model probably still represents the leading edge of management theory, perhaps awaiting the formulation of a successor model.

While the fit, both chronologically and substantively, is not precise, close linkages between evolving organizational forms and evolving management theories can be seen. The earliest statements of the Traditional model provided a rationale for the vast accumulation of resources in Type I (owner-managed) organizations. Later, the scientific management movement, many of whose tenets fit neatly into or flowed directly from the Traditional model, provided guidance for the development of Type II (functionally structured and centrally controlled) organizations. Task specialization and supervision along functional lines, promoted by Taylor (1911) and others, required close coordination and therefore increased the number of levels of management. Thus, the classic Type II organization emerged: tall (many hierarchical levels), narrowly structured along strict functional lines, and closely regulated by rules, procedures, and budgets.

If the Traditional model guided the builders of Type II organizations, the Human Relations model offered prescriptions for maintaining such structures. Type II organizations, with their sequentially organized technologies, were highly vulnerable to recalcitrant employee behavior; a breakdown in the flow of operations at one point could bring the entire system to a halt. Thus, management efforts, in line with Human Relations prescriptions, to make people feel as if they were important to the organization, to see the larger picture, and to feel a sense of loyalty and belonging to the corporate family, were all designed to keep the cost-efficient Type II organization running according to plan. Members were allowed to move up narrow, specialized career ladders, maximizing their expertise in a specific functional area.

Just as the Human Relations model met the needs of the mature Type II organization, the Human Resources model was essential to the operation of a Type III (divisionalized) organization. The "chicken-egg" question of whether Human Resources assumptions influenced the architects of early Type III structures at General Motors, Du Pont, Sears, and so forth, or whether this managerial theory emerged as a rationalization for the success of these firms is interesting to consider but probably unanswerable and to some extent unimportant. However, it is clear that Sloan at General Motors, Pierre Du Pont at Du Pont, Wood at Sears, Teagle at Standard Oil, and others were all more willing to delegate decision-making authority to subordinates than had been their predecessors. Giving newly developed general manager offices full authority to operate essentially autonomous divisions required the belief that capability for effective decision making was widely distributed within the managerial hierarchy.

Nevertheless, the first clear descriptions of the Human Resources model were not made until three decades after these pioneering organizations began their experimentation with the Type III structure. Elements of a Human Resources philosophy were offered by Sloan (1964) and other executives during the thirties and forties, but it was not until the fifties that the model began to be well articulated. James Worthy (1950), a former vice-president at Sears, published a widely read article in 1950 extolling the impact of that organization's flat, decentralized structure on both employee morale and performance. Four years later, Peter Drucker (1954) drew on his experience and studies at General Motors, Sears, and other leading organizations to produce a widely read and quoted book, *The Practice of Management.* Drucker's arguments for decentralization and "management by objectives" rather than by rules clearly reflected a belief that many, if not most, organization members were both capable of and motivated to contribute to organizational goals. Finally, in 1960, Douglas McGregor (1960) offered an even more explicit treatment of the Human Resources model in his book, *The Human Side of Enterprise.* McGregor drew on many of the same sources as Drucker, but he made especially clear the assumptions about human capabilities (at even the lower levels of the organization) underlying his version of the Human Resources model. Therefore, whatever the causal direction, it was during the same decade (1950s) in which these and a growing stream of related writings were published that Type III organizations proliferated rapidly, drawing on the structural models established by pioneering firms and using Human Resources language to justify their new forms.

Linking the Strategic Typology to Management Theory

Are there identifiable linkages between an organization's strategic type and the management theory of its dominant coalition? For example, do top executives in Defenders profess Traditional beliefs about management and those in Prospectors a Human Resources philosophy? The answer to this question is, in our opinion, a bit more complex than simply yes or no.

Empirically, the hospital study described in Chapter 13 suggests that management theory is related to organizational strategy and structure in the manner indicated above: Traditional-Human Relations managerial beliefs are more likely to be found in Defender and Reactor organizations, while Human Resources beliefs are more often associated with Analyzer and Prospector organizations. The findings on hospitals presented there, however, are only suggestive and may not be representative of all organizations. There are, in fact, numerous examples of Human Resources policies and practices flourishing in organizations with narrow market domains and functional structures. What then *is* the relationship between managerial philosophy and organizational form?

As described in Chapter 13, the relationship between management and type of organization appears to be constrained in one direction. That is, it seems highly unlikely that a Traditional or Human Relations manager can function effectively as the head of a Prospector organization. The prescriptions of the Traditional model simply do not support the degree of decentralized decision making required to create and manage diversified organizations. (It might be possible for a Traditional or Human Relations manager to function as the chief executive of a mature Prospector firm but only after divisional autonomy has been so firmly entrenched that major interventions are widely perceived as illegitimate.)

On the other hand, it is quite possible for a Human Resources manager to lead a Defender organization. Of course, the organization's planning and control processes under such leadership would be less centralized than if the organization were managed according to the Traditional model. Using the Human Resources philosophy, heads of functional divisions might either participate in the planning and budgeting process or simply be delegated considerable autonomy in operating their cost centers. (Note, however, that in Defender organizations operated according to the Human Resources philosophy, human capabilities are aimed at cost efficiency rather than product development.)

Reactor organizations frequently provide the best examples of conflict between management theories and organizational needs in the area of strategy and structure. Recall that in Chapter 7 and at the beginning of this chapter, we suggested that the dominant coalition at Fortress Insurance appeared to be highly resistant to the idea of following their competitors in the creation of semiautonomous, full-service regional offices. We indicated that this resistance was understandable, even predictable, when viewed through the perspective of management theory. Top Fortress executives held beliefs compatible (though not necessarily optimal) with the needs of their Defender organization. The progress of these executives through the system to their present positions had been accomplished by giving close attention to detail and focusing primarily on issues related to their functional specialties. Now at the top, they continued to involve themselves closely in all operating activities. Their subordinates, reared in the same environment, expected their superiors to review all decisions and seldom questioned their judgment. The Traditional-Human Relations beliefs of most members of the dominant coalition, reinforced by experiences which were structured to provide only confirming evidence for their managerial theories, made it extremely difficult for them to believe that real decentralization of operating decisions could work effectively. Thus, while at one level top Fortress executives could accept the need for new market behaviors and even for some realignment of structure to match strategy, they had neither the motivation nor the skill to put those changes into effect.

It is, of course, perfectly understandable for management to be cautious in the implementation of new organizational structures and processes with which they have had little, if any, experience. As noted earlier, Chandler described many examples of pioneering Type III organizations advancing and then retreating in their movement toward new structures. However, when this necessary caution solidifies because of a firm allegiance to management theories that question employee capabilities to operate in these new structures, delay may be prolonged into dysfunction.

The fit between management theory and the strategy, structure, and process characteristics of Analyzers is perhaps more complex than with any of the other organization types. Analyzers, as described previously, tend to remain cost-efficient in the production of a limited line of goods or services while attempting to move as rapidly as possible into promising new areas opened up by Prospectors. Note that the organization structure of the Analyzer does not demand extensive, permanent delegation of decision-making authority to division managers. Most of the Analyzer's products or services can be produced in functionally structured divisions similar to those in Defender organizations. New products or services may be developed in separate divisions or departments created for that purpose and then integrated as quickly as possible into the permanent technology and structure. It seems likely to us, though our evidence is fragmented and inconclusive, that various members of the dominant coalition in Analyzer organizations hold moderate but different managerial philosophies. That is, certain key executives believe it is their role to pay fairly close attention to detail while others appear to be more willing to delegate, for short periods, moderate amounts of autonomy necessary to bring new products or services on line rapidly. Obviously, if these varying managerial philosophies are "mismatched" within the Analyzer's operating units—if, for example, Traditional managers are placed in charge of innovative subunits—then it is unlikely that a successful Analyzer strategy can be pursued.

Holding together a dominant coalition with mixed views concerning strategy and structure is not an easy task. It is difficult, for example, for managers engaged in new product or service development to function within planning, control, and reward systems established for more stable operations, so the Analyzer must be successfully differentiated into its stable and changing areas and managed accordingly. Note, however, that experimentation in the Analyzer organization is usually quite limited. The exploration and risk associated with major product or service breakthroughs are not present, and thus the interdependencies within the system may be kept at a manageable level. Of course, such would not be the case if Analyzer organizations attempted to be both cost-efficient producers of stable products or services and active in a major way in new product and market development. Nevertheless, numerous organizations are today being led or forced into such a dual strategy (multinational companies, certain forms of conglomerates, many organizations in high-technology industries, etc.), and their struggles may well produce a new organization type (Type IV) and demands for a supporting theory of management. We will offer our perceptions of these emerging trends in the next chapter.

CONCLUSIONS

We have traced the evolutionary process in the areas of organizational form and management theory to suggest that the two are at least related, if not closely intertwined. We have shown, first, that the major organizational forms that have emerged over time (Type I, II, and III as described by Chandler and labeled by Fouraker-Stopford) still exist in many industries in various forms, along with a hybrid type that we have called the Analyzer and an unstable type called the Reactor.

Secondly, we have described a similar evolutionary process that has occurred in management theory. Although it is difficult to discern whether management theory was the impetus for the development of the most recent organizational forms or simply a means for rationalizing their success, it is clear that the evolution of organizational forms is related to the evolution of theories of management. Moreover, though our evidence is inconclusive, it appears that some forms of organization require certain types of management whereas others are less constraining. Specifically, we believe that Prospector organizations require

Human Resources management whereas Defender organizations allow but do not require it.

For most purposes, our discussion is now complete. We have described and illustrated a model of how organizations adjust to their environments (the adaptive cycle). In addition, we have shown how organizations, as determined empirically in our studies, move through the adaptive process. Specifically, we have argued that there are four types of strategic behavior, three of which are viable in the long run while the other is much less so. We then demonstrated how this theoretical framework can be used for diagnostic purposes, developing in the process a list of key questions that could aid managers in changing the strategic nature of their organizations. Last, in this chapter, we brought management theory squarely into the picture, for it is our belief that no form of organization can be operated effectively unless it has an appropriate accompanying managerial theory.

To this point, we believe that our framework and discussion have provided the major *necessary* components for successful organizational diagnosis and change. At the same time, however, our discussion has not explicitly provided *sufficient* "answers" for the full range of strategy-structure situations which the modern organization might face. Therefore, in the following chapter, we will explore some environmental conditions which may increasingly prevail in the future, and we will sketch the requirements of an organizational form and an accompanying management theory that can deal with these conditions.

Chapter 9

Mixed Strategies and Structures

Throughout the previous chapters, we focused attention on the organization's continuing tasks of maintaining an effective alignment with environmental conditions and managing the intraorganizational interdependencies resulting from the chosen alignment strategy. Utilizing our research findings, we described a set of internally consistent patterns of organizational adaptation to environmental demands, patterns in which the form of alignment (strategy) was complemented by the approach used to manage internal interdependencies among technology, structure, and process. For example, where the alignment task is simplified by the choice of a narrow, stable product-market domain, top management can devote much of its attention to constructing policies and plans that permit centralized coordination of functional divisions (the Defender pattern). At the other extreme, where the alignment task is made complex by a strategy of product or market diversification, the management of interdependencies is simplified, or at least reduced in scope, by the creation of self-contained product or regional divisions, each facing a limited domain and responsible for its own internal coordination (the Prospector pattern).

The question before us here, raised at the close of Chapter 8, is whether an understanding of the organizational patterns already described provides sufficient guidance for the design of strategies and structures to meet emerging environmental conditions. We shall explore this broad question in the following sections. First, we describe some of the complex task environments being faced by a growing number of organizations today, and then we examine the fit between existing patterns of adaptation and the demands of these task environments. Second, we explore some emerging response patterns to these environmental conditions which combine mixed strategies with mixed structures and processes. Third, we describe and discuss an organizational form that is the logical extension of these mixed strategies and structures, the *market-matrix* organization. Finally, we outline the managerial philosophy and practices required by the market-matrix organization.

COMPLEX TASK ENVIRONMENTS

In the following paragraphs, we will briefly describe a few of the unusually complex environments faced by numerous organizations through choice, unanticipated developments, pressure from constituents, and so forth. Our belief is that the environmental conditions faced by these organizations may be a precursor of situations likely to be faced by an increasing number of organizations in the future.

Conglomerates

The growth of conglomerates has been a highly visible phenomenon in the past two decades. Conglomerates, complex organizations constructed through the merger or acquisition of existing firms, take many forms. One form results from *horizontal* growth through merger or acquisition simply to expand product lines and/or markets *within* a given industry. Conversely, *vertical* growth through the acquisition of suppliers or consumer outlets can be undertaken to assure the cost-efficient production of a limited product line. However, the most interesting form, and perhaps the only one that truly deserves to be called a conglomerate, is an organization in which mergers and acquisitions occur *across* industry lines primarily for the purpose of financial synergy. For example, a "pure" conglomerate might well acquire one organization in an industry with only limited potential for growth but a sizable cash flow and a second organization in a risky segment of another industry characterized by large growth possibilities but limited current profitability.

Mergers and acquisitions in any of these three types of conglomerates inevitably force the dominant coalition to make important strategy, structure, and process decisions. However, these decisions are most difficult in the latter, interindustry case, particularly if management attempts to achieve synergistic effects beyond the financial area, such as the interdivisional rotation of managers or the creation of a centralized research and development group.

Aerospace Firms

The modern aerospace industry traces its origin to the early part of this century, but much of its product development has occurred within the past three decades. A prime characteristic of this industry is rapid technological change: today's prototype is tomorrow's standard product. Many aerospace firms attempt to operate at several points on the technology continuum. To the extent that they succeed, they tend to allocate some portion of their resources to fairly stable environments demanding standardized (though perhaps still highly sophisticated) products and other portions to edge-of-the-art activities such as designing and building components for space vehicles and facilities. The strategy and structure decisions necessary to adapt simultaneously to these quite different task environments are in all instances difficult but particularly so in those cases where a close technological and/or personnel synergy is sought between the two operating segments.

Educational Institutions (and Other Public Agencies)

Increasingly over the past decade, some constituents have demanded that public agencies provide them with expanded or unique services in addition to traditional services, even though the agencies' budgets have been stabilized or even diminished. Educational institutions in particular have sought means of expanding their offerings, experimenting with new subject areas and curricula designs, while limiting their investment in new faculties and facilities. Agency or institutional leaders have had to make complex strategy and structure decisions in order for their organizations to be both responsive and cost-efficient.

Multinational Companies

As is the case with conglomerates and aerospace firms, multinational companies (MNCs) have expanded dramatically in number and operating scope within the past two decades. Typically, MNCs have initially sought foreign markets for their domestically produced products in order to further utilize productive capacity. If their products sell well in host countries, the parent firm may then establish regional marketing operations in these areas to assure a continuing market. Finally, in order both to achieve transportation economies and to further relations with host governments, production facilities may be constructed in these host countries through direct investment or joint ventures. Successful operation in one or two foreign arenas frequently leads to expansion into other countries, and the fully developed MNC may have marketing and/or production facilities located throughout the world. Strategy and structure decisions become increasingly difficult as the number of host countries increases, each with its own particular characteristics, and as the organization moves toward worldwide markets with dispersed facilities. In the fully developed multinational company, tremendous planning, coordination, and control problems arise as regional variations in production technologies and product designs increase.

USEFULNESS OF CURRENT RESPONSE PATTERNS

To what extent does an understanding of the adaptive patterns described in the earlier chapters prepare an organization for the complex and often ambiguous adaptation demands faced by conglomerates, aerospace firms, educational institutions, multinational companies, and so on? We believe that the strategic typology can provide management with necessary, but perhaps not in all instances sufficient, guidance.

Areas of Close Fit

Conglomerates   In our judgment, the descriptive and diagnostic materials presented earlier can provide useful insights for the management of some types of conglomerates. Conglomerates formed primarily for market coverage within the same or related industries take on much the same form as the multidivisional Prospector firm. To the extent that corporate management allows the individual companies to operate as self-contained units, problems of interdependency are minimized, and corporate executives are left relatively free to scan the horizon for additional opportunities. These opportunities can be pursued by creating new product or service divisions or by acquiring companies already operating in the target areas. Clearly, conglomerates of this type can respond quickly to a wide spectrum of opportunities, but they run the risk of failing to develop the full profitability of their operating companies since few resources are centralized to achieve economies of scale. Moreover, these conglomerates also run the risks of antitrust action and over-extension of capital resources.

Alternatively, conglomerates formed through acquisition of supplier and/or outlet organizations face alignment and internal interdependence problems similar in type, if not in magnitude, to those faced by Defender organizations. To the extent that supplier and outlet operations can be blended with the parent organization's core technology through formal planning, interdependencies can be centrally managed. That is, corporate executives can afford to spend considerable time on these interorganizational and intraorganizational operating problems because the entire organization is directed toward a limited product-market domain.

Aerospace Firms, Public Agencies, and MNCs   Where conditions are appropriate, an extension of the Analyzer type of organization provides useful guidance to the managers of organizations such as aerospace firms, public agencies, and MNCs, which attempt to operate in both stable and turbulent environments.

Recall that Analyzers allocate most of their organizational resources to a set of reasonably stable task environments while at the same time conducting somewhat routinized scanning activities in a limited product-market area. In the main, Analyzers monitor product or market innovations developed by Prospector organizations, imitate and improve on the most promising of these developments, and then incorporate these innovations as rapidly as possible into the stable, standardized segment of the organization.

Aerospace firms, public agencies, and MNCs can follow variants of the Analyzer pattern providing they (1) have a well-developed core technology directed at a stable area of operation and (2) can exercise discretion concerning the size and scope of the new activities and/or arenas they address. For example, the aerospace organization which is free (because of the profitability of its main activities) to limit the size, nature, and number of the prototype projects it undertakes can jointly deal with its tasks of alignment and interdependency management. Small projects can be administered as largely self-contained units without creating important interdependence problems. Of these projects, only those which are being fed into the stable portion of the organization justify more intensive, though temporary, attention by the dominant coalition. Finally, where the organization can choose among alternative projects and can pace its involvement with them, careful planning can minimize interdependence issues.

In a similar fashion, public agencies or schools can respond to demands for innovation by using the Analyzer pattern if they (1) can pace their experiments to match the cyclical expenditure of resources in their stable operations and/or (2) can anticipate the incorporation of successful prototype programs into the routine operating segment of the organization. Multinational companies can also follow the Analyzer pattern to the extent that they avoid the complexities involved in joint ventures and/or host-country production facilities. In other words, if regional variation between products and technological processes is avoided, an MNC can employ a single centralized production technology and disperse only the marketing function.

At this point, it should be noted that most Analyzer organizations have extensive experience with incorporating new areas of activity into their essentially stable structures. For example, product development teams have been utilized for many years in the appliance industry to speed the process of moving a design idea from the drawing board to the assembly line. Management temporarily draws a team leader, design and process engineers, toolmakers, machinists, and others away from their permanent roles and gives them a time schedule in which to get on line a product that will have the same or improved features as those in a competitor's new product. Similarly, in the consumer packaged goods industry, product managers (usually based in the marketing department) provide a mechanism for keeping these essentially stable organizations (a single core production technology) responsive to the particular market needs surrounding a large number of products. The product manager's task is to monitor developments in the market(s) for his particular brand or group of brands, to initiate planning for changes in design necessary to match these market developments, and to propose advertising and marketing programs to maintain or expand market share. The authority of these product managers varies considerably from company to company, but in all instances their success depends primarily on developing effective relationships with key personnel in R&D, production, and sales.

As noted earlier, an Analyzer organization, even when augmented by scanning and/or coordination mechanisms such as those described above, strikes a fine balance between the joint needs of environmental alignment and interdependence management. Whenever either of these tasks moves out of the limits for which established routines are available, the dominant coalition may become overloaded.

Areas of Lesser Fit

In the situations discussed above, organizations faced complex and difficult environments, but we believe that our strategy-structure framework provides guidance for organizations which are attempting to respond to these or similar environmental conditions. However, there are circumstances for which our framework may be less helpful.

Multi-industry Conglomerates The dominant coalition of the multi-industry conglomerate faces some of the same alignment and interdependence management problems faced by the single-industry, horizontal-expansion conglomerate. If each of the organization's separate divisions can be independently managed, corporate management can devote a sizable portion of its time to opportunity scanning (the Prospector pattern). However, because the operating companies in a multi-industry conglomerate face quite different task environments (peculiar to each of their own industries), corporate management's task of evaluating the performance of the various companies is magnified. Efforts to produce and apply uniform performance criteria may lead corporate executives toward decisions that are logical in an overall sense but perhaps inappropriate to a particular industry setting. Conversely, utilizing only industry-relative performance criteria makes it difficult for corporate management to evaluate competing demands from operating-company managers for capital funds. Finally, to the extent that corporate management achieves its goal of financial synergy—for example, taking funds from profitable operations for investment in growth firms—the bases and motivation for self-guidance by operating-company managers may be blurred or diminished.

While the theoretical framework developed in this book does not offer specific recommendations to corporate management with regard to these complex issues, it does provide insights into the cost-benefit dynamics associated with alternative organizational behaviors. Specifically, the framework provides a set of cautionary signals. For example, to the extent that corporate management directly manipulates performance-evaluation criteria, divisions' market orientations, and capital funding flows, it takes on the internally oriented role of management in a Defender type of organization despite the fact that the basic structure of the organization and its task environments are more in line with that of the Prospector type. Extending the framework to include the case of the multi-industry conglomerate, adaptability might be enhanced if a conglomerate acquired only Defender (or only Prospector) organizations across several industries. Having done so, corporate management might then develop a central staff of highly specialized internal "consultants" who could apply their knowledge and skills toward upgrading the performance of the acquired organizations. Of course, the central staff of a Defender conglomerate would be composed of specialists of very different kinds from the staff of a Prospector conglomerate (e.g., financial experts versus market researchers). However, in conglomerates that choose to acquire a mix of different types of organizations in various industries, top management must recognize that energy and attention devoted to managing internal interdependencies reduces that available for product and market scanning, and vice versa.

Aerospace Firms, Public Agencies, and MNCs   As noted earlier, the dominant coalition is likely to become overloaded whenever organizations attempt to operate intensively in two environments, one requiring responsiveness and the other stable, cost-efficient performance. Of course, such organizations can choose to focus mainly on one of these arenas, either minimizing the more turbulent environment and retrenching toward the Defender response pattern, or moving predominantly into the more turbulent environment with a Prospector strategy and structure. Where organizations cannot or choose not to move to a pure solution, how can alignment and interdependence management requirements be met simultaneously?

In many aerospace organizations, some public agencies and schools, and in a limited number of multinational companies, some interesting strategy-structure innovations have emerged over the past several years. These innovations, broadly defined as matrix management and structures, can best be understood by examining them against our continuum of existing organization types.

AN EMERGING ADAPTIVE PATTERN: THE MATRIX ORGANIZATION

Although matrix organizations have several forms (Sayles, 1976), most can be placed into one of two categories: dual assignments for certain managers or a joint-planning process that spans the stable and responsive portions of the organization (Davis, 1976).

Dual Assignments

In many organizations, efforts are made to facilitate the tasks of environmental alignment and interdependence management by assigning a high-level manager dual responsibilities. For example, in an aerospace firm, the head of the electrical engineering design department may also be given responsibility for managing a major "one-shot" project, usually one which will draw heavily on his own technical training and experience. Similarly, in a public agency or school, a department head or a senior professional from a permanent department may be given the additional assignment of managing an innovative or experimental program or curriculum. Or, in a multinational company, a senior manager may be given the dual assignment of managing a given product group for worldwide distribution and overseeing the operation of a regional marketing division in a foreign country (which may handle several of the MNC's product groups). In each of these examples, the organization is attempting to compartmentalize the alignment task (by breaking it into smaller though still heterogeneous pieces) and to provide a focal point for interdependence decisions and information. Presumably, through their dual roles as members of the dominant coalition in both the stable and turbulent portions of the organization, high-level executives can initiate decisions and policies that both resolve conflicts and tap synergistic potential. Thus, for example, in his role as a regional marketing manager, the MNC executive might become aware of design characteristics of the firm's products which cause them to be less attractive to customers in that region. Later, during his regular meetings with managers of other product groups, he can draw on his knowledge of the product design process to suggest design modifications that could increase sales in his own region (and perhaps in other regions) without seriously disturbing the stability of existing production techniques. In this instance, the manager's dual role produces the orientation of a Prospector seeking the freedom to respond quickly to perceived opportunities.

The reverse situation is, of course, of equal potential value. From experience obtained as the head of an experimental project, the public administrator may gain insight into his other role as the head of a functional department. He may become aware of information and expertise present in other departments that could significantly increase the efficiency of his own department's operations—the Defender orientation. Again, he has the opportunity in his dual role to seek agreement among other departmental managers for his proposal. Of course, given that any one manager has actual decision-making authority only within relatively narrow limits, he is highly dependent on his own persuasive ability to obtain the support necessary to establish new channels of communication and new avenues of cooperation. Where he cannot obtain this support, his only recourse is to appeal to a higher level of authority. If such appeals are numerous, overload can occur at the top of the organization.

Joint Planning

An alternative to the dual-assignment matrix approach is the joint-planning approach. Organizations following the latter approach would first establish separate but roughly equivalent managerial roles (in terms of salary, status, and hierarchical level) in both the stable and turbulent portions of the overall organization. In the aerospace firm, heads of major functional departments would be of roughly equivalent stature to the heads of major projects or programs. In the public agency, heads of standard service departments (or professional groupings) would be of roughly equivalent stature to heads of major programs or projects. And in the multinational company, the manager of a product group would be of roughly equal rank to regional and functional managers.

All of these managers would be expected to behave primarily as advocates of their particular units, building plans which maximize the likelihood that their units will accomplish ongoing assignments. For example, the manager of a product group in an MNC ideally would attempt to sell nearly identical products across as many regions as possible so that scale economies could be achieved in manufacturing and distribution. Conversely, a regional manager in the same organization might be interested in varying product design to maximize sales in his particular region, emphasizing some products over others which he believes have less appeal in his region. The regional manager might also enter into a joint agreement with a host-country firm in his region to manufacture one or more of the firm's products, thereby assisting the host economy and perhaps improving his company's image and relationships with customers and regulatory agencies.

Similarly, in an aerospace firm, the head of the electrical engineering design department would be encouraged to plan for the long-term personnel needs of his unit based on projections for research and development activities and his estimates of the personnel to be drawn from his unit for special projects now in progress or anticipated. At the same time, the firm's project managers would be estimating the personnel that each project will need to draw from the various functional units, including the electrical engineering design department.

As expected by organizations following the joint-planning model, many points of divergence and conflict emerge as the plans and forecasts of the product group are compared with those of the regional office. Voluntary bilateral resolution of these conflicts is encouraged, and many points of disagreement between product and regional (or functional and project) managers are resolved directly. Nevertheless, the priorities of the two parties are seldom closely related, and disagreements are frequently turned over to a joint planning committee for resolution. This committee, made up of representatives of the two management groups (product and regional or functional and project) plus key members of higher management, makes the final decisions necessary to bring the two sets of plans into general agreement for the coming operating period (typically 6 months or a year). When major conflicts arise which were unforeseen during the resolution process, the joint planning committee may be reconvened. Minor disagreements that emerge during the operating period are expected to be resolved by mutual agreement among the managers involved.

The joint-planning approach has as its key component the creation of a specific mechanism for the resolution of interdependence problems that would otherwise require full-time attention from top management. Freed from these problems, top management can devote much of its time to the difficult tasks of monitoring the organization's present alignment with its different task domains and of surveying the environment for alternative opportunities. Interdependence-management mechanisms of the type described here tend to work as long as the planning horizons of the major organizational units can be generally interwoven and as long as resources are available to accommodate the inevitable planning mistakes. Clearly, however, the ability of adaptive (regional or project) units to behave in a true "prospecting" manner will be constrained under this system, as will the efforts of more stable (functional or product) units to organize themselves for maximum cost efficiency, that is, to behave as pure Defenders.

THE MARKET-MATRIX ORGANIZATION: A NEW ORGANIZATIONAL FORM?*

The "dual-assignment" and "joint-planning" matrix systems described above might be viewed as rudimentary versions of a new type of organization that could simultaneously accommodate stable and changing areas of operation. These matrix forms are rudimentary in that they exist as appendages to current forms of organization. Specifically, such matrix forms might be called Type III-A organizations, diversified organizations trying to accommodate some areas of flexibility within the framework of an overall operating plan.

Where interdependence problems extend beyond the capacity of the dual-assignment and joint-planning approaches, however, some organizations have moved toward a matrix system regulated by internal market mechanisms. Such a move usually occurs when issues of resource allocation are large enough in number and important enough in content to warrant a major shift in managerial thinking and a major investment in constructing and maintaining a highly sophisticated system for managing intraorganizational interdependencies. As suggested earlier, the market-matrix system might be the precursor of a new form of organization, the Type IV structure.

In a fully developed matrix system, resources are diverted from stable areas of operation and allocated among more uncertain (and more temporary) programs, projects, or arenas through direct buyer-seller negotiation. To illustrate how market mechanisms operate under this approach, we will examine separately applications in aerospace firms, public agencies, and MNCs, those organizations which we believe are already facing many of the environmental conditions of tomorrow's world.

*The discussion in this section draws heavily on concepts and explanations offered by Robert Biller. See, for example, Biller (1976).

An Aerospace Example

We are not aware of any organization that employs a fully developed market-matrix system, but an example can be created by combining the present and planned practices of several real aerospace companies.

Apex Aircraft Instruments is a division of a major aerospace firm, and it has over 7,000 employees, including nearly 4,000 involved in the production of a well-established line of new and replacement instruments for both the civilian and military aircraft markets. In addition to producing for this relatively stable (for the aerospace industry) market, Apex regularly engages in research and development projects in conjunction with military and/or space-exploration contracts, either directly or as a secondary contributor to prime contractors. At the moment, Apex has six major projects, each involving over 100 employees and stretching over 2 or more years, and four minor projects under contract and waiting to be initiated. In addition, Apex has three major internally funded R&D projects under way, each aimed at the development of a new commercial product.

Each of the managers of these projects except one (who was hired from a competitor) has been drawn out of a regular assignment in one of the permanent departments of the organization, usually an engineering unit. Project managers are invited to accept such posts by the project planning committee, a group of senior top-level executives drawn from both the stable (functional) and more variable (project) areas of the organization. Invitations are handled confidentially, and managers are free to decline (though pressure may mount when particular expertise is badly needed). In addition, managers invited to head projects are expected to review and bargain over project budgets (dollar and time schedules) and the perquisites related to their own role as project directors (e.g., a bonus for bringing the project in on or ahead of schedule). When a manager accepts the invitation to serve as project director, his permanent position is filled on a temporary basis, and he is thus assured of having a role to which he can return when the project is completed.

Role of the Project Manager   Once the project manager has accepted that position and agreed to the project budget, he begins the difficult task of building the project team, starting with his own personal staff: an assistant project manager and a budget officer. The project manager can choose anyone he wishes for these or other project posts; there are no rules governing such appointments.

The manager first inquires about a desired individual's interest in serving on the project. If there is interest, the project manager approaches the individual's boss and begins the process of negotiating for that person's release from his or her present assignment, usually a role in a functional department. The standard negotiated "deal" between a project manager and a functional department head calls for the project manager to transfer funds from his project budget to the department budget to cover the present salary and benefits of the sought-after individual (plus, frequently, a small overhead charge). The project manager may purchase all or part of an individual's time, depending on project needs and the individual's willingness to serve. Once the deal is completed, the individual's job is filled temporarily, so that he too has a permanent role to which he can return (the overhead charge covers extra administrative expense associated with position changes).

When a standard exchange of the above sort is negotiated, a project manager is behaving as a willing buyer seeking out the skills needed for his project for the time period required. If he is an efficient buyer (prompted by a tight project budget), he is motivated to purchase the least expensive talent appropriate to the project, perhaps a few days of the time of an experienced professional and several weeks from a junior engineer. However, if the buyer is satisfied, what about the seller? Why is a functional department head willing to release a presumably valued member of his unit? In a market-matrix structure, the answer is straightforward: the functional department head sells talent from his unit because he has to in order to cover his unit's salary budget.

Role of the Functional Manager   To understand why the functional department manager is motivated to sell talent from his unit, we must back up a step and examine how his unit's salary budget has been set (through negotiation with the project planning committee). The functional unit manager is expected to maintain a collection of human resources in his department sufficient to meet long-term product and development needs as well as the needs of contracted and in-house-funded projects. Product, and some major project, needs can be predicted with reasonable accuracy through the intermediate run (1 to 3 years), but many specific project needs cannot be precisely estimated. It is the project planning committee's task to estimate the overall level of project activity for a given planning period (e.g., 2 to 5 years), to further estimate the general types of talents that will be needed, and to review and revise these estimates regularly. Out of these projections come the present personnel quotas and future projections for each functional unit. These quotas and projections provide guidance to the unit manager concerning what sorts of individuals he is responsible for acquiring, maintaining, and developing. For example, a unit manager may be expected to expand his present pool of 48 professionals and technicians by six members over the next 2 years, with special attention to building up skills in the area of quality control. However, while the functional unit manager is expected to hire and develop to these limits, he is provided a salary and benefit budget that will actually fund only a portion of the total schedule, say, 80 percent. The proportions of the unit's salary and benefit budget which are funded and not funded reflect the estimated proportion of that unit's personnel which will be requested for project service (in this instance, 20 percent).

Thus, with only 80 percent of his personnel budget funded, the functional unit head is motivated to respond positively to requests by project managers to purchase the time of individuals in his department. Further, he is also motivated to allow and encourage members of his unit to maintain and develop skills that will make them more salable (through joint career planning with his subordinates, assignment shifts and rotations, running department problem-solving seminars, etc.). To the extent that the members of a functional unit *are* highly desirable for project service, the unit manager builds an argument for enlarging his staff (and thus his own status). Conversely, to the extent that the project demands for personnel from his unit fail to meet expected levels, the functional unit manager will face pressure to reduce his personnel schedule.

An Appeals Mechanism   Given that we now have willing buyers and sellers, do we expect that all projected negotiations between project managers and functional unit heads will be routine? A moment's thought suggests the answer must be "no." The individual a project manager feels is essential to the accomplishment of his objectives may be the same individual to whom the functional unit manager has given an important product-development assignment within the unit, and the release of this individual to project duties would require either delaying completion of his assignment or using larger amounts of less experienced talent to replace him. Nevertheless, a deal may still be made, if the project manager is willing to cover the unit's added expense by transferring project funds in excess of the desired individual's actual salary and benefits to the functional unit's budget. In the market-matrix system, as indicated above, no restrictions are placed on the actual amounts agreed to in such negotiations.

Similarly, a project manager may discover that an individual he needs for his project has just been acquired by another project manager. Again, negotiations are in order. If a project manager, by the price he is willing to pay, can convince another manager to relinquish an individual and seek out more units of less effective talent, a deal can be made. Again, no restrictions are placed on such deals. Project managers are intimately aware of what their project needs are and what their budgets will withstand. If they pay a premium for one individual, they will need to acquire less expensive talent to fill other slots. Similarly, functional unit managers are aware of their own budget needs and departmental workloads. In sum, negotiations are free in that they are not directly monitored, but they are clearly constrained by departmental and project requirements and budgets.

While the project planning committee does not monitor the negotiations undertaken by project managers and functional unit heads to allocate resources, the committee is constantly available for appeal. With everyone having the right to appeal concerning the negotiating stand (or lack of negotiation) by any other member, one might imagine that the project planning committee (or its appeals subcommittee) would be quickly overloaded and forced to do what it is specifically designed not to, that is, manage specific internal project assignments. In fact, in a fully developed matrix system, appeals are few in number. Most managers are motivated either to continue negotiations or to shift acquisition targets, for once an appeal is made, the decision is completely out of their hands; they may be awarded all that they requested, but they may also lose completely with no further avenue for compromise.

Other Essential Characteristics of a Market-Matrix System   In addition to an appeals mechanism, sparingly used, a market-matrix system has three other essential properties, all of which have been mentioned in the example above but which deserve further emphasis. The most important of these properties is the complete freedom of project managers and functional unit heads to make whatever personnel exchanges meet their needs. Any restrictions on this requirement have the same effects as interventions in any free-market mechanism. Particularistic interventions (e.g., voiding a negotiated deal) are always viewed by the players as inequitable and thus undermine the market mechanisms, and across-the-board constraints damage the guidance properties of a market (e.g., if price limits are set, real demand priorities are not exercised).

The second crucial property is the requirement that all project personnel be drawn out of permanent functional unit positions. If projects are to be efficiently completed and terminated, their members must have the security of a valued role to which they can return. Without this assurance, project members will be motivated to extend the project's lifetime, stringing out the work until they find other positions. On rare occasions, subject to the approval of the project planning committee, a project manager may be allowed to go outside the organization to acquire some unique knowledge or expertise. Every effort is made, however, to keep outside hiring to a minimum, for when such individuals are brought in, they too tend to be motivated to extend the life of a project. Moreover, placing the project manager in the role of external recruiter minimizes the importance of the functional unit manager's role in that area.

The third essential property is voluntarism, the right of any individual to veto his participation in a given project. This produces conditions within the organization which approach an optimal free-market allocation of human resources. That is, voluntarism permits the most competent organization members to gravitate toward those projects which present them with the greatest professional challenge, thus yielding a highly productive allocation of talent within the system as a whole. However, when an individual moves into a project assignment, he runs the risk of being overlooked for important assignments (and even promotions) within his unit. The project manager must therefore accept some responsibility for guiding the individual's development and pressing for appropriate rewards through recommendations to the individual's permanent boss and special memos to the project planning committee (subcommittee on selection and salary review). Project managers unwilling to fulfill these obligations will develop reputations that will make it difficult for them to staff their projects. Paralleling this requirement is the need to reflect an individual's worth in his standard "price" (i.e., in his salary). Real or perceived inequities occur when individuals for whom special deals are regularly negotiated (with payments in excess of their salaries) are not rapidly and appropriately rewarded, that is, if their salaries are not brought closer into line with their internal market value.

If the conditions cited here are met, a market-matrix system can be relied on to handle many of the interdependence-management problems occurring in an organization that is attempting to operate simultaneously in both a stable market area and a more turbulent, less predictable domain. With a mechanism for efficient internal resource allocation, highly responsive to both project and functional unit needs, top management can devote much of its time to scanning activities in both domains. Clearly, a matrix system of this sort is not easy to develop or maintain. Higher-level managers must learn how to create "markets" rather than how to make specific resource-allocation decisions, and lower levels of management must become increasingly sophisticated in budget building and management, negotiating skills, and effective long-term buyer and seller behavior. We will have more to say on these points shortly.

Public Sector Applications

In recent years, a host of public agencies have experimented with matrix mechanisms that approach the fully developed system of Apex Aircraft Instruments described above. Two examples will illustrate the directions these experiments have been taking.

Colleges and Universities   Increasingly, colleges and universities are facing the need for diversification to respond to the rapid growth of new areas of study and student demand for special curricula. Frequently, diversification efforts cannot be easily handled within existing departments structured around established scientific disciplines (such as biology) and professions (such as business administration). New curricula or research targets may cut across the domains of two or more existing departments or fall at the boundary between units.

One solution to the diversification dilemma faced by colleges and universities approaches a market-matrix system. A program or curriculum director is appointed and provided with a salary and benefit budget but no permanent faculty positions. This program director is expected to "purchase" faculty members from permanent units in order to offer courses in the new or redesigned area. Just as was the case at Apex Instruments, program directors first contact faculty members to determine their interest in the new curriculum and then negotiate with them and their superiors (deans or department head) for their time.

Program directors are, in this instance, willing buyers carefully shopping for appropriate talents and interest. Again, however, there must be some benefit to the "sellers" (heads of permanent units) if a free and willing exchange is to occur. In many cases, the benefit to the permanent unit is the opportunity to bring in visitors, lecturers, or other part-time faculty, using the funds transferred from the program director to the department's budget for the permanent faculty member's time. With many permanent departments facing steady if not declining budgets, the opportunity to enrich their faculty mix, even temporarily, may be welcome. Furthermore, there is the possibility that new offerings, if they prove successful, may well be housed eventually in the department from which their faculty has been drawn.

Similarly, within large departments some experimentation has begun toward the creation of a matrix system composed primarily of program directors and permanent department heads. For example, in a business school, the directors of undergraduate, M.B.A., and Ph.D. programs may be given a budget designed to fund a particular number of courses and then be expected to negotiate with heads of various groups (accounting, marketing, etc.) for the use of particular faculty members. To our knowledge, none of these intradepartmental matrix systems yet operates as freely as the interdepartmental programs, but some do make substantial use of quasi-market mechanisms.

Public Agencies   A growing number of governmental units are experimenting with matrix systems along the lines described in the preceding examples. For example, a welfare department in a middle-sized city decided that instead of increasing the size of existing units it would experiment with a special target family program. The general charge given to the target family program director was to provide integrated assistance to a selected number of families whose members were heavy users of the specialized services offered by the various permanent units in the department. Again, the program director was given a budget but no permanent personnel slots. He was expected to recruit his staff from among the professional personnel and other employees of the permanent units, negotiating with their unit heads for their release and transferring funds to pay for their time from his budget to their department. Unit heads, operating under the assumption that heavy use of personnel from their units for the experimental program would strengthen their future budget requests, were at least to some extent willing sellers.

Multinational Company Applications

In the largest multinational companies, pressures are mounting for the development of improved mechanisms for interdependence management, and numerous experiments toward fully developed matrix systems are under way (e.g., Davis, 1976; Beer and Davis, 1976; Prahalad, 1976). In the following paragraphs, we will discuss some areas where increased reliance on market devices may be desirable.

As indicated earlier, some forms of multinational operation are, at least in the abstract, simple extensions of domestic structures, and the resulting alignment and interdependence-management issues have relatively clear-cut solutions. For example, the movement of a department store chain into a foreign market demands heavy reliance on the regional manager's knowledge of local conditions to make merchandising decisions. But such reliance differs primarily in degree, not in kind, from that which the organization places on domestic regional managers who order from centrally purchased stock in accordance with expected buyer behavior in their areas. Similarly, the single-product organization (e.g., a soft drink company) may be required to work out complex franchising agreements for foreign operation, but the basic structural format for such agreements is usually already in place. Linear extensions of domestic operations into foreign arenas are characteristic of the food, beverage, container, automotive, farm equipment, pharmaceuticals, and cosmetics industries (Davis, 1976).

Major strategy and structure complications emerge, however, when product organizations begin both manufacturing and marketing operations in foreign countries subject only to some degree of domestic control. The problems accelerate for multiproduct MNCs operating in a large number of foreign areas. For these organizations, the efforts of group product managers to achieve integrated, cost-efficient worldwide production and distribution may conflict with regional managers' desires for variation in product design and joint-venture production to promote product acceptance.

Intraorganizational market mechanisms may be designed to deal with such product-region interdependencies (though their actual operation may be greatly complicated by tax and currency exchange considerations). For example, some organizations are experimenting with varying degrees of freedom in the interchanges between group product and regional profit centers. Group product managers may be allowed to offer regional managers attractive transfer prices in order to promote the initial distribution efforts of selected products. Similarly, regional managers may be allowed to subsidize less efficient foreign production and distribution mechanisms in order to promote acceptance of their full line of products.

However, looking beyond these arrangements, it may well be that the appropriate matrix design for the complex multiproduct MNC is three-dimensional rather than two-dimensional (Davis, 1974). On one axis is the worldwide group *product* manager and on another is the *area* (or regional) manager. On the third axis are the *functional* specialists in charge of production, engineering, research and development, and so on. A highly sophisticated system can be designed to allow all three sectors of the organization to pursue their special interests with their interactions guided by internal market mechanisms (although, to our knowledge, no such fully developed system is now in operation). In such a system, both regional and group product managers could contract with the functional units for their services. Scale economies would generally be expected to work in such a manner that costs for regional product development and production would be higher than central development and production. Nevertheless, guided by market-expansion opportunities, regional managers in some instances might be willing to absorb some of these costs. Group product managers and regional managers would be expected to negotiate prices at which excess foreign production would be exchanged or shortfalls covered.

Clearly, a system of this sort is complicated and fraught with potential for mismanagement. Nevertheless, the present means of handling internal interdependencies through nonmarket, hierarchical decision making (giving decision power to one of the three contending factions) is also subject to costly delays and mismanagement (Prahalad, 1976). Without question, the design and operation of a complete matrix organization with freely operating internal markets would, as suggested earlier, require new managerial skills and major rethinking of the roles of top- and middle-management personnel.

MANAGEMENT OF A MARKET-MATRIX ORGANIZATION

Many years will probably pass before it is known whether or not the market-matrix organization can be called a truly new organizational form—the Type IV structure. However, imagining for the moment that it is, what developments in management theory will be necessary to facilitate the effective use of this type of system?

Recall that in Chapter 8 we discussed concurrent developments in management theory and alternative forms of organization. The Traditional and Human Relations theories of management, both of which supported functional specialization and the centralization of important operating decisions, were highly compatible with Type I and Type II organizations. The Human Resources model, which recognized a far greater potential for self-direction and self-control among individuals and groups, appeared to be a necessary complement to the development of the Type III organization with its much heavier utilization of general managers in charge of largely autonomous units.

One might imagine that because the market-matrix system is designed to allow organizations to pursue mixed strategies with mixed structures it demands a complementary mix of managerial philosophies and practices. That is, Human Relations managers might well direct some portions of the system and Human Resources managers other portions. In the short run, such an arrangement might well work, assuming that present measurement and placement skills could accomplish it. In the longer run, however, we expect that the effective management of a matrix organization, particularly the more sophisticated forms outlined here, will require an even more pronounced shift toward the Human Resources theory of management.

This shift in management theory will not come about easily. Over a decade ago, Forrester (1965, p. 5) anticipated many of the managerial requirements of today's emerging organizational forms, but he also noted that these managerial philosophies and practices were unlikely to be adopted readily: ". . . in matters of social organization we usually propose only timid modification of conventional practice and balk at daring experiment and innovation." Why is this the case? In our opinion, the primary reason managers do not experiment extensively with new organizational designs, even though these are necessary and have been articulated (e.g., Drucker, 1974b; Sayles, 1976), is that most require widespread use of Human Resources values and practices. Most of the research on management theory, however, suggests that the Human Resources philosophy is not widely accepted or practiced. Top managers may well express confidence in the self-direction skills of their division mangers (for the short run at least), but such "confidence" is frequently bolstered by close monitoring of (and potential intervention into) the types of decisions that need to be made independently by division managers in a freely operating matrix system. Moreover, division managers represent a focal point of responsibility, handy points of leverage if top management is dissatisfied with any aspect of divisional performance.

In the market-matrix system, large numbers of managers are expected to participate in the pursuit of unit goals, engaging in resource-allocation negotiations with numerous other managers at various levels throughout the organization. If all such negotiations are to be approved by top management, overload is inevitable. However, if these negotiations are to be governed by market mechanisms, confidence in subordinates' decision-making abilities well beyond that usually shown must be exercised. Just as top managers had to learn at least to restrain their interventions into divisional and regional decision making if the benefits of a Type III organization were to be attained, they must learn even greater restraint in market-matrix or Type IV organizations.

Top management, of course, does not give up control in a matrix system. The dominant coalition is very much a part of the decision making that sets up the internal market. As is the case with a central government, top management can subsidize certain operations it wishes to develop (or maintain) and tax others which have achieved fortuitous, windfall returns. Moreover, top management serves as an appellate court for market inequity contentions and may, if clever, influence market behavior through investments and shifts in alignment without directly monitoring or interfering with internal negotiations. In such a system, as suggested earlier, top management is judged not by the quality of the operating decisions it makes but by the quality of decisions that emerge from the system it has constructed.

In addition to these changes in top management's role and behavior, substantial changes in the orientation and behavior of middle managers will be required. In particular, managers at this level will need assistance in learning negotiating skills and the effects of exploitative market behavior. Market mechanisms inevitably produce short-run monopsonistic and monopolistic positions. Managers need to recognize the longer-lasting costs of exploiting such positions and to develop the skill to assist their colleagues in avoiding dysfunctional behaviors.

In sum, fully developed matrix organizations operate under the assumption that structures and processes can be designed to provide personnel with the information needed to guide their behavior toward appropriate organizational goals and to make it imperative that they interact effectively with other organizational units. The belief that many, if not most, organization members are competent to operate within such systems—the key assumption of the Human Resources model—seems clearly essential.

CONCLUSIONS

It is our view that complex, new alignment and interdependence management problems are facing many modern organizations. The adaptive strategies described in this volume—Defender, Reactor, Analyzer, Prospector, and the emerging mixed strategy-structure forms—are visible to a greater or lesser extent within each of the industries we have studied and probably are common to all industries. It is our belief that successful organizations of the future will be those which develop the capability (frequently with outside aid) to examine their own pattern of strategy, structure, and process; to recognize its costs and benefits; and to make adjustments in the pattern when change is desired or required. At this point, the dynamics of the four current strategic types are much clearer than those of the emerging organizational form. However, we believe that an understanding of the properties of these basic types will prove useful in the design and operation of more complex organizations.

Chapter 10

Conclusions and Extensions

Final chapters can be troublesome. Both author and reader need a sense of completion, but this is difficult to achieve in a book that has ventured into relatively unexplored territory. At this point, we have arrived at a position analogous to that of mountain climbers part way up an un-climbed face, pausing to compare the route traveled against the ascent plan and having to estimate the remaining terrain and distance. Like the climbers, we now have information not available at the start, but we have become so immersed in our immediate task that the once-clear overall route may have become blurred. Moreover, to continue the climbing analogy, it would be time consuming (and perhaps dangerous) to step far enough back to regain that clear perspective. Nonetheless, our intent in this chapter is to summarize and comment on the major points offered in the first nine chapters and to speculate about some future problems and issues in the area of organizational adaptation.

ORGANIZATIONAL ADAPTATION:
THEORY, PROCESS, AND MANAGEMENT

We sought to achieve five major objectives in this book: (1) to develop an understanding of the adaptive process, (2) to provide an explanation of the alternative forms of organizational behavior that exist today, (3) to link these forms of organization to past and present theories of management, (4) to explore the process by which organizations as entire socio-technical systems can be diagnosed and changed, and (5) to create a conceptual foundation for the examination of emerging organizational forms.

The Adaptive Cycle

In Chapters 1 and 2, we argued that the process of organizational adaptation is neither an uncontrolled phenomenon nor a process involving perfectly rational and efficient choice. Instead, adaptation occurs through a series of managerial decisions, the effectiveness of which hinges primarily on how consistently managers' choices are integrated. Until recently, managers have lacked guidance in making total-system strategic choices because relevant concepts and theories tended to deal with only a portion of the overall adaptive process and to treat adaptation in a static manner. Our model of organizational adaptation, called the *adaptive cycle,* was intended to portray the full adaptive process and to suggest the dynamics through which adaptation takes place. In our view, organizational adaptation is essentially composed of three broad problems requiring continuous top-management attention and decisions: the entrepreneurial problem (selecting a viable market domain and a set of objectives relative to it), the engineering problem (creating a technological process for serving the selected domain), and the administrative problem (developing an organization structure and a set of managerial processes to coordinate and control the selected technology, and, further, to direct those innovative activities necessary for maintaining the organization's continuity). As stressed throughout the book, solutions to these three problems must be properly related to each other if an effective adaptive cycle is to be completed.

Strategic Types

In Chapters 3 through 6, we described four different types of organizations, each of which has its own unique pattern of adaptation. These *strategic types,* called the Defender, Prospector, Analyzer, and Reactor, help define a continuum of adaptive behavior along which most existing forms of organization can be arrayed. Three of these organization types, the Defender, Analyzer, and Prospector, are consistent and stable. That is, each has a set of response mechanisms that can be consistently applied when a change occurs in the environment. As these mechanisms are refined over time, the organization develops a unique set of strengths upon which it can rely (and an associated set of weaknesses which it must protect against). These strengths form a stable base from which the organization responds to its environment. The Reactor, on the other hand, is an inconsistent and unstable type of organization. Because it lacks a set of response mechanisms which can be reliably called upon to cope with a changing environment, the Reactor often exists in a continual state of instability. Unless the Reactor's environment is especially benign, management will at some point be forced to move the organization to one of the other three types.

Management Theory

We believe that these two major components of the theoretical framework, the adaptive cycle and the strategic typology, can be profitably employed in diagnosing and changing organizational behavior. In Chapter 7, we discussed and illustrated how the diagnostic and change process might proceed. A major conclusion of that chapter was that successful organizational diagnosis and change is heavily influenced by managers' beliefs concerning how human resources can and should be managed. Therefore, in Chapter 8, we discussed management theory, pointing out the implications of the various organization types for management philosophy and practice. Viewing organization and management theory from an historical perspective, it seemed logical to conclude that any new developments in organizational strategy and structure must be accompanied by similar developments in managerial philosophy and practice if organizations of the future are to be effective.

Emerging Organizational Forms

Future environmental conditions, organizational forms, and management theories were the focus of attention in Chapter 9. In the main, our research dealt with existing patterns of organizational behavior. However, there are a growing number of organizations for whom these current adaptive patterns are insufficient to meet emerging environmental demands. We discussed some of these organizations—aerospace firms, multinational companies, and some conglomerates and public institutions—and suggested that the response mechanisms which they are now developing may be precursors of a new organizational form. Of course, our crystal ball is not infallible, but these organizations appear to be moving toward what we envision as the *market-matrix* organization, a type of organization that can be both flexible and efficient and one that taps a broad range of human capabilities.

SOME KEY POINTS REVISITED AND EXPANDED

The basic theme running through our early chapters was that of patterned behavior, the tendency of organizations to discover, develop, and maintain a set of consistent responses to various environmental events. As Cyert and March (1963) described, and as the organizations in our studies confirmed, once an organization achieves a viable adaptive strategy, search for new approaches tends to decline. Below, we review the dynamics of limited search and its costs and benefits. Then we explore how the dysfunctional aspects of limited search might be avoided, examining the requirements for expanded search to foster organizational learning.

Limited Search: Underlying Dynamics

First, there are forces in an organization's environment that inhibit major shifts in the organization's strategic behavior. As Thompson (1967) pointed out, an organization does not determine its domain unilaterally; each of the major actors in its task environment (customers, suppliers, competitors, regulatory agencies, etc.) builds up its own expectations concerning the role that a given organization has played and will or should play in the future. Apart from the economic constraints and consequences involved, an organization must expend considerable effort simply to establish a new role. As is the case with an individual, when an organization attempts to change its "image," it frequently finds that it is difficult to convince the actors in its environment that the change is real. Thus, these actors almost unwittingly assign a role to the organization that may be difficult to alter.

Second, there are powerful forces inside the organization working against major changes in any satisfactory pattern of behavior. In fact, in both economic and psychological terms, limited search makes good sense. The search process itself is costly, and search activities must compete with other proposals for scarce organizational resources. Psychologically, limited search produces overall continuity and predictability in the activities of organization members, and it does not require managers to conceive of the new and difficult adjustments which would be necessary if the organization were to alter its direction substantially. Finally, the existing pattern of behavior has been created by, and thus presumably serves the interests of, those persons who might have the power to change it.

Benefits of Limited Search

As a result of limited search, the organization develops a set of "distinctive competences" that allows it to maintain itself and perhaps compete aggressively in its industry. These organizational strengths are bolstered by placing certain types of specialists in key executive slots and by shaping the organization's structure and processes to enhance strengths and minimize weaknesses related to its particular pattern of market behavior. Over time, "system-specific" knowledge and expertise accumulate and managers are under strong pressure to reinforce the resultant organization design since, in most cases, organizational success comes from doing better what one is already doing.

Costs of Limited Search

But limited search also imposes at least two significant costs. The first and more obvious cost is that limited search tends to create an organization that is unable to deal with fundamentally different problems. Because the search for solutions to new problems does not extend much beyond already known solutions, the organization is motivated to transform ill-defined problems into a form that can be handled with existing routines (Cohen, March, and Olsen, 1972). Unfortunately, organizations periodically face problems that are resistant to remodeling and require solutions not contained in the organization's repertoire.

The inability to solve new or significantly different problems derives from a larger and usually hidden cost of limited search: the retardation of organizational learning. In order for an organization to learn, that is, to increase the number and kinds of adaptive behaviors it possesses, substantially new forms of behavior may be required from organization members. According to Argyris (1977), most organizational behavior involves "single-loop" learning that occurs only within the confines of the existing system. Individuals or groups are seldom encouraged or permitted to question the ongoing practices of their organizations. In order to expand the set of effective organizational behaviors, "double-loop" learning, where present behavior and its underlying causes are directly confronted, must occur. Organizational learning of this sort is obviously difficult for it requires management to examine in a systematic fashion not only the outcomes of decision making but the processes by which these decisions are reached and to conduct limited experiments in selected areas to extend the organization's capabilities and determine its deficiencies.

An Appropriate Indictment

It is not our intent to indict managers for engaging in limited search. Attempting to reduce uncertainty, attain goals, and gain the cost effectiveness associated with logical operating procedures are appropriate managerial behaviors. However, if managers engage in limited search without periodically examining the consequences of their behavior, that is, if they are not aware of the potential costs of limited search and do not take action to protect against these costs, then a charge of managerial parochialism can be leveled.

More pointedly, despite the fact that limited search is a natural and useful activity, the organization that does not develop mechanisms to protect against the inevitable dysfunctions associated with limited search is behaving irrationally. Such mechanisms, as we have continually stressed, are nothing more than insurance against risks that are quite predictable, at least in the aggregate. The required number and form of these "insurance" mechanisms are, of course, dependent on the organization's unique pattern of strategy, structure, and process. Some strategic types are inherently more prone to certain risks than others (e.g., the Defender to major market shifts and the Prospector to cost inefficiencies and overextension of resources), but all are subject to some level of threat. For example, as pointed out in Chapter 7, the Analyzer's ability to move rapidly into profitable markets may be compromised as technological sophistication increases. Thus, in all cases, limited search is an interesting paradox of organizational behavior, a useful but potentially dangerous activity.

EXPANDED SEARCH: THE LEARNING ORGANIZATION

It seems clear that, whatever its present strategic type, the organization that has invested in risk-protection mechanisms—that has developed the capacity for "double-looped" learning—is likely to have a substantial advantage over its competitors during critical periods of environmental change. Therefore, how can risk-protection mechanisms be constructed, or, more broadly, how can the capacity for expanded search be developed and maintained?

An organization, as noted above, is a deliberately focused mechanism. It survives to the extent that it does a limited set of things well. At the same time that an organization develops its distinctive competence, however, it is exposing itself to risks associated with those things which it does *not* do well. Therefore, learning targets must be identified and pursued which allow the organization to expand its search process. If an organization is a Defender, it needs to develop the ability to scan the environment outside of its particular domain and to assimilate the information thus collected into its long-range plans. Conversely, if the organization is a Prospector, it needs to develop the capacity to be cost-efficient in its more stable areas of operation.

In our view, the learning process must include a language that allows new information to be processed and incorporated into a growing repertoire of organizational behaviors. An organization must know what type it is in comparison with other organizations in its industry or group, it must understand the strengths and weaknesses usually associated with this form of organization, and it must set appropriate learning targets for reducing the impact of these weaknesses on the organization. Building on earlier discussions, particularly in Chapter 7, two key factors appear to characterize effective risk-protection activities of this sort: first, a means of generating and then attracting dominant-coalition attention to *extrasystemic information* concerning the effectiveness and efficiency of the organization's present alignment with its environment, and second, some form of *learning laboratory* in which alternative approaches to market strategy, organization structure, and managerial processes can be explored without interfering with the operation of the central system.

Extrasystemic Information

There are a number of means by which organizations can obtain information and perspectives generally not available, or at least not visible, within the ongoing system. Among these are outside consultants, external members of the board of directors, and venture capital committees.

Outside Consultants   In Chapter 7, we emphasized the usefulness of outside consultants as sources of information and points of view which an organization is unlikely to be able to generate internally. The outside consultant can draw on his experience to transfer information and insights from one organizational setting to another, and he can often bring to the smaller organization analytical skills that are too expensive to develop and maintain within the system. As also noted in Chapter 7, however, a single consultant seldom possesses the complete range of insights and skills needed to examine the total adaptive characteristics of an organization; special expertise may be required across such diverse areas as market analysis, methods engineering, employee training and development, and so on. Therefore, it is imperative that top management understand the overall adaptive process so that it does not fragment outside advice by implementing recommendations in one area without tying these changes into related parts of the organizational system.

Although there are a growing number of consultants who have the capability to assist the organization in acquiring the full range of external assistance needed, the outside consultant's persistent dilemma is that of probing far enough into the existing organization to understand its strengths and weaknesses without becoming so deeply enmeshed that his or her perspective is obscured. As we have pointed out elsewhere (Miles, 1975, p. 164), the normal consultancy model may not enhance organizational learning to any great extent since only a limited segment of the management of the client organization is actively involved in the definition of the organization's problems. If consultants apply prepackaged solutions no matter what the problem, or present organization members with cures for ailments which some of them believe do not exist, or simply accept management's diagnosis of the situation and give the organization the "solution" it wants, then little useful organizational learning will occur, and covert if not explicit resistance to the consultants' prescriptions is guaranteed. On the other hand, where consultants develop an action-research program—helping organization members formulate the questions they want to ask and then aiding them in gathering the information required for an answer—client learning is much more likely to take place. As noted in Chapter 7, management must become skilled not only at determining the type of consulting skills it needs but also the type of consulting approach needed for particular issues.

External Board Members   An organization's board of directors is a potentially valuable mechanism for obtaining extrasystemic information and perspectives, but this mechanism is almost always underutilized. Boards dominated by internal members, with external members chosen only for their links to valued institutions (banks, governmental agencies, etc.), may not achieve the level of risk protection a well-designed board could provide. Outside members with broad experience, unencumbered by specific representational requirements, can play a role akin to that of the external consultant.

Obviously, such external members can function only as effectively as board procedures allow. Those boards whose roles are limited to policy review and crisis intervention offer little opportunity for organizational learning. Moreover, a single isolated external member may not have an impact equal to his or her expertise. While research evidence is limited (e.g., Mace, 1971; Drucker, 1974a, Chap. 52), those organizations which give careful attention to the development of their boards appear to be investing in a useful learning mechanism.

It should be emphasized that we are specifically directing attention here to the neutral outside director. Directors appointed to represent specific interest groups—consumers, for example—clearly may also provide useful perspectives to the organization, but the very nature of their role (and frequently their experience and orientation) limits their ability to offer insights concerning adjustment of the total organizational system. Similarly, while many European governments have presented a strong argument for mandatory worker representation on boards, we believe that the issue of industrial democracy should be dealt with separately from that of developing expanded-search capacity. To the extent that workers have insights concerning system inconsistencies (as is likely), their ideas should be sought by the board whether or not their membership is required by law.

Venture Capital Committees   Increasingly, management is realizing that more good ideas are likely to be present in the system than will ever be processed through normal channels. In fact, numerous anecdotes (and some hard evidence) attest to major product, service, or technological innovations which were substantially delayed or missed entirely by presumably well-managed organizations.

As one approach to the dilemma, there have recently been calls for, and some experimentation with, the creation of venture capital committees composed partially of individuals not directly connected with the organization (Hutchinson, 1976). A venture capital committee is designed to evaluate innovative ideas from organization members outside formal suggestion systems or other development programs. For example, an engineer engaged in work on one project may spot a product innovation not being addressed by his group or by any other organizational unit. Ordinarily, there would be no clear route for this idea to take toward development. However, where a venture capital committee exists, the engineer is encouraged to present his idea to that group with the hope of rapid action. Ideas that are funded for development and testing usually bring their originators monetary rewards in addition to recognition.

The argument for outside representation on such committees or boards recognizes that even units aimed at innovation are prone to limited search. Internal members, such as those who sit on Scanlon Plan or similar committees, may simply not have the information or insight to appraise objectively ideas that radically depart from the organization's conventional wisdom.

The appropriate composition and operation of venture capital committees have not yet been determined. Clearly, such factors as the desirable range of skills and experience are closely dependent on the organization's industry, domain, and technology. At the same time, it is also clear that if external members are truly to expand the organization's search capacity, they (as is the case with members of the board) must be present in sufficient numbers to avoid internal domination and must not be selected on the basis of narrow representational criteria.

Having outside members present, of course, does not guarantee that venture capital committees will in fact be venturesome. Some that we are familiar with operate under such highly constrained and poorly financed conditions that they play only a small role in the development of risk-protection mechanisms. Nevertheless, outside membership on these committees does appear to be highly beneficial to those organizations seriously attempting to develop their learning ability.

Attention to Extrasystemic Information   As suggested above, no matter what mechanisms are in place for the collection of extrasystemic information, there is no guarantee that significant action will be taken and, by extension, that organizational learning will occur. Consultants, as illustrated in Chapter 7, can be employed and then ignored, outside board members can be co-opted or contained, venture capital committees can be little more than window dressing, all as part of the natural process of limited search.

Although current knowledge precludes a full treatment of the conditions necessary for effective development and utilization of extrasystemic information, some crucial aspects should be mentioned. Organizations are most likely to "hear," assimilate, and take action on extrasystemic information to the extent that:

1   top management is aware of its own inherent tendency to defend the organizational system it has helped design;

2   key sources of defensive behavior are recognized and corrected (e.g., reward and control systems that heavily penalize mistakes while failing to reward successful innovation);

3   a number of outside information sources are developed and utilized on an ongoing basis, not simply when crises occur;

4   outside information is used to develop future actions rather than to indict current inefficiencies; and

5   consultants and other outside information sources focus on problem finding rather than answer giving (i.e., collaborating with management to define problems instead of selling modifications of preconceived solutions).

Learning Laboratories

In most organizations a number of learning laboratories, areas within the system in which alternative strategies, structures, and processes can be explored without interfering with the operation of the main system, exist or can be created.

Isolated Divisions, Departments, Regions   Some years ago, Ritti (1970) showed that engineers' feelings of accomplishment and influence were directly related to the distance of their unit from corporate headquarters. Ritti's findings suggested that distant groups were freed from many of the constraints of the existing system and possibly were able to experiment more easily with new methods and approaches. Certainly in multinational corporations there are innumerable examples of regional organizations experimenting with market strategies (and supporting structures and processes) with a degree of freedom that probably would not be possible in the larger domestic system. However, geographically separated divisions of domestic corporations frequently develop their own styles of operation with some more effective than others. In fact even within a single plant, as the Michigan surveys (e.g., Likert, 1967) have regularly shown, considerable variations can and do exist in managerial processes and informal structures.

To thoughtful managers, the differences in patterns of behavior that develop naturally across departments, divisions, or regions will be viewed as spontaneous experiments from which much can be learned that is of value to the total organization. The tendency in many organizations, however, is either to ignore the data flowing from successful variations (by attributing success to chance or favorable circumstances) or to respond by taking action to bring strategies, structures, and processes back into line with overall system standards even when alternative approaches are producing superior results. Obviously, no learning takes place when such actions occur except that the individuals involved learn that they must, in the future, take greater care to conceal even their successful experiments from higher management.

Almost equally unfortunate are those instances in which natural experiments produce successful new approaches that are recognized, copied, and pushed hurriedly into application in the larger system without any clear understanding of why and how these approaches succeeded. Without this understanding, efforts to "spread the gains" are frequently unsuccessful and the wrong lesson is learned, namely, that the new approach does not work.

The process by which organizations might learn more effectively from natural experiments is obviously complex (see March, 1971, for some provocative suggestions). It does seem likely, however, that many approaches to systematizing such learning will only drive experimentation further underground. (On the other hand, the Scanlon Plan and its variants appear to have the capability to bring forth at least some experimental data. See Donnelly, 1977.) At a minimum, organizations concerned with learning how to obtain protection from major risks ought to be devoting attention to the problem of how to make use of information and ideas generated by variation within normal operations.

Subsidiaries Subsidiaries can frequently be used to enhance overall organizational learning without disrupting the existing system. Diversification through acquisition or through internal creation of self-contained divisions is a relatively well-understood technique in most large Prospector organizations. In smaller organizations, however, acquiring or developing a subsidiary system is an issue of much greater magnitude and one for which the parent firm, whether Prospector, Analyzer, or Defender, is far less well prepared. In order to maximize risk protection and learning, the small organization might be encouraged to acquire subsidiaries whose strategy-structure-process pattern differs from its own. (Clearly, acquisition is more reasonable than development in such instances, since the small organization is probably less likely to have excess managerial capacity). For either the large or small organization, however, the dilemma is how to maintain the autonomy of the subsidiary while still learning from its experience.

Given current knowledge and practice, we believe that well-designed royalty arrangements such as that being planned by Alpha Electronics (in Chapter 7) probably have the best chance of solving the autonomy-learning dilemma. Recall that Alpha planned to "sell" to its subsidiary (which had the right to refuse to buy) the license to produce and distribute certain low-priced, standardized versions of Alpha's exotic test equipment. Royalties would then be paid to the parent firm, and a predetermined portion returned to the division that developed the product. Over time, Alpha's management should come to understand the properties that make for a commercial success in the new market without running the risk of attempting to develop and manage products outside the company's basic competence. More important, such an arrangement allows the subsidiary truly to operate its own business without the fear that Alpha will skim off funds needed for product development. Further, the subsidiary should also learn through this arrangement, that is, become increasingly familiar with the parent firm's technology and thus able to create new products on its own. At that point, Alpha will be faced with a new set of problems, but hopefully it will have learned not only in the areas of marketing and engineering, but also in the area of administration, so that it can develop an enlarged financial and control arrangement beneficial to both systems.

Even in the large multidivision corporation, corporate-division financial arrangements frequently reduce division incentive to innovate and restrict interdivisional knowledge transfer (Pitts, 1974, 1977a). If divisions were allowed to receive some payoff on their development activities, again perhaps a royalty on processes adopted by other divisions, total corporate learning might be enhanced. Whatever the arrangements required in a given setting, however, it would appear that conscious attention to the use of subsidiaries and/or divisions as learning arenas for administrative as well as entrepreneurial and engineering problems is a valuable investment of management time. Moreover, reward and control systems that enhance rather than discourage learning are already available (see Miles, 1975, Chap. 8).

To this point, the discussion of organizational learning—the development of the capacity for expanded search—has focused on the problems and opportunities associated with existing types of organizations. How does organizational learning of the sort discussed above apply to emerging organizational forms?

THE ORGANIZATION OF THE FUTURE—TYPE IV

We believe that planned and managed organizational learning can speed the development of a new organizational form capable of responding to simultaneous demands for product-market innovation and cost efficiency. As noted in Chapter 9, the slow development of the market-matrix organization, characterized by bold organizational experiments followed by hasty retreats when threats to existing administrative know-how occur, is not the result of a lack of basic management creativity. Indeed, managers have demonstrated the capacity to invent numerous variations on the matrix structure (Sayles, 1976), complete with multi-dimensional properties (Prahalad, 1976). The barrier to the articulation and development of a true Type IV organization is the threat such a system implies for existing managerial norms and behaviors.

The market-matrix organization, as it appears to be emerging, will disperse information and decision-making responsibility well beyond the limits visible in even the most aggressive Prospector organization of today. The market-matrix organization employs internal market mechanisms to which decision makers throughout the system respond, thus reducing upper management's "hands on" control. At the same time, the market-matrix structure imposes a new set of roles and skill requirements on higher managers which are far more demanding than those present in today's organizations. Some of the behaviors with which middle and lower managers will have to become proficient were described in Chapter 9 (e.g., integrative bargaining, voluntary restraint of exploitative behavior, etc.). Less attention, however, was given to the new role requirements of top management.

The "Mini-Economy"

Top managers of a true market-matrix organization will be required to view their role as that of governing a mini-economy. This role requires that top managers understand the overall system thoroughly, not in terms of *what* decisions ought to be made but in terms of *how* decisions should be made. It is their task to develop consensus for a direction which the system will take and for the right to tax and transfer funds to maintain that thrust while designing and operating conflict resolution mechanisms to handle competing claims.

Note that in the market-matrix structure, top management does not reserve to itself the opportunity-scanning function or the responsibility for cost efficiency in existing operations. Instead, these are built in as components of the system. A key role of top management in such new structures will be that of providing and maintaining learning opportunities. The components of a matrix system have the properties of existing organization types: Defenders in functional departments and stable divisions, Prospectors in project areas or divisions operating in turbulent markets. Top managers who have learned the properties of these types, who can articulate their benefits and costs, would appear to be most capable of success in this new role (particularly in its teaching function). Moreover, most of the requirements for organizational learning discussed above are central elements of the market-matrix system. That is, personnel regularly move from stable, relatively permanent units to changeable, temporary groups and back again, broadening their behavioral repertoire in the process.

Similarly, managers whose basic orientation, like that of the Defender organization, is toward cost efficiency (e.g., production managers, worldwide product managers, etc.) must bargain and/or jointly plan with Prospector managers (e.g., project managers, regional managers, etc.) whose orientation is toward innovation and market responsiveness. In the process, each has the opportunity to learn the costs, benefits, and demands of the other's orientation.

However, while learning opportunities for individuals, units, and the larger organization itself are abundantly available in the market-matrix system, they may not be realized. Initially, at least, top management will find it difficult to govern and regulate the system without exerting hierarchical authority. Pressure will come not only from top management's own preference for direct control and for a return to familiar ways of operating, but also from subordinates' expectations that decisions which concern resource allocation should be made by top management. To the extent that top management is able to facilitate rather than control and to convince lower managers that they can—and in fact must—accept broader responsibility, learning will occur. However, more often than not, today's top managers appear unable (or unwilling) to perform this function. Most mechanisms in today's organizations do not provide full self-governing information, and resource-allocation decisions are still made hierarchically, with cost-efficiency priorities dominating at one time and effectiveness at another. The basic lessons learned by managers in such circumstances are the familiar ones of self-protection, short-run exploitation, and the immediate appeal to higher authority in times of conflict.

Concurrent with a lessening of direct control, top management must develop competence in *systems diagnosis.* It must acquire the skill not only to determine which component of the system is operating ineffectively but also to ascertain why this malfunction is occurring. To the extent possible, top management needs the skill to spot such malfunctions before they occur, to recognize, for example, when a prototypical project or operation is moving out of the experimental stage and when it ought either to be given permanent status or allocated to an established unit. Conversely, top management must be able to identify (or help functional managers identify) the point at which stable operations are losing their traditional market base so that new structures and processes can be arranged within the unit or these operations spun off from it.

Finally, top management must develop the broad and somewhat nebulous ability to maintain a *balance of desirability* in all areas of the organization. One of the main difficulties of matrix management is that many employees find their "permanent" homes less desirable than project assignments. Preference for projects occurs, in part, because project structures and processes virtually demand Human Resources management while stable operations can be managed in Traditional or Human Relations modes.

We predict that in the long run successful market-matrix organizations will tend toward Human Resources management in both their stable and changing areas. (Note: this prediction does not mean that the same structures and processes will exist in both areas, only that the same commitment to maximum development and utilization of member capabilities will be present.) Moreover, an investment in Human Resources management in areas where it is not a necessity is likely to be viewed by the progressive organization as further "risk protection."

A FINAL WORD

Our intent in this book has been to provide a means by which scholars and managers can describe, discuss, and increase their understanding of the dominant behavioral characteristics of modern organizations. Our theoretical framework is in no sense complete, as modifications and extensions will undoubtedly occur. Nevertheless, our experience with both students and managers has confirmed that where discussions proceed along lines offered here, learning does occur, learning which we believe is conducive to the improved operation of existing systems and absolutely essential to the development of tomorrow's organizations.

The knowledge that our approach appears to aid the learning process allows us to end the book on a rather positive note. To complete our opening analogy, we have climbed as far as we can with our present map and equipment. We did not reach the summit, but we have a good idea where the best route lies.

Part Two

Industry Studies

Chapter 11

Strategy in a Single Industry: The Case of College Textbook Publishing

This chapter describes the first of three studies that contributed to the development of the theoretical framework presented in this book. The bulk of this study was conducted in 1972. Then, in 1975, three of the original participating firms were revisited to provide follow-up evidence in certain areas. Thus, in the sections below, we will refer periodically to the first and second "phases" of the study. We begin by discussing the original research problem, the methodology used in the first phase of the study, and the initial set of findings. Then we discuss the purpose and results of the follow-up study. Last, we briefly summarize the objectives and results of both phases of this research.

ORIGINAL RESEARCH PROBLEM

The general purpose of this study was to investigate how an organization responds to conditions in its environment. In many ways, the study was exploratory, since at that time there was no readily available theoretical framework which took the organization in its environment as a unit of observation and analysis.

Two previous works largely formed the conceptual basis of this study. First, Lawrence and Lorsch (1967), in a study of 10 industrial firms in three widely differing industries, analyzed the degree of uncertainty associated with three "sectors" of each firm's environment: (1) the market sector, (2) the technoeconomic sector (the production process), and (3) the scientific sector (the state of the arts in the industry). Their unit of analysis was not the total organization but three major organizational subunits that corresponded to the three environmental sectors: marketing, production, and research and development. Within each subunit, the authors measured managers' perceptions of environmental uncertainty and then correlated these with measures of organization structure and several individual characteristics. In general, Lawrence and Lorsch's findings involving organizational subunits were consistent with those of an earlier interindustry study by Burns and Stalker (1961) that involved entire organizational systems. That is, subunits facing the most uncertain environments were the least structured ("organic"), while subunits facing more predictable environments were highly structured ("mechanistic"). Thus, it appeared from the Lawrence and Lorsch study that organization structures and managers' perceptions of the environment were related.

However, shortly after the study by Lawrence and Lorsch, Weick (1969) raised the possibility that managerial perceptions might not be strongly related to the "actual" conditions in the organization's environment. Weick introduced the concept of environmental enactment, the idea that managers choose to focus their attention on only certain portions of the environment and thereby generate the conditions to which their organizations respond. If enactment was a valid concept, then managers perceived their own "relevant" environment, and this enacted reality was the basis for organizational response.

Combining the findings from the Lawrence and Lorsch study with Weick's concept of enactment, the fundamental problem guiding this particular study was: "Does an organization's form of enactment—its selection and development of a particular domain within the larger environment—produce predictable patterns in managerial perceptions and in organizational structure and process?" More specifically, two of the important questions derived from this problem were the following:

1   Is there a relationship between managers' perceptions of the environment and environmental conditions that have been determined "objectively"?

2. Are organizational structure and process consistent with either the objectively determined environment or with managerial perceptions?

RESEARCH DESIGN

Industry Setting

Data for this study were collected in 16 college textbook publishing firms. Only one industry was chosen so as not to confound managerial perceptions and the objective measures of the environment. Presumably, a sample that included different types of organizations would have contaminated the measurement and understanding of environmental influences and the organizational variables selected for the study. Furthermore, it was believed necessary to examine an industry that was undergoing some amount of market change. The reasoning here was that changing environments are likely to produce greater uncertainty than static environments, and it was hoped that diversity among managerial perceptions would be fostered by a certain amount of market turbulence. Finally, industries which were so large and complex as to inhibit an understanding of changing market conditions and their associated organizational responses were to be avoided. Our desire was to locate an industry in which the behavior of the major firms could be compared and contrasted with each other. Based on information from several sources, the college textbook publishing industry appeared to be an appropriate setting for this research.

Historical Development of the Industry   College textbook publishing is only a portion of the printing and publishing industry which produces books, maps, newspapers, magazines, sheet music, postcards, calendars, printed advertising, and playing cards. Primary products for the college market include textbooks, laboratory manuals, workbooks, tests, and audiovisual materials, and these are sold to college students in both 2-year and 4-year schools in the United States and abroad.

At the turn of this century, no publisher had a separate college department, due mainly to the fact that there were less than 350,000 college students at that time. Henry Holt and Company (now Holt, Rinehart, and Winston) had published several distinguished college texts, but the first college department was established in 1906 by The Macmillan Company.

Shortly after the end of World War II, college textbook sales increased dramatically. Returning servicemen, taking advantage of the GI Bill, enrolled in colleges and universities in large numbers. This spurt in enrollments, combined with predictions of an increase in the postwar birthrate, gave rise to great optimism about the college textbook business in future years. Therefore, during the 1950s, several companies were determined to shed the "cottage" or "country club" image of the industry. For example, Prentice-Hall became widely recognized as the first college publisher to view publishing as a *business* when, in the early fifties, it aggressively began to secure manuscripts and to promote their sale in the college market. Other publishers quickly followed suit, most notably McGraw-Hill and Holt, and by continually attempting to improve the methods by which authors were located and their books produced and marketed, these and other publishing houses showed steadily increasing sales and profits.

Next came the "golden sixties," a period of rapid industry growth stimulated primarily by the maturation of the World War II baby boom and by heavy federal aid to education. During this period, in which domestic sales more than tripled (from $97 million to $324 million), the compounded annual sales growth rate of 13 percent was well in excess of the rates in most other areas of the economy, and to obtain the needed capital for such rapid expansion, a number of firms considered merging and/or "going public" (i.e., selling stock on the open market). In the early sixties, mergers, acquisitions, and public stock offerings reached almost feverish proportions for an industry considered to be relatively conservative and unsophisticated in its management. Also, many new firms entered the industry, and by the end of the decade there was heavy competition for the college textbook dollar.

The flower of the sixties quickly lost its bloom in 1970 when the textbook sales growth rate fell substantially, due mainly to a decline in college FTE (full-time equivalent) enrollments and students' per capita expenditures on books. Because of the abolition of the draft and the turmoil created by the Vietnam war, students were not entering colleges in as large numbers as in the 1960s, and those who did simply were not buying as many textbooks. Moreover, a number of other forces developed which tended to offset the previously high demand for college texts, including student sharing of books, improved efficiency of used-book dealers, and increased use of copying machines. Finally, and perhaps most important in the long run, traditionally clear-cut demarcations of both markets and products were breaking down. Curricular changes in many colleges and universities made "standard" textbooks less appropriate if not obsolete for many courses (particularly in the social sciences), and many "trade" books (books of general interest) began to be regularly adopted for classroom use.

These environmental conditions produced a very poor year for college textbook publishing companies in fiscal 1971 (April 1971–April 1972), and due to the subsequent recession and inflation that plagued the economy, 1972 and 1973 were only marginally better. However, just when publishers' concerns were being more frequently and openly expressed, college enrollments increased markedly in the fall of 1974, particularly among part-time and female students. This enrollment increase, combined with higher per capita expenditures on texts and a general price increase reflecting the rapidly escalating cost of paper, produced substantial revenue and profit figures for many textbook publishers in fiscal 1974. In fall 1975, the increase in the overall enrollment rate was the highest among 4-year colleges and universities since 1970; the increase in the freshman enrollment rate was the highest in 10 years. However, it is still too early to tell whether or not the 1974–1976 enrollment growth rate represents a trend in the industry.

Given present enrollment projections, a view of cautious optimism might be generally appropriate for college textbook publishers today. The straight-line projection of current college enrollments might provide cause for alarm, for an absolute decline in total college enrollments is predicted in 1983 (from 9.2 million students to 8.9 million). However, if certain changes occur (a change in the student body mix to include more part-time students, minorities, and continuing education students; more federal aid to education; more rapid responses by universities to meet demands for new programs; etc.) then large opportunities may await those publishing companies which accurately perceive and respond to the growth areas. Although no one foresees a return to the heyday of the sixties, college publishers appear to have moderate to good profit opportunities in the intermediate run if they are solidly managed. In sum, publishing companies seem to have moved from the leisurely conduct of business during the fifties, through the rapid growth and large profits of the sixties, to a period where opportunities are available to those companies which move consistently and aggressively in a well-conceived direction.

Organizational Sample and Data Collection Procedure

For the reasons stated above, the college textbook publishing industry appeared to provide an appropriate arena for the planned research. However, in order to investigate the possibility further, a pilot study was conducted in one of the better-known publishing houses. This pilot study, consisting of numerous interviews with the company's eight top managers over a period of approximately 2 months, yielded three conclusions that were important to the remainder of the study. First, as one descended the hierarchy in this organization, managerial perceptions tended to be directed more and more inward. Only such top executives

as the president, college division director, editor-in-chief, and national
sales manager continually and intensively scanned the environment in
search of opportunities for and potential threats to the organization.
Thus, if the impact of the environment on the organization was to be
assessed, the perceptions of these individuals appeared to be most crucial. Second, these top executives agreed unanimously that market factors (consumer buying behavior, competitors' actions, identification of
new markets, etc.) were the key uncertainties affecting their company.
That is, although numerous elements of the environment had to be taken
into account in decision making, market factors were weighted most
heavily by these executives. Finally, each of the executives in this organization agreed that the industry was continuing to undergo a good deal of
change and that the responses of their competitors were quite varied.
Therefore, it appeared that both managerial perceptions of and organizational responses to the changing conditions in this industry were heterogeneous, a desired feature of the study.

The college textbook publishing industry is composed of approximately 75 firms with total sales of $564 million in 1976. However, of
these 75 organizations, about 20 companies account for the vast majority of textbook sales. The sample ultimately selected for this study
included 16 organizations: 11 of the largest 20 and 5 randomly selected
small publishers. Size, in terms of number of employees in the college
department, ranged from 40 to 700. Data were obtained from interviews
with 62 upper-echelon executives in the 16 companies. In each firm, an
attempt was made to interview three key people: the college division
director, the editor-in-chief, and the national sales manager. In addition,
knowledgeable industry observers such as investment analysts, trade
association executives, and private consultants were interviewed.

Variables and Measures

Based on the results of the pilot study, it was decided that only market
uncertainty would be measured specifically. In each firm, managers'
perceptions of the predictability of product demand and competitors' behavior were assessed using interview items. These perceptions were then
categorized as low, moderate, or high perceived market uncertainty.

Alternatively, "objective" measures of market uncertainty were
constructed based on two key dimensions which had been hypothesized
in the literature as likely to produce uncertainty: homogeneity-
heterogeneity and stable-changing (Thompson, 1967). These objective
measures, developed for each firm by taking a random sample of 100 of
its textbook titles from the *Publishers' Trade List Annual,* were not dependent on managers' views of the market environment. Instead, these

measures simply indicated whether a company published narrowly or broadly in the total market (homogeneous-heterogeneous) and whether the domains in which it did publish were stable or changing (based on rankings from academics and publishing executives).

Each organization's general response to market uncertainty was hypothesized to vary primarily at the input and output ends of the organization. Thus, appropriate measures were constructed that assessed (1) the organization's attempts to control variability in its primary input (i.e., manuscripts), and (2) the intensity of the organization's market research efforts. In addition, the process by which several major publishing decisions were made was examined in order to determine the degree to which decision-making authority was centralized or decentralized.

In sum, the study examined the effects of perceived versus objective market uncertainty (the environmental variables) on control of input variability, intensity of market research, and centralization of decision making (the organization variables). In addition, numerous questions were asked about the development of the organization's structure, production processes, relations with subsidiaries, and so on. The purpose of these additional questions was to explore the context in which these focal variables operated.

Hypotheses

All of the specific hypotheses that were examined in this study can be summarized in the following manner:

1   Organizations in which top managers perceive a high degree of market uncertainty will make greater efforts to control input variability, will exhibit more intensified market research, and will have less centralized decision-making processes than organizations in which top managers perceive a low degree of market uncertainty.

2   Organizations in heterogeneous and changing market environments will make greater efforts to control input variability, will exhibit more intensified market research, and will have less centralized decision-making processes than organizations in homogeneous and stable market environments.

3   The three organizational variables (control of input variability, intensity of market research, and centralization of decision making) will correlate more closely with managers' perceptions of the market than with the objective measures of heterogeneity and change.

FINDINGS

According to the results presented in Table 11-1, all but two of the relationships fell into the predicted pattern, but none was particularly strong.

Table 11-1   Relationships Between the Three Measures of Market Uncertainty and the Organization Variables[a]

Organization variable	Perceived market uncertainty	Objective measures of market uncertainty	
		Homogeneous-heterogeneous	Stable-shifting
Centralization of decision making	−.30 (p<.20)	.00	.45 (p<.05)[b]
Control of input variability	.48 (p<.05)	.37 (p<.15)	.37 (p<.15)
Intensity of market research	.36 (p<.20)	.35 (p<.20)	−.37 (p<.20)[b]

N = 62

[a] Degree of association was determined by using the contingency coefficient C and level of significance by chi-square analysis.
[b] Relationships which did not occur in the predicted direction.

The initial interpretation of these results was that organizations in uncertain market environments tended to have organic rather than mechanistic structures and that these features of the organization were more closely aligned with managerial perceptions than with objective indicators of environmental conditions. However, based on the remaining interview data, it was clear that these general linkages among environment and structure did not fully reflect the actual relations that existed between these organizations and their environments.

The most apparent discrepancy between the data in Table 11-1 and the larger pool of data from the interviews was that managers' perceptions could not be weighted equally. That is, in order to explain why a company had undertaken a particular course of action in response to environmental change, it was necessary to take into account the power and influence patterns within the organization and to relate these patterns of influence to organizational responses. In some companies, for example, the college division director had risen through the ranks from the financial and production/distribution areas, and, given his or her background, perceived the environment very differently than did counterparts in other companies who had come from the marketing and editorial ranks. These contrasting backgrounds of the top executives affected their perceptions, the decisions they made, the subordinates they chose, etc., and our perceptual measures did not account for these differences in power and influence across top-management groups.

Furthermore, many of the managers who were interviewed wanted to express their perceptions in much more specific terms than was suggested by the interview items. Several managers felt that their perceptions were best expressed in terms of specific projects (e.g., trying to develop new markets was always seen as a very uncertain type of activity), and many more believed that their perceptions at the moment were substantially different from their perceptions of the year before. Thus, it appeared that our attempt to categorize and compare reactions of managers and organizations by asking standardized questions was, in many instances, distorting the complexity and richness of these managers' views.

Finally, it was apparent that most managers' perceptions were closely tied to the development of their particular company, and they replied to the questions in the context of their organization's specific strengths and weaknesses. For example, in replying to a question about changes in the demand for college textbooks, many managers answered only from the standpoint of their company's ability to take advantage of changes in demand. In a significant number of cases, it was extremely difficult to get managers to speak in terms associated with overall industry conditions. To these managers, divorcing the company from its place in the industry was difficult to do conceptually and, consequently, was regarded as a somewhat artificial exercise.

These factors—different influence patterns across managerial groups, the complex and frequently changing nature of perceptions, and the close relationship between perceptions and company characteristics—suggested that an expanded and more refined concept of the organization and its environment was needed. It was clear that the perceptions of individual managers could not simply be aggregated to obtain the organization's overall view of the environment, nor could a particular action taken by the organization be predicted from any one individual's views. It seemed that even within this relatively small sample of 16 companies there were different types of organizational behavior that could be identified. Therefore, the data were reinterpreted from this perspective, resulting in the construction of the organization typology presented in the book. These four patterns of behavior were called *strategic types* to suggest that the entire organization adopts an *orientation* toward its environment, and this orientation determines the lines along which the organization is designed. This orientation is what Weick (1969, 1977) calls enactment, and managerial perceptions conform relatively closely to the overall form of enactment.

FOLLOW-UP STUDY

Because this study did not originally set out to develop a typology of strategic behavior in organizations, the initial phase of the research lacked the necessary data to describe in much detail the characteristics of each of the four types of organizations. Therefore, in 1975, we returned to three of the original companies that most closely fit the three "stable" strategic types (i.e., a Defender, an Analyzer, and a Prospector). It was hoped that a more complete specification of the features of these organizations would lead to a larger, more systematic study at some later date.

The three follow-up firms were selected by first listing those companies that appeared, based on the original data, to be representative of the types of organizations in our framework (including the Reactor). This list contained five organizations: a Defender, a Reactor, an Analyzer, and two Prospectors. This list, along with a brief description of the four types, was sent to the president of a marketing company in the textbook industry, and his evaluations corresponded exactly to ours. Using an interview format, the same procedure was followed with the president of one of the firms in the original study (which was not chosen for the second phase). His views were in basic agreement with ours and the other president's, although he found it more difficult to "type" entire organizations in this manner. Thus, on the basis of our own beliefs and those of two external observers, we felt sufficiently certain of our three choices to proceed. During the course of the follow-up interviews, we solicited two more independent opinions (from a high-level official in the publishers' trade association and an investment analyst who closely monitors publishing firms), both of which essentially supported our choice of the three organizations.

Ten upper-level managers in the three companies were interviewed (five of whom were also respondents in 1972). When their evaluations of their own firm and the other two were combined with the four external opinions, all 14 respondents agreed unanimously that the companies chosen as the prototypical Defender and Analyzer were appropriate. Ten of the 14 respondents agreed with the Prospector choice (the other four called this firm an Analyzer).

The follow-up interviews focused on three areas: (1) the company's choice of a product-market domain and its development of the domain over time; (2) the organization's core technological process for moving manuscripts from the identification and development stage through production to distribution; and (3) major structure-process characteristics such as descriptions of the organization chart, market research efforts, discretion allowed key individuals such as editors, and so forth. (The reader will note that these three categories correspond to the entrepreneurial, engineering, and administrative portions of the adaptive cycle discussed in Chapter 2. However, at this time we did not have much knowledge of the dynamic nature of this cycle.)

In the following pages, we will describe how these three organizations operate in the college textbook publishing industry.

The Defender

The Defender is a highly successful firm that is over 70 years old. Since its inception, the company has limited its product-market domain to the fields of business and economics. The growth of the organization has closely paralleled the expansion of business education generally. Beginning with a single bookkeeping text, the company added books in spelling, law, typewriting, penmanship, and salesmanship. In the early days, sales were largely to private business schools because high schools and colleges were not offering business courses to any large extent.

After World War I, however, there was a significant expansion in business courses in high schools and colleges. During the 1920s, the company realized the necessity of publishing different books and materials to satisfy the needs of high schools, private schools, and colleges and universities. By 1930, the expansion program was well under way, and today the organization has three separate departments that publish materials for each of the three types of schools.

The Entrepreneurial Problem Throughout its history, this company has not had any serious market problems. Its very first textbook filled a specific market need, and the fields of business and economics have consistently remained healthy market areas to this day. At the time of the second visit to this organization in 1975, management had no plans other than to take full advantage of the recent (and projected) influx of students into business and economics.

This company is almost unmatched in its ability to meet rapidly and effectively all needs for instructional materials in business at the high school and community college level. With a shift in student enrollments toward the 2-year colleges expected to continue through the seventies, the company can anticipate increased growth in a market segment in which it is already the most dominant firm. Thus, for over 70 years this Defender has continued to penetrate the business and economics market, and environmental forces have consistently favored its choice of domain.

Four-year colleges and universities, however, are a market segment in which the company is relatively weak. There appear to be two major reasons for the company's lower visibility at this level: (1) the organization's "image" as a publisher of lower-division textbooks, and (2) a policy of publishing only one book in each subject area. The first factor seems to be the price the company is paying for its success at the other market levels, while the "one-book" policy does not offer professors at the 4-year schools much opportunity to experiment with different teaching materials. Over the last few years, the Defender has been attempting to make greater inroads into the 4-year schools by having its editors and sales representatives make more contacts with professors, but the company does not wish to publish "experimentally" for this market because its very successful list of titles might become diluted by poor-selling texts. Thus, it may be some time before the Defender is an important force in the 4-year colleges and universities market.

The Engineering Problem   The Defender has a production and distribution system that is entirely consistent with its narrowly defined product-market domain. Because of its one-book publication policy, most of the production people work on revisions within the company's current list of titles. The production staff is composed of talented individuals (many with advanced degrees in English) who attempt to make each book easily readable and, they hope, the leader in its field. No manuscript is published until it has been carefully researched, written, revised, and edited through the close cooperation of the authors, the editorial department, consultants, and the sales department. Unlike some other publishing houses, however, the Defender does not have an elaborate art and design group among its production staff. Almost none of the books published by this company contain color photographs or figures, and the overall design format is very straightforward. In general, this Defender's production process is relatively simple and very efficient. In addition, by avoiding some of the expensive art and design activities used by other publishing companies, the Defender operates on a lower production-cost curve.

An equal amount of managerial attention has been devoted to increasing the efficiency and productivity of the sales and distribution system. A very high proportion of the company's sales representatives are former business teachers, and their teaching background helps in selling to the business and economics market. Further, the company's limited range of products allows each sales representative to know fully what he is selling and how it compares with the books of competitors. Finally, the representatives of this company call on virtually every school that is a potential user of the company's products. Many schools that are given, at most, perfunctory attention by representatives from other companies provide a valuable source of revenue for this organization.

The Administrative Problem   The consistency of this company's product-market domain (narrow, stable) and its production and distribution technology (efficient) extends through the administrative structure and processes of the organization. This company is very tightly controlled by the president and executive vice-president. The president is a financial specialist and is essentially in charge of finance and data processing, plant and shipping, and personnel. Most operating responsibilities belong to the executive vice-president, who is in charge of the sales and marketing, editorial, and production departments. Thus, the dominant coalition in this organization is composed of two people between whom a very efficient division of responsibilities has evolved. The executive vice-president runs the company on a day-to-day basis, freeing the president to deal with financial matters and to improve distribution efficiency. Other key managers, for example, the general sales manager, editor-in-chief, and production manager, all reported that they usually have less decision-making discretion than their counterparts in competing firms, but each expressed his or her feeling of pride in working for a company that "knows what it's doing." Over the course of the 3-year study period, the only major managerial change was to hire a new sales manager for the college department, as the company was attempting to make greater inroads into the 4-year colleges and universities. The new sales manager reported that the company had a history of "hoarding information" (another way of saying that information was centralized), and one of his first objectives was to convince top management of the need for making more information and resources available to his unit if it was to investigate the 4-year market effectively. Before this individual was hired, very little scanning of the environment took place beyond the company's familiar domain. Finally, another characteristic of the Defender's dominant coalition (and, indeed, the entire organization) was its stability and permanence. Over half of the company's employees have been there for at least 10 years, and a number have served as many as 40 years. In both the central office and field staffs, promotions are almost always made from within.

The organization is structured along functional lines, which distinctly separate the sales, production, and editorial departments. As noted earlier, the editorial department works mostly on revisions of the company's current books, so this department does not contain nearly as many field editors (individuals who search for new manuscripts) as other companies' similar departments. The sales staff, also as noted earlier, is very aggressive and thorough, and it has been the company's practice to hire business teachers out of high schools and community colleges to sell to these markets. Because of their personal backgrounds and the fact that the company produces few books, these sales representatives know their product well enough to operate without extensive coordination and supervision.

Finally, the production department complements the sales and editorial departments with its ability to transform efficiently a manuscript into final form. This department is composed largely of talented specialists who make copy readable, and they generally perform activities associated with molding a product (books, tests, filmstrips, etc.) to fit a target market exactly. It is important to note that the only significant committee that has been created to coordinate activities among sales, editorial, and production is headed by an individual from the production department.

The organization's major managerial processes conform nicely to its specialized and formalized structure. Early in the organization's development, the central offices were moved close to the company's primary printer and other sources of supply. Ninety percent of the printer's business comes from this publishing firm, and the two organizations have worked together closely to integrate scheduling, upgrade equipment and processes, etc. Thus, planning tends to be a somewhat routine activity that is centered around printing schedules. Many economies of scale (and thus cost savings) are achieved by this close relationship between publisher and printer, and other important planning needs can be more easily woven into this basic relationship than is the case with publishing companies that work with many independent printers.

Once basic plans have been set, yearly operations typically flow smoothly. Financial and production information, as noted earlier, is centrally controlled, so deviations from plan are quickly spotted and corrected. With the exception of the committee that coordinates the sales, editorial, and production departments, few significant lateral relations occur in this organization. Thus, information and conflict resolution tend to be handled through normal hierarchical channels. In general, the organization operates as a well-directed and efficient mechanism, the epitome of a Defender.

The Analyzer

The Analyzer organization was in many ways a Reactor at the time of the first visit to this company. Although the firm was a large, successful, and respected publisher of high-quality educational materials, management was coming to the conclusion in the early seventies that it had allowed the company to drift to the point where it was in danger of becoming significantly out of step with changes in the college market. Unlike the Defender, which is a "specialty" publisher, the Analyzer is a "general" publisher with a product-market domain that spans most of the major academic fields and disciplines. The company's basic strengths, however, were in the areas of natural sciences, mathematics, and computers, and these disciplines accounted for over half of the firm's business. Second to the hard sciences in sales volume were the humanities and social sciences. The company's business and economics titles ranked a distant third in total sales, while the vocational-technical area represented the smallest portion of the company's overall business. According to top management, however, this market profile was the exact opposite of predicted areas of future growth. The projections of industry experts indicated that the business-economics and vocational-technical areas should expand during the seventies, while sales in the hard sciences and humanities-social sciences should decline.

Therefore, in 1972, a new college division director was appointed (the former national sales manager) and charged with the task of bringing this organization more into line with current and projected market developments. It was information about the changes he was making in late 1974 and early 1975 that led us to consider this organization as an Analyzer. In 1975, we asked this particular individual and several others to reconstruct the reorganization of this company's college division.

The Entrepreneurial Problem As indicated, the company faced a potentially serious entrepreneurial problem in the beginning of the seventies: the product-market focus of its college division appeared to be inconsistent with market trends. The college division had been formed as a separate division in 1968 with the objective of publishing in most academic fields from the freshman through first-year graduate student market, and it began active publication of texts primarily in the company's previously strong areas of science, mathematics, and computers. Then, in 1971, a small, wholly owned subsidiary was formed and located in California. Although not large, this subsidiary was intended to be a full-service publisher (i.e., not limited to a few disciplines) and was specifically created to give the New York-based parent company West Coast representation. Moreover, the subsidiary was to experiment with publishing briefer, better written, and more colorful books on certain core topics in a wide variety of disciplines. Many of this subsidiary's books were to be supplemented with films and other audiovisual materials in order to form complete "learning packages." In the 4-year period between 1971 and 1975, the company published a number of successful new books in the sciences, mathematics, computer sciences, business, and psychology.

In 1972, a second subsidiary was established in California. This company was to publish both textbooks and professional and reference books in the fields of information science, accounting, library science, and computer applications. This second subsidiary was to be a "fully vertical" publisher in that it would cover the first-year college to professional market.

Midway through 1974, it was obvious to the college division director that the division was not making a clearly directed effort at tapping the business and economics market. Textbooks for this market were being published by the two subsidiaries and by the college division business group itself, and the overlap of three sets of editors all searching for new manuscripts in the same field caused tremendous planning and coordination problems. Therefore, in late 1974, the director made three important entrepreneurial decisions: (1) to maintain publication of quality textbooks in the hard sciences and humanities-social sciences but not to grow significantly in these areas; (2) to focus heavily on the business and economics markets; and (3) to publish only marginally in the vocational-technical market for the time being since this area required substantially different expertise from that the division possessed. These entrepreneurial decisions subsequently had a major impact on the structure and operations of the college division.

The Engineering Problem   The engineering changes that were made to implement the desired changes in domain fit neatly into the Analyzer model. The company's stable area of business—hard sciences, computers, mathematics, social sciences, etc.—remained largely unchanged except that new titles were sought less actively. However, the company's new growth areas, business-economics and vocational-technical, were dramatically reorganized and largely separated from the traditional areas. The second subsidiary was dissolved and its operations absorbed into the original subsidiary. In addition, the entire business-economics group from the parent company in New York was moved to California to form a single combined company.

Although this consolidation of three separate operations into a single subsidiary was primarily a structural change, it greatly altered the company's overall technology for producing textbooks and other educational materials. Where formerly all production was performed at the company's New York headquarters, now only books in the stable areas of science, mathematics, etc., were produced there. In the business-economics and vocational-technical areas, the company now used smaller and more flexible technological processes that could be rapidly adjusted to meet the particular needs of these two markets. The California subsidiary was thus free not only to develop books but also to produce them, and this technological flexibility permitted quicker and more effective market entry than if every project had to go through production at the New York headquarters.

The Administrative Problem   Besides the consolidation of the two subsidiaries and the parent company's business-economics group, other administrative changes were made that were rapid, synergistic, and successful. In April 1975, the company purchased the entire product line of another publisher. Although this publisher's list of titles was mostly in predicted slow-growth areas such as mathematics and the humanities, the list was also one of the most profitable, and the acquisition afforded instant and visible entry into several fields where the company had not been active. Moreover, by purchasing the product line but not the personnel or other assets of the acquired firm, the Analyzer was able to increase sales and profits quickly without adding substantially to overhead. These cost savings were then available for allocation to the publishing programs in the business-economics and vocational-technical areas.

Today this organization is structured very much along the lines of the Analyzer model. Instead of the previous functional structure, where the editorial, production, and marketing groups were separate, the new structure is a decentralized product organization with resources allocated to four publishing groups that report to the college division director. Reporting to the head of each publishing group (natural sciences, humanities-social sciences, business-economics, and vocational-technical) are field editors in relevant disciplines and a marketing specialist. This reorganization allows each of the four publishers (as they are called) to determine the needs for his or her area, to control the field editors in their efforts to locate and develop publishable materials, and to market and control the inventory of all books and materials in his or her area through the marketing specialist. Except for the business-economics and vocational-technical groups, which have their own technological capabilities, the sales, production, and service operations remain centralized for purposes of efficiency and cost control.

The Prospector

The Prospector is a large, successful, general publisher whose strengths lie in the humanities and social sciences, although this company is a respected publisher in many other fields.

The Entrepreneurial Problem   This company is widely recognized throughout the industry as a leader in product and market innovation. The most striking difference between this organization and the Defender described above is that the Prospector's management does not agree unanimously on what the company's product-market domain is or should be. During the second phase of the study, several key managers discussed the chronology of the organization's domain development over the past decade.

Although the company apparently had been a Prospector at least since the early fifties, it was during the tumultuous sixties that the organization's domain changed most rapidly. During the sixties, many colleges and universities experimented with curricular and program changes that enabled some publishers to conduct an almost continuous program of innovation. Short paperback books on certain core topics, films and other audiovisual materials to augment texts, commissioning of authors to write books that were largely defined by the publisher, pairing academic authors with newspapermen and other professionals to write "more relevant" books—these and a variety of other publishing innovations were pursued by this firm. Of course, every one of these experimental efforts did not ultimately pay off in financial terms. Nonetheless, several managers commented on the beneficial aspects of building capabilities into the organization that would be available if and when they became necessary, and they also stressed the importance of maintaining the firm's image as one of the industry's major innovators.

During the first half of the seventies, the company engaged in a more deliberate development of some of the markets that it had skimmed in the sixties; one executive referred to this process as "crack filling." Whereas in previous years, individual editors' intuition and expertise provided most of the impetus for product and market development, the firm began to supplement the editors' personal capabilities with a computerized data base containing relevant information about all of the company's significant markets. The twin objectives of this computerized data bank were to guide the editors' decisions in areas that needed to be developed more fully while simultaneously freeing them to do investigative work in areas not yet explored by the company. A by-product of this computerized market research system was that new editors with a particular expertise desired by the company could be hired and quickly brought up to date on where and how market "cracks" could be filled. By 1975, the system had not been fully put into operation and tested, but, if successful, it may allow this company to behave somewhat like an Analyzer, that is, to take full advantage of the organization's more stable and healthy areas while retaining its prospecting capabilities.

During the study period from 1972 to 1975, this company's domain underwent fewer specific changes than that of the Analyzer organization described above. However, using a longer time perspective, the Prospector presents a picture of almost continuous transformation in its mix of products and markets. During the sixties, the organization expanded its domain considerably. During the seventies, it reevaluated this broadened domain and began to emphasize certain areas more heavily. Thus, viewed over time, the organization appears to be in a constant state of flux: entering new markets and leaving others, developing new products and dropping others, and changing emphases in established areas.

The Engineering Problem In order to maintain flexibility for properly servicing a changing domain, the company has created a loosely structured process for producing many of its textbooks and other educational materials. This company was among the first to create the position of publisher (mentioned above), and it has perhaps given these individuals the greatest freedom to allocate resources as they desire. Currently, the three publishers in this company's college division have editorial and marketing capabilities within their units. At the time of the study's second phase in 1975, management was considering making each publisher's unit a full-fledged "profit center" with budgets reflecting production as well as editorial and marketing activities.

In the meantime, each publisher relies on a mix of in-house production people and external free-lance specialists to produce the materials developed in that unit. Unlike the Defender and the Analyzer, the Prospector has a relatively small production unit so that the various projects coming from publishers are not delayed or homogenized by having to pass through a single-core technology. However, the three publishers still do not feel that this combination of in-house and subcontracted production allows them enough control over quality or the ability to coordinate projects for effective market timing. The Prospector's management is philosophically opposed to acquisition, so it appears that internal "subsidiaries" will be formed around each publisher, including at least some production capabilities.

The Administrative Problem This organization's diverse and dynamic product-market domain and its multiple, decentralized technologies require an administrative structure and process much different from that of the Defender. The most obvious difference lies in the composition and tenure of the top-management group. Unlike the Defender organization where power was centralized and permanently vested, power in this organization tends to be much more broadly diffused and somewhat transitory. In the first phase of the study, several managers in this company were reluctant to draw and discuss an organization chart, arguing that it would only convey general relationships and not a true picture of how responsibility and authority were distributed throughout the organization. In 1975, only one of the five individuals interviewed in 1972 was still in the position he held then, and this particular person was not a manager. These shifting relationships made it difficult to specify a single power base in the organization; power seemed to flow according to the company's current projects. For example, when management decided to develop the computerized market research system mentioned above, it hired a specialist from one of the firm's major competitors, a company known for its marketing and sales expertise. The statements of other executives indicated that this individual quickly began to wield substantial influence within the organization.

The fact that this executive was hired from outside the company reflects another characteristic of a Prospector's dominant coalition, its typically cosmopolitan nature. When the Defender hired its new college sales manager from outside, this move represented a major departture from normal practice, undertaken to facilitate entry into a relatively new market. However, the Prospector hired its market research expert from outside as a matter of course. It simply believed that he was the person best suited for this job. In general, the Defender's desire to improve efficiency suggests that it look internally for individuals who know "our system." Conversely, the Prospector's desire to improve effectiveness suggests that it also should consider outsiders for key jobs, those who know the industry. The examples used here were not isolated cases. Whereas the Defender maintained a highly stable top-management team, the Prospector exhibited a steady flow of personnel changes from both within and outside the company.

As noted above, this organization's structure and several of its major processes are built around the role of publisher. This role was created in order to focus intensively on particular market segments, and over the past several years increasing resources have been allocated to the publisher to perform this role in its entirety. However, as also noted above, the three publishers in this company did not as yet have full production capabilities in their respective units. Thus, the firm is not completely organized along autonomous product lines, although the publishers' demands seem to be pushing the organization in this direction.

In order to decentralize decisions and resources to the publishers, several process changes have been required. The process most affected has been planning. As the company has moved toward autonomous subunits, the planning process has been changed to allow more major decisions to be made within the publishers' groups. At first, the company attempted to maintain its 1-3-5-year planning format, but it found that the publishers' actions often diverged significantly from their formal plans. At the time of the study's second phase, several key managers believed that too many people involved in planning regarded it as an exercise to be endured rather than a useful management tool, and alternatives were being explored that would permit general targets to be set without locking the subunits into a predetermined course of action. At the time of the follow-up study, however, it was not clear what form the planning process would take in the future.

The nature of the organization's planning system necessarily affected the control process, particularly the use of budgets. Just before the follow-up study was conducted, the three publishers were invited to participate much more actively in the development of budgets. Top management recognized that it would be necessary to continue adjusting the budgetary process and anticipated that once the decision was made concerning production capabilities in the publishers' groups, the planning and control systems could be designed to conform with complete autonomy in these units.

In sum, it should be emphasized that the administrative structure and process of this company or any other Prospector are not likely to remain constant for very long due to the changing nature of these organizations' product-market domains. Therefore, even though this description presents the essence of a Prospector organization, it is also probably true that the description is already somewhat dated.

CONCLUSIONS

The primary purpose of this chapter has been to describe organizational strategy, structure, and process in more detail by examining the behavior of organizations in a single industry. As indicated, the study began in 1972 with an attempt to link managerial perceptions of the market with such important organizational features as controlling the variability of inputs, performing market research, and the process of making several key (publishing) decisions. However, this attempt to capture the relationship between an organization and its environment was only partially successful. After analyzing the data, it became obvious that the original research design did not adequately address the powerful influence of the organization's history, differences across firms in the composition of the top-management group, and the intricate relationship between managerial perceptions and the distinctive competences of the organization. Thus, at the conclusion of the first phase of the study, we realized that in addition to studying the perceptions of individual managers, we needed to explore the context in which these perceptions occurred. This realization led us to develop a typology of organizational form that encompassed the types of companies encountered in the college textbook publishing industry. This typology included the three stable forms of Defender, Analyzer, and Prospector, and a relatively unstable type called the Reactor.

Although this typology was helpful in reinterpreting the original data, it was clear that we needed to know much more about the characteristics of each of the organization types before we would be able to claim that the typology was a valid and useful framework. We therefore began a procedure for selecting representative examples of the three stable organization types. After identifying three appropriate organizations, a small-scale follow-up study was conducted in these companies. This research enabled us to describe the organization types more completely, and it suggested some general problems and directions for future research. A larger and more systematic study of several of these problems and issues is discussed in Chapter 12.

Interindustry
Comparisons of Strategy:
Electronics and Food Processing

At the conclusion of the first phase of the publishing study, it appeared that (1) the top managers of firms in the publishing industry had substantially different perceptions of the challenges and opportunities facing their organizations; (2) aspects of organizational structure and process were related to these managers' views (though not in ways easily measured); and (3) both managerial perceptions and structure-process characteristics might well be associated with a persistent pattern of response to environmental demands. The second study was, not surprisingly, influenced by these observations. Among the questions addressed in this study were the following: Would the variation in managerial perceptions of the environment observed in the college textbook publishing industry also be present in other industries? If so, would these variations in environmental perceptions be reflected in key structure-process characteristics—the composition of, and patterns of influence and resource allocation within, the organization's dominant coalition? Finally, would the organizational types identified in the publishing industry be observable in other settings and thus help to explain the relationship between managerial perceptions and organizational structure and process?

In order to answer these questions, it seemed useful to examine managerial perceptions and dominant-coalition characteristics in industries different both from each other and from college textbook publishing. Two industries, electronics and food processing, were selected for their diverse markets and technologies. Within firms in each industry, various characteristics, perceptions, and actions of the dominant coalition were investigated. These included functional areas perceived to be of strategic importance to firms within the industry, the extent to which subunit power reflected the strategic prominence of these different areas, the allocation of certain organizational resources, and the nature of the organization's search or scanning process.

The chapter is divided into three main sections. The first section on research design discusses the study's conceptual framework, the major variables examined, the sample of organizations, data-collection procedures, and the research hypotheses. The second section presents the findings on managers' perceptions of the environment and their relation to other dominant coalition characteristics and to type of organization. The implications of these findings for a broader view of organizational behavior are discussed in the final section.

RESEARCH DESIGN

Conceptual Framework

The conceptual framework that guided the present study relied heavily on theory and research offered by Child (1972), Miles, Snow, and Pfeffer (1974), Hinings et al. (1974), Pfeffer and Salancik (1974), and Cyert and March (1963). That is, the organization was viewed as engaged in dynamic interaction with its environment, with the strategic choices of the dominant coalition substantially influencing the form of this relationship (Child, 1972). Following Miles, Snow, and Pfeffer (1974), the organization was expected to respond to its environment in a relatively consistent manner over time. Depending on the organization's response pattern, managers' perceptions of critical environmental contingencies were expected to vary, and those organizational subunits charged with reducing crucial uncertainties were expected to be the most powerful (Hinings et al., 1974). That is, in line with managers' perceptions of the locus and extent of environmental uncertainty, certain organizational functions would be regarded as having greater strategic importance than others. Subunits charged with carrying out these strategic functions would thus be expected to be relatively powerful.

To the extent that an organizational subunit is powerful, it should be able to command resources in proportion to its power (Pfeffer and Salancik, 1974). Thus, it was expected that a highly valued managerial resource—larger budgetary allocations—and other indicators of the ability to obtain resources would be associated with powerful subunits.

Finally, the process by which organizations scan or search their environments for both threats and opportunities should reflect their managers' views concerning uncertainty, strategic functions, subunit power, and resource allocation. That is, to preserve the general alignment of the organization with its environment, the dominant coalition is apt to develop a consistent approach to searching the environment for potential threats and opportunities (Cyert and March, 1963). For example, one means of reducing environmental uncertainty is to select a narrow and relatively stable product-market domain. Under these conditions, such "stable" organizational subunits as production, finance, and maintenance would probably be the most powerful and would receive the largest allocation of organizational resources, and thus, relatively little attention might be devoted to searching for new market opportunities. Conversely, if the dominant coalition initially chose to steer the organization toward new product and market development, then marketing, research and development, and other "adaptive" subunits would tend to become powerful and attempt to reinforce their position by continuing to scan the environment for further areas of opportunity. In the first type of organization the search process would probably be directed inward toward the organization's operations, and, consequently, top management would not perceive much environmental uncertainty. In the second type, the search process would be directed outward toward new markets, and top managers would perceive a high degree of environmental uncertainty as a result. Thus, the conceptual framework used in this study can be diagrammed as follows:

$$\text{Perceived environmental uncertainty} \rightarrow \text{Strategic functions} \rightarrow \text{Subunit power} \rightarrow \text{Resource allocation} \rightarrow \text{Search process}$$

Variables and Measures

Perceived environmental uncertainty refers, as indicated, to the predictability of conditions in the organization's environment. In this study, perceived environmental uncertainty was measured using questionnaire items that corresponded to six major sectors of the industrial organization's environment: (1) relations with raw materials suppliers, (2) competitors' product price, quality, and design changes, (3) customer demand, (4) relations with financial suppliers, (5) relations with governmental regulatory agencies, and (6) relations with labor unions. These environmental dimensions were suggested by previous theory and research by Dill (1958), Katz and Kahn (1966), Lawrence and Lorsch (1967), and Thompson (1967).

The concept of *strategic function* refers to those functional areas within the organization considered by members of the dominant coalition to be of strategic importance to successful competition in their industry. Eleven functions common to most organizations, including electronics and food-processing companies, were ranked by the president or general manager in order of their importance for competing effectively within the industry: sales and marketing, finance, accounting, personnel and labor relations, engineering, production, research and development, long-range planning, purchasing, equipment maintenance, and quality control. Functions such as sales and marketing, research and development, and long-range planning were classified a priori as "external" in orientation.

Subunit power results from the ability to cope with crucial environmental uncertainties or contingencies. In this study, the president or general manager ranked his or her subunits according to their influence on policy-level decision making. In addition, other measures that may reflect power were examined: (1) the location of the organization's most innovative managers, (2) the location of managers with integrative skills, (3) the president's concept of the appropriate functional background of a new chief executive if one were to be appointed, and (4) subunit representation on the long-range planning committee.

We expected the organization's *resource allocation* to be consistent with perceptions of both environmental uncertainty and subunit power. For each organization, resource allocation was measured by asking the president or general manager to indicate (1) where he or she would currently invest new managerial talent, (2) which subunit would get a requested 10 percent increase in its operating budget if only one request could be granted, (3) where new capital funds would be invested if they became available, and (4) the order in which subunit budgets would be cut if required. Each of these four resource-allocation decisions was classified according to whether it favored adaptive or stable subunits. In addition, the base salaries of the president's immediate subordinates (obtained from the personnel manager) were used as an indicator of the subunit's ability to garner organizational resources. For purposes of analysis, subunits were divided a priori into those which could be considered as *adaptive* (concerned with external effectiveness) and those which could be considered as *stable* (concerned with internal efficiency).

Adaptive subunits included those with responsibility for marketing, research and development, and long-range planning, while stable subunits included finance, production, and purchasing.

Finally, the organization's *search process* refers to the areas in which the organization searches for new opportunities and for solutions to its adaptive problems. A rough approximation of this complex process was attempted by measuring two factors only. First, the president and the personnel director were asked to describe for the previous 5-year period the areas in which the organization had directed most of its attention. These areas were divided into two categories, *external* (such as new products and markets) and *internal* (such as more efficient manufacturing equipment and processes). Second, the president was asked to indicate whether he would prefer information about the external environment or about internal operations if he were able to receive a 25 percent increase in useful information coming directly to him.

Hypotheses

The principal hypotheses examined in this study can be summarized in two broad statements:

Organizations in which the chief executive perceived a high degree of environmental uncertainty would (1) consider externally oriented strategic functions as most vital to competitive success, (2) exhibit more powerful adaptive subunits than stable subunits, (3) allocate resources primarily to the adaptive subunits, and (4) search externally for growth opportunities and for solutions to adaptive problems.

Conversely, organizations in which the chief executive perceived a low degree of environmental uncertainty would (1) consider internally oriented strategic functions as most vital to competitive success, (2) exhibit more powerful stable subunits than adaptive subunits, (3) allocate resources primarily to the stable subunits, and (4) search internally for growth opportunities and for solutions to adaptive problems.

In addition to testing specific relations between aspects of managers' perceptions of their organizations' environments and internal power and process characteristics, this study sought to explore the extent to which the strategic typology developed in the publishing industry study would be useful in explaining and predicting behavior in two different industries. It was hoped that knowledgeable observers would be able to apply the typology in each industry. If so, it was expected that the identification of "typical" strategies would broaden our understanding of uncertainty-structure-process relationships.

Organizational Sample and Data Collection Procedure

The industries chosen for this study, electronics and food processing, were, as indicated, selected for three major reasons. First, electronics and food processing appeared to differ substantially in terms of market and technological change. That is, the products and the technologies used in the electronics industry seemed to be much more variable than those used in the food-processing industry. Organizations within these two industries, therefore, were presumed to face significantly different market and technological environments (Lawrence and Lorsch, 1967). Secondly, as was true of the textbook publishing companies, electronics and food-processing firms typically were not so large as to inhibit an adequate understanding of their overall operations within their respective industries. Finally, numerous organizations in both industries existed within a single greater metropolitan area, thereby creating the potential for making comparisons across organizations that were operating within the same general environment.

Approximately 100 organizations in the two industries were contacted initially, and 49 of these agreed to participate in the study. Data were obtained from 22 electronics firms (most of which made semiconductors and integrated circuits) and 27 food-processing companies (mostly engaged in the processing and/or canning of fruits and vegetables). The size of the food-processing companies, in terms of number of employees, ranged from 20 to 35,000, while the size of the electronics firms varied from 200 to 33,000. In terms of age, the sample ranged from a 3-year-old electronics company to a food-processing organization that was over 100 years old. According to executives in these companies, the 49 organizations ultimately included in the sample were generally representative of organizations in both industries with respect to characteristics such as size, age, and methods of operation. The large size of this sample permitted a more systematic comparison of top-management characteristics across organizations than was possible in the publishing study, and the acquisition of data from firms within the two different industries provided an opportunity to explore, at least partially, the generalizability of the theoretical framework described in this book.

Data were collected by means of interviews and a short questionnaire. In each organization, interviews were held with two key individuals, the president (or general manager in the case of a division) and the personnel director. The interview with the personnel director was designed to elicit background information about the organization including: number of employees, number and types of operating units, major capital investments and reorganizations over the previous 3 years, the composition of the long-range planning and budget committees (if any), the key subordinates of the president and their base salaries, and so on.

The interview with the president was considerably more extensive. Broadly speaking, questions were directed toward finding out: (1) which functions had the greatest strategic importance in the industry (marketing, finance, research and development, etc.); (2) which subunits of the organization were most powerful in terms of influencing policy-level decisions; (3) how resources were allocated to these subunits; and (4) ways in which the organization scanned or searched its environment. In addition, the president was asked to "type" his organization and those of his competitors (from a prepared list) using descriptions of the Defender, Reactor, Analyzer, and Prospector types.

The questionnaire, which was completed by the chief executive officer, measured this individual's perception of the environmental conditions faced by his organization during the previous year. Various aspects of relations with environmental elements were rated according to how well the organization could predict their behavior. The questionnaire items used to measure perceived environmental uncertainty are shown in Figure 12-1.

FINDINGS

Variations in Perceived Environmental Uncertainty

The results of the environmental uncertainty questionnaire, presented in Table 12-1, generally support the view that managerial perceptions vary from organization to organization within an industry. In the food-processing industry, top executives perceived competitors' actions and customers' demand for current and new products to be the most uncertain portions of their organizations' environments, followed by the behavior of governmental regulatory agencies, raw materials suppliers, labor unions, and, finally, financial suppliers. Furthermore, within the food-processing industry, there was frequently considerable variation in managers' perceptions of environmental conditions (particularly with respect to the behavior of regulatory agencies, as illustrated by the sizeable standard deviations for those items).

In the electronics industry, a somewhat different pattern of managerial perceptions emerged. Here, as in the case of food processing, top executives perceived competitors' actions to be the most uncertain environmental factor. Unlike food-processing executives, however, electronics managers saw few differences in the predictability of behavior among labor unions, governmental regulatory agencies, financial suppliers, raw materials suppliers, and customers. Furthermore, electronics

We are interested in your company's relationships with various sectors of the external environment (e.g., suppliers, customers). Specifically, we would like you to rate the characteristics or behavior of various sectors on the degree of their predictability, where 1 = highly predictable and 7 = highly unpredictable.

	Predictable Unpredictable (circle one)

1. Suppliers of your raw materials and components:
   a. their price changes are 1 2 3 4 5 6 7
   b. quality changes. 1 2 3 4 5 6 7
   c. design changes. 1 2 3 4 5 6 7
   d. introduction of new materials or components. . 1 2 3 4 5 6 7
2. Competitors' actions:
   a. their price changes are 1 2 3 4 5 6 7
   b. product quality changes. 1 2 3 4 5 6 7
   c. product design changes. 1 2 3 4 5 6 7
   d. introduction of new products 1 2 3 4 5 6 7
3. Customers:
   a. their demand for existing products is. 1 2 3 4 5 6 7
   b. demand for new products 1 2 3 4 5 6 7
4. The financial/capital market:
   a. interest rate changes:
      1. short-term debt 1 2 3 4 5 6 7
      2. long-term debt 1 2 3 4 5 6 7
   b. changes in financial instruments available:
      1. short-term debt 1 2 3 4 5 6 7
      2. long-term debt 1 2 3 4 5 6 7
   c. availability of credit:
      1. short-term debt 1 2 3 4 5 6 7
      2. long-term debt 1 2 3 4 5 6 7
5. Government regulatory agencies:
   a. changes in laws or agency policies on pricing
      are. 1 2 3 4 5 6 7
   b. changes in laws or policies on product stan-
      dards or quality 1 2 3 4 5 6 7
   c. changes in laws or policies regarding financial
      practices. 1 2 3 4 5 6 7
   d. changes in labor (personnel) laws or policies . . 1 2 3 4 5 6 7
   e. changes in laws or policies affecting marketing
      and distribution methods. 1 2 3 4 5 6 7
   f. changes in laws or policies on acceptable
      accounting procedures. 1 2 3 4 5 6 7
6. Actions of labor unions:
   a. changes in wages, hours, and working condi-
      tions. 1 2 3 4 5 6 7
   b. changes in union security 1 2 3 4 5 6 7
   c. changes in grievance procedures 1 2 3 4 5 6 7

Figure 12-1 Questionnaire items measuring perceived environmental uncertainty.

executives' perceptions varied less from company to company than did the perceptions of food-processing executives (as evidenced by the generally lower and relatively similar standard deviations across questionnaire items).

In sum, therefore, these results corroborated the expectation that managerial perceptions of the environment would vary across organizations *within* an industry. However, we were surprised to find that managerial perceptions did not vary more substantially *across* industries in the expected manner.

Perceptions Across the Two Industries   If we examine the aggregate means for all the items on the environmental uncertainty questionnaire (Table 12-1), it is clear that there was almost no difference between the perceptions of electronics and food-processing executives (3.2 versus 3.3). Inspection of the overall means for each of the six major environmental factors also revealed no substantial differences. Thus, it seems clear that these perceptual data do not support the widely held belief that substantial differences exist between environmental conditions in the electronics and food-processing industries.

In our view, there are at least three possible explanations for this somewhat surprising finding. First, there may have been methodological problems associated with the attempt to measure managerial perceptions of the environment. Each president or general manager was asked to use the previous 1-year period as the basis for estimating environmental uncertainty. This relatively short time framework may have served to compress the dynamics present in either of the industries into such a short period that homogeneity in perceptions was inevitable. A longer reference period, perhaps 1 to 3 years, might have elicited more variations in managers' perceptions of environmental conditions.

A second possible explanation for these similarities in managerial perceptions is more substantive in nature. Despite the interindustry similarities in the questionnaire data, our interpretation of the interview comments of executives in both industries suggested that substantial environmental differences did indeed exist between electronics and food processing. Therefore, it is conceivable that individuals in one or both groups of executives might have "misperceived" the conditions in their respective organizational environments. Given the relatively large size of the sample, however, such widespread misperception seems unlikely. (In retrospect, objective indicators of environmental uncertainty clearly would have been helpful in resolving this issue.)

A third, and in our view, highly plausible explanation is that, despite the actual environmental conditions, top managers in these indus-

Table 12-1 Managerial Perceptions of Environmental Uncertainty (by Industry)

Questionnaire item	Food Processing			Electronics		
	Mean	Standard deviation	N	Mean	Standard deviation	N
1. Raw materials and components suppliers:						
a. price changes	3.9	1.92	26	3.1	1.41	21
b. quality changes	3.3	1.83	27	3.2	1.66	21
c. design changes	2.6	1.35	25	2.6	1.18	21
d. introduction of new materials	3.8	2.18	27	3.1	1.33	21
Overall mean	3.4	1.82	27	3.0	1.40	
2. Competitors' actions:						
a. price changes	4.2	2.11	27	4.6	1.99	22
b. product quality changes	3.4	1.79	25	3.4	1.49	22
c. product design changes	3.7	2.01	25	4.1	1.33	22
d. introduction of new products or components	4.4	1.96	26	3.9	1.63	22
Overall mean	3.9	1.97		4.0	1.61	
3. Customers:						
a. demand for existing products	3.1	1.73	27	3.1	1.66	22
b. demand for new products	4.3	2.07	26	3.0	1.52	22
Overall mean	3.7	1.90		3.0	1.59	
4. Financial/capital market:						
a. interest rate changes						
1. short-term debt	3.6	1.91	24	3.6	1.46	20
2. long-term debt	2.8	1.82	24	3.3	1.52	19

Item						
b. changes in financial instruments available						
1. short-term debt	2.5	1.23	22	3.0	1.65	19
2. long-term debt	2.6	1.44	22	3.4	1.38	19
c. availability of credit						
1. short-term debt	2.2	1.29	24	2.4	1.39	20
2. long-term debt	2.8	1.75	24	3.0	1.53	20
Overall mean	2.8	1.57		3.1	1.49	
5. Government regulatory agencies:						
a. changes in laws or agency policies on pricing	3.7	2.57	21	2.8	1.68	15
b. changes in laws or policies on product standards or quality	3.2	2.02	27	2.9	1.63	18
c. changes in laws or policies regarding financial practices	3.5	2.22	24	3.4	1.42	18
d. changes in labor (personnel) laws or policies	3.8	1.67	26	3.6	1.82	22
e. changes in laws or policies affecting marketing and distribution methods	3.4	1.98	26	2.6	1.30	18
f. changes in laws or policies on acceptable accounting procedures	4.0	1.89	26	3.7	1.96	21
Overall mean	3.6	2.06		3.2	1.64	
6. Actions of labor unions:						
a. changes in wages, hours, and working conditions	2.5	1.27	25	2.3	1.09	4
b. changes in union security	2.2	1.27	25	3.0	1.22	4
c. changes in grievance procedures	2.6	1.57	25	2.8	.83	4
Overall mean	2.5	1.37		2.7	1.05	
Aggregate mean for all items	3.3	1.79		3.2	1.48	

tries had simply grown accustomed to them over time. Asked to evaluate environmental conditions on a questionnaire, managers chose similar scale points to describe objectively different conditions. Such an explanation relies heavily on the notions that managers develop a tolerance for uncertainty and that their own industry is the primary referent for their perceptions of the environment.

Perceived Uncertainty and Organizational Adaptiveness   In order to explore this latter explanation further, the data on organizations in each industry were analyzed so that the degree of organizational adaptiveness could be ascertained. That is, if the organization had successfully created and maintained subunits designed to cope with environmental uncertainty, then its top executive might well have perceived only moderate amounts of uncertainty in what might in fact have been a turbulent environment. Thus, as indicated in the previous section on research design, the organization's critical or strategic functions were divided into those which were oriented externally toward the environment or internally toward existing operations (e.g., marketing versus production). Similarly, organizational subunits were divided into those which were adaptive (concerned with external effectiveness) and those which were stable (concerned with internal efficiency). The proportion of strategic functions that were considered to be externally oriented and the proportion of adaptive subunits and resources allocated to them are shown in Table 12-2.

These results clearly show that electronics firms were more oriented toward external effectiveness than were food-processing companies. That is, compared to the typical food processor, an electronics organization was much more likely to emphasize externally oriented strategic functions (95 percent versus 59 percent), have more powerful adaptive subunits (66 percent versus 49 percent), and allocate more resources to these adaptive subunits (47 percent versus 38 percent). (The data suggest, however, that with respect to search processes, differences between the two types of organizations were less substantial.) Thus, in this sample of organizations at least, electronics firms were more adaptive than food-processing companies. Perhaps because of this general orientation, top executives in electronics organizations reported that they perceived approximately the same amount of environmental uncertainty as did food-processing executives. The data presented in Table 12-2 do not, of course, "prove" this contention, but they do lend weight to the possibility that adaptive organizational subunits may absorb some environmental uncertainty for the top executive.

Table 12-2   Strategic Function, Subunit Power, Resource Allocation, and Search Process: Proportion of Organizations Exhibiting High Adaptiveness (by Industry)

Organizational variables	Food processing		Electronics	
Strategic function	59%		95%	
Subunit power as ranked by CEOs	33		64	
Other indicators of subunit power:				
Location of most innovative managers	70		77	
Location of most integrative managers	48		59	
Involvement in long-range planning	44		64	
Functional background of a new chief executive	52		64	
Overall subunit power (mean percentage)		49		66
Resource allocation:				
Salaries of key managers	41		41	
Investment of new managerial talent	63		82	
Investment of capital funds	22		36	
Increase in operating budget	33		41	
Priority during budgetary reduction	30		36	
Overall resource allocation (mean percentage)		38		47
Search process:				
Areas of new business (last 5 years)	48		59	
New information priority (internal or external)	67		50	
Overall search process (mean percentage)		58		55
Aggregate percentages	47%		59%	
Sample size	27		22	

Managerial Perceptions and Dominant Coalition Characteristics

Even though electronics firms, as shown above, appear to place greater emphasis on externally oriented (adaptive) activities than do food-processing firms, the key questions as to whether and how managerial perceptions of environmental conditions are related to subunit importance, power, resource allocation, etc., among the organizations within each industry still remain.

In approaching these questions, it is useful first to compare directly the perceptions of chief executives in the two industries as to which strategic functions are vital to their competitive success. Accordingly, the

Table 12-3   Chief Executives' Rankings of Top Three Strategic Functions (by Industry)

Food Processing	Electronics
Sales and marketing	Sales and marketing
Production	Research and development
Long-range planning	Product engineering

top-ranking strategic functions for each industry are shown in Table 12-3.

As shown, chief executives in the food-processing industry ranked the three most important strategic functions as follows: (1) sales and marketing, (2) production, and (3) long-range planning. This ranking is consistent with the view that food companies, particularly the producers and/or canners of fruits and vegetables observed in this study, operate in mature markets in which continuity and growth require increased market penetration or the creation of new markets for existing products. We believe that research and development and product engineering were ranked low by food-processing executives because the likelihood of developing new products that will sell in high volume is low, and profit margins are slim. On the other hand, the production and distribution of existing products on a more efficient basis were heavily emphasized.

Thus, in the typical food-processing organization, internally oriented strategic functions were perceived to be most vital to competitive success by the chief executive. Although sales and marketing ranked first, interview comments suggested that sales planning and promotion for current products heavily overshadowed the marketing of new products. Similarly, production was ranked high because of the emphasis upon efficiently producing existing items. Third, although long-range planning had been classified a priori as an externally oriented function, the bulk of the planning performed in these food-processing firms appeared to be internally oriented—directed at sales projections, harvesting operations, production quotas and schedules, and so on.

Chief executives in the electronics industry presented a different view of the functions considered to be of strategic importance to competitive success. They ranked the three most important strategic functions as: (1) sales and marketing, (2) research and development, and (3) product engineering. This ranking is consistent with interview comments suggesting that products and markets are less mature in electronics than in food processing, that the return on resources invested in new product development is greater, and that R&D and product engineering represent ongoing efforts to improve the design and quality as well as reduce the costs of existing products (which are all relatively new, especially compared to most processed foods). Thus, the functions perceived to be of strategic importance in the electronics industry tended to be externally oriented. Greater emphasis was placed on marketing than on sales, and R&D and product engineering were emphasized more than efficient production. However, as mentioned earlier, there was considerably less agreement among electronics executives regarding this ranking of strategic functions than among food-processing executives.

Hypothesized Relationships

This study predicted that the chief executive's perceptions of uncertainty in his or her organization's environment would be related to characteristics of the dominant coalition—strategic function, subunit power, resource allocation, and search process—with greater emphasis on adaptiveness under perceptions of high environmental uncertainty (PEU), and on stability under low PEU. The pertinent findings are shown in Table 12-4.

Food Processing In the food-processing industry, there was a moderately strong relationship between chief executives' perceptions of uncertainty and the functions regarded as critical to competitive success ($C = .34$, $p < .05$). That is, under conditions of low perceived uncertainty, more emphasis tended to be placed on internally oriented functions such as production, accounting, finance, and quality control. Conversely, under conditions of high perceived uncertainty, more emphasis was typically placed on externally oriented functions such as sales and marketing.

Under low perceived uncertainty, the overall pattern of subunit power found in food-processing organizations followed logically from the overall strategic emphasis placed on internally oriented functions ($C = .49$, $p < .01$). Chief executives typically ranked stable subunits such as production, accounting, finance, and quality control as most powerful ($C = .58$, $p < .01$). When asked where they would want the most innovative managers, these executives again specified the stable subunits ($C = .32$, $p < .05$). The same pattern applied to managers with integrative skills, but this result was less significant ($C = .25$, $p < .10$). When perceived uncertainty was low, the long-range planning committee was clearly dominated by production and financial specialists ($C = .53$, $p < .01$). Finally, in the judgment of many of these respondents, a new chief executive should come from one of the stable subunits, although this result, too, was not statistically significant ($C = .19$, $p < .25$).

The overall allocation of resources under low uncertainty appeared to follow the same pattern ($C = .54$, $p < .01$). Consistent with the idea

Table 12-4   Relationships Between Perceived Environmental Uncertainty (PEU) and Strategic Function, Subunit Power, Resource Allocation, and Search Process (by Industry)*

Dependent variable	Perceived environmental uncertainty		
	Food processing	Electronics	Total sample
Strategic function	.34 ($p<.05$)	.02 ($p<.48$)	.18 ($p<.15$)
Subunit power as ranked by CEOs	.58 ($p<.01$)	.03 ($p<.48$)	
Other indicators of subunit power:			
Location of most innovative managers	.32 ($p<.05$)	.36 ($p<.05$)	
Location of most integrative managers	.25 ($p<.10$)	.11 ($p<.35$)	
Involvement in long-range planning	.53 ($p<.01$)	.38 ($p<.05$)	
Functional background of a new chief executive	.19 ($p<.25$)	.03 ($p<.48$)	
Overall subunit power	.49 ($p<.01$)	.24 ($p<.15$)	.42 ($p<.01$)
Resource allocation:			
Salaries of key managers	.48 ($p<.01$)	.25 ($p<.15$)	
Investment of new managerial talent	.41 ($p<.01$)	.30 ($p<.10$)	
Investment of new capital funds	.03 ($p<.45$)	.16 ($p<.25$)	
Increase in operating budget	.23 ($p<.15$)	.25 ($p<.15$)	
Priority during budgetary reduction	-.01 ($p<.49$)	-.21 ($p<.15$)	
Overall resource allocation	.54 ($p<.01$)	.35 ($p<.05$)	.48 ($p<.01$)
Search process:			
Areas of new business (last 5 years)	.38 ($p<.03$)	.43 ($p<.03$)	
New information priority (internal or external)	.08 ($p<.35$)	.42 ($p<.03$)	
Overall search process	.12 ($p<.35$)	.38 ($p<.05$)	.28 ($p<.03$)
Sample size	27	22	49

*Degree of association was determined by dichotomizing Perceived Environmental Uncertainty (PEU) scores at the mean and calculating the contingency coefficient C. Positively signed correlations indicate an emphasis on adaptiveness under high PEU and on stability under low PEU.

that subunit power attracts additional resources, the salaries of these chief executives' subordinates were highest in the stable subunits ($C = .48, p<.01$), and these subunits were likely to receive a requested increase in their operating budgets ($C = .23, p<.15$). No relationship was obtained between perceived uncertainty and the investment of new capital funds, or the order in which subunits' budgets would be reduced.

Finally, under low perceived uncertainty, the areas of opportunity pursued over the previous 5-year period suggested internally oriented search processes ($C = .38, p<.03$). That is, these firms had avoided the development of new products and markets and concentrated instead on the improved ability to deliver existing products to present markets. Surprisingly, however, this search behavior was not reflected in answers to the question concerning new information priority—these top executives were divided as to whether they would prefer more information about environmental conditions or about internal operations.

Electronics   In the electronics industry, most results were in the predicted direction, but few of the relationships were as strong as those in food processing. This was due, in part, to the fact that a substantial majority of the firms in the electronics sample displayed adaptive characteristics (see Table 12-2) irrespective of whether the chief executive perceived environmental conditions as certain or uncertain. One possible explanation for this result is that electronics firms may attempt to maintain flexibility in their structure and operations, even when it does not appear to be necessary, to insure against a sudden shift in the industry's comparatively volatile markets and technological processes. In any event, the findings discussed below must be regarded as more tentative than those obtained for the food-processing organizations.

There was no relationship between electronics executives' perceptions of uncertainty and the functions that they considered to be of strategic importance in their industry ($C = .02$, $p<.48$). However, this finding came as no surprise, since 95 percent of the firms placed greater emphasis upon externally oriented functions (see Table 12-2).

The relationship between perceived uncertainty and the overall pattern of subunit power was also less clear in electronics firms ($C = .24$, $p<.15$). When an uncertain environment was perceived, the chief executive generally preferred to have more innovative managers in adaptive subunits such as marketing and R&D ($C = .36$, $p<.05$), and the long-range planning committee tended to be dominated by members of these units ($C = .38$, $p<.05$). However, the other indicators of subunit power, particularly the executives' own rankings, did not reflect a clear pattern of subunit power being lodged in the adaptive subunits under conditions of greater uncertainty.

As with subunit power, the relationship between perceived uncertainty and the resource allocation pattern was less clear-cut in electronics firms. Overall, when more uncertainty was perceived, a larger share of resources tended to be allocated to adaptive subunits ($C = .35$, $p<.05$). However, none of the individual resource allocation decisions was strongly associated with the chief executive's perceptions of the environment. On the other hand, the search process of organizations perceiving more uncertainty did have a definite external orientation. That is, over the previous 5 years, these electronics firms maintained their continuity and growth principally through the development of new products and the location of new markets. In addition, if new information were to be made available to him, the chief executive generally expressed a preference for information about conditions in the environment rather than about internal operations.

Thus, it appears that there are linkages between perceived environmental uncertainty and the other variables examined in this study—strategic function, subunit power, resource allocation, and search process. In each organizational sample, only one correlation between uncertainty and adaptive characteristics did not fall in the predicted direction. Perceived uncertainty proved a better predictor of adaptation among food-processing firms (where 7 out of 13 correlations were significant at the .05 level or better) than it did among electronics firms (where only 4 correlations achieved this level of significance).

Managerial Perceptions, Dominant Coalition Characteristics, and Organization Strategy

As indicated earlier, in addition to examining the specific links between environmental perceptions and the structure of (and processes within) an organization's dominant coalition, we hoped to apply the organizational typology developed in the publishing industry study to determine whether it might be valid and useful in electronics and food processing. We believe that the result of this exploration is a highly qualified "yes".

Two approaches were used to type the organizations in this sample. The first approach involved the interviewer attempting to place each organization in one of the four categories based on the total information available from the two interviews. Within our research group we felt quite confident of our placement of many of the organizations—executives' statements about their organizations' market behavior coupled with our knowledge of industry activities persuaded us that we could easily type a number of the firms in each industry, particularly those used as case examples in the early chapters of this book. However, for many of the organizations in the sample, our knowledge beyond the interview schedule data was minimal. Since we had little or no opportunity to corroborate our judgments, we felt it was unwise to attempt a systematic analysis of the links between researcher-designated organizational types and dominant coalition structure and process.

The second approach used to type organizations initially appeared more promising. We asked the chief executive in each organization to type both his own organization and other firms within the industry with which he was familiar. However, this approach, too, achieved only moderate success.

On the positive side, 27 organizations—14 in food processing and 13 in electronics—were typed by at least two chief executives from other firms. The ratings reflected a modest level of agreement concerning the strategic type of these firms; overall, 39 percent of the ratings for the 27 organizations fell in the modal type of each firm.

It should be noted, however, that the 27 organizations for which a minimal outside evaluation was available represent only slightly more than half the total sample. Further, a comparison of the externally typed organizations with the full sample suggests that these electronics firms may not have been representative of the organizations in that industry. Of the 13 externally typed electronics firms, 10 were below the median in overall perceived environmental uncertainty—a highly disproportionate figure for which no ready explanation was apparent. Finally, slightly over half the 27 externally typed organizations (15) were classified as Analyzers, while only 5 were classifed as Prospectors, 5 as Defenders, and 2 as Reactors (the proportions were roughly equivalent in both industries.).

The difficulties encountered in obtaining clearly corroborated external typings (a point to which we will return shortly) discouraged extensive analyses employing the strategic categories. Nevertheless, the limited analyses that were undertaken suggested that behavior patterns consistent with the strategic typology might be present. When Prospectors and Analyzers were grouped and compared to Defenders and Reactors in each industry, the following pattern was apparent:

Prospectors and Analyzers, by a ratio of 14 to 6, were classifiable as adaptive in terms of their chief executives' rankings of strategic functions, the subunits in which key subordinates were located, membership on long-range planning committees, subunits in which chief executives wished to invest new talent, areas in which increased information was desired, the units in which CEOs wished to have their most innovative managers, the units from which the next CEO was expected to emerge, and the organization's orientation toward new product development over the past 5 years.

Conversely, employing this same set of factors, Defenders and Reactors, by a ratio of 5 to 2, were classifiable as low in adaptiveness. That is, their chief executives tended, overall, to rate functions such as production as most strategic, to view their key subordinates as located in production or finance rather than in marketing or research and development, to desire new information related to internal rather than external issues, and so forth.

However, when other items from the questionnaire were examined, no relationships were apparent between external typings and chief executives' statements about their own organizations. For example, CEOs in

Prospector and Analyzer organizations were no more inclined to favor adaptive units than stable units with increased operating budgets.

In sum, this exploratory analysis of the usefulness of the strategic typology in two additional industries (which differed both from the publishing industry and from each other) generated some interesting observations, many of which could be interpreted as consistent with the overall theoretical framework. It was clear, however, that these findings were merely suggestive and that no broad generalizations were warranted.

At the same time, it appeared that the strategic typology might have considerable explanatory potential if samples could be structured to permit more extensive external categorization of organizations in terms of their pattern of environmental enactment. While the external ratings generated in this study were less complete and less consistent than we had hoped, our sampling approach may have contributed to such results. That is, while electronics and food processing are meaningful industry groupings for many purposes, each industry is, in fact, quite heterogeneous. Many of the executives in this study felt confident to rate only a few of the organizations on their industry list (a factor that may also have contributed to the seemingly disproportionate number of organizations placed in the middle category, the Analyzer). In fact, a number of executives noted that many of the organizations "in their market" (those with which they competed directly and thus knew best) were located outside the area covered in this study. Thus, while this study was well designed for its basic purpose—to elicit environmental perceptions in two different technological and environmental settings—it may not have been well structured to compare organizations in direct competition for the same basic markets.

CONCLUSIONS

This study brought our understanding of how organizations adapt to their environments into somewhat sharper focus. Building on the publishing study and other research, it provided additional insights about how the impact of environmental change and uncertainty on organizational structure and process is mediated by the perceptions, decisions, and actions of the dominant coalition. More specifically, the study indicated that organizations operating in ostensibly similar environments may in fact perceive the environment differently. Differences in managerial perceptions across organizations within the same industry are then reflected (to varying degrees) in the composition of, and influence patterns within, the organization's dominant coalition. This pattern was quite clear in organizations in the food-processing industry, less so in organizations in the electronics industry. (Environmental perceptions across the two industries were quite similar in this study, an unexpected finding for which three possible explanations were advanced.)

The findings of this study suggest some support for the hypothesis that when the organization faces high environmental uncertainty, it places greater emphasis on externally oriented functions such as market research and product development. Of course, cause and effect in such cases are seldom clear—an organization actively engaged in product and market development is more likely to face high uncertainty than an organization whose products and markets are relatively stable. Nevertheless, it appears plausible to argue that high perceived uncertainty tends to produce a sequence of internal organizational patterns that can be identified. When the dominant coalition emphasizes external strategic functions, adaptive organizational subunits (such as marketing) tend to wield more power within the dominant coalition. These subunits are able to attract a larger share of the organization's monetary and human resources, and thus these subunits are able to encourage search processes designed to detect external opportunities and threats.

Conversely, when an organization faces low uncertainty, internally oriented functions (such as production) assume strategic importance. As a result, stable organizational subunits become powerful, the dominant coalition allocates a larger share of resources to these subunits, and search processes are designed to detect opportunities for increasing production efficiency and threats to internal stability.

Although this study did not directly extend the characteristics of the strategic typology to a large extent, it did furnish confirming evidence for an important premise upon which the typology is based: even though organizations within the same industry may exhibit considerable variation in the environmental perceptions of their chief executives and in their internal structures and processes, these characteristics do not vary randomly but tend toward internally consistent patterns. Moreover, the limited inferences about the relationships between externally categorized patterns of response to environmental events (strategic types) and internal structure and process characteristics were not inconsistent with the theoretical framework emerging from the literature and the publishing industry study. While the findings based on this study are inconclusive, they suggest that studies with samples chosen to allow clear external typings may produce valuable insights. This point clearly influenced the design of the hospital study reported in the following chapter.

Chapter 13

Management and Strategy: The Case of the Voluntary Hospital

This chapter describes the last in the series of three studies that contributed to the development of our theoretical framework. The publishers study tended to confirm an insight that had been obscured by much of the research on relations between organizations and their environments: it suggested that ostensibly similar organizations situated in the same general environment may enact quite different task environments and pursue markedly different strategies within them. The study of electronics and food-processing organizations revealed associated variations in intraorganizational structure and process and provided some further insights concerning the explanatory power of the strategic typology.

A group of voluntary hospitals provides the setting for the third study. First, the strategic typology is used as a basis for examining differences in managerial perceptions and organizational adaptation, and then strategy is related to management theory and organizational decision making. In the following sections, we describe the research design, present our findings, discuss some relationships between organizational strategy and management theory, and illustrate strategy-related responses to two significant developments in the health care industry.

RESEARCH DESIGN

Generally speaking, this study focused on organizational adaptation to the environment—a process through which the dominant coalition first becomes aware of changing conditions in the organization's task environment and then makes adjustments in anticipation or in response. More specifically, the research investigated relationships among organization strategy, managerial perceptions of the environment, type of adjustment, management theory, and the influence of organization members on decision making.

As noted throughout the book, adaptation usually occurs in a gradual and evolutionary fashion, making it a difficult phenomenon to explore with a cross-sectional research design. The approach used here was to look for an industry whose environment was undergoing rapid and substantial change. We believed that such conditions would accelerate the process of adaptation and accentuate the differences between those organizations that were adapting successfully and those that were struggling to maintain a viable alignment between environmental conditions and organizational structure and process.

Based on the criterion of environmental change, hospitals appeared to provide an appropriate setting for the research, so exploratory interviews were conducted with knowledgeable observers in order to test the relevance of the theoretical framework and to develop an understanding of these organizations. We found that not only does the health care industry have a history of turbulence, but that two current developments—the malpractice insurance crisis and the impending legislation of some form of national health insurance—had destabilized conditions even further. Given this favorable prognosis with respect to environmental change, a pilot study was conducted in three voluntary hospitals. Its objectives were to test and improve measures of the research variables and to develop sampling and data collection strategies.

Subsequently, we selected a research sample of organizations that were as similar and as geographically proximal as possible. There are three basic types of hospitals: (1) voluntary hospitals, which are private, nonprofit corporations; (2) federal, state, and local governmental hospitals, which generally treat either unique patient populations or specific diseases; and (3) proprietary hospitals, which are privately owned and operated for profit. We chose to restrict our study to voluntary general hospitals because this type is preeminent in terms of both numbers and importance within the health care system. The special-purpose, long-term, for-profit, and governmental hospitals thus excluded differed from the sample in such fundamental respects as administrative structure, extent of external control, medical technology, patient characteristics, and sources of financial support. After contacting 28 voluntary hospitals within a single metropolitan area, we secured the cooperation of 19. These organizations appeared to be representative of the voluntary hospitals within the study area.

Data Collection Methods

The complex and changing nature of adaptation experienced by the three hospitals in the pilot study raised a dilemma in deciding how to collect data. On one hand, in order to draw general conclusions, we needed to collect information about adaptation in a relatively large number of hospitals. We could meet this requirement most efficiently by using questionnaires or by analyzing archival data. On the other hand, in order to understand the full complexity and dynamic nature of the adaptive process, we needed to collect a large volume of information concerning institutional history, goals, and structure within specific hospitals. To meet the second requirement, an intensive field-study approach seemed best.

To resolve this dilemma, we developed a data collection program that included elements of both approaches. We asked two independent groups of judges to classify the sample hospitals according to strategic type (Prospector, Analyzer, Defender, or Reactor). One group was composed of local health professionals with no affiliation to any single hospital: members of health-planning agencies, officers of the local medical society, hospital consultants, administrators of health-oriented foundations, and professors of hospital administration. The other group was composed of the chief administrators of the sample hospitals.[1]

The next step was to schedule a preliminary interview with each hospital's chief administrator. Although partly open-ended, the interview was based primarily on a set of predetermined questions dealing with the history of the hospital, recent changes in structure and process, and other aspects of internal operations. At the conclusion of the interview, we left the administrator a set of instructions for diagraming the hospital's task environment and a questionnaire that elicited his views about how decision influence was distributed among key groups in the hospital, his attitudes regarding the future utility and probability of adjustment, and the theory of management he endorsed.

After these materials had been returned by mail, a second interview was scheduled. In this interview, the administrator described the precise manner in which the hospital had responded to each of two significant health care developments in this metropolitan area: a month-long phy-

---

[1]Because prior exposure to the strategic typology could have biased administrators' other responses, these data were gathered at the conclusion of the final interview and after all questionnaire data had been returned.

sicians' strike and new federal health-planning legislation that threatens to reduce the autonomy of individual hospitals. The administrator also described anticipated shifts in the mission or goals of the hospital and answered any questions raised by his or her responses to the questionnaire or in the previous interview. Thus, the questionnaire data allowed us to make systematic comparisons across hospitals in the sample while the interview data provided specific descriptions of adaptation within individual hospitals.

Variables and Measures

Organization strategy, as discussed in Chapters 3 through 6, is a distinct pattern of organizational response to the opportunities, threats, and demands that originate from the external environment. Each hospital's strategic type was determined by pooling the judgments of health professionals and practicing hospital administrators. These raters were presented with brief written descriptions of the four strategic types and asked to use this typology to classify those sample hospitals with which they were familiar.[2]

Despite their different vantage points, the judgments of the health professionals and the hospital administrators tended to converge on a single typological classification for each hospital. Although the extent of agreement was clearly higher for some hospitals than for others (it ranged from .92 to .40, with a mean of .59), we believed that these results were sufficiently consistent to classify five hospitals as Prospectors, five as Analyzers, three as Reactors, and six as Defenders.

Task-environment perceptions were defined as the specific elements comprising the task environment and the extent to which organizational decision making was perceived to be contingent upon these environmental elements. Every organization faces uncertainties stemming from its interdependence with the task environment. According to Thompson (1967), the organization can attempt to absorb these uncertainties in three major ways: (1) by reducing the impact of the task environment through buffering, (2) by adjusting to external actions that can be predicted, and (3) by influencing environmental actors (agencies, groups, organizations, etc.) to behave according to the organization's preferences.

Following Thompson, we theorized that the degree to which hospital decision making is contingent upon the task environment is determined jointly by environmental impact, environmental predicta-

---

[2]Each administrator's classification of his or her own hospital was deleted in computing these evaluations. All administrators said the strategic typology made sense, and they found the task of rating other hospitals reasonably straightforward. However, many administrators believed that their own hospitals were "unique" and did not fit neatly into any of the strategic types.

bility, and the hospital's ability to influence the environment. In other words, contingency is greatest when the hospital's operations are affected in strong but unpredictable ways by environmental elements that the hospital is comparatively powerless to influence.

In order to determine the task environment that each hospital had enacted, the chief administrators were asked to diagram or map the most prominent entities within their hospitals' task environments. (One administrator's map is reproduced in Figure 13-1.) Next, for each entity listed on the map, we asked respondents to use a five-point scale to register their perceptions concerning impact, predictability, and influence. By combining these scores across all environmental elements for a particular hospital, we were able to construct a task environment contingency index for each organization.

Organizational adjustments refer to a broad spectrum of changes in organizational structure and process that are undertaken to maintain or improve the hospital's alignment with its task environment. A scale consisting of five categories that represent changes of successively broader scope and greater impact was used to classify organizational adjustments (see Figure 13-2). The scale ranges from minor adjustments in work pro-

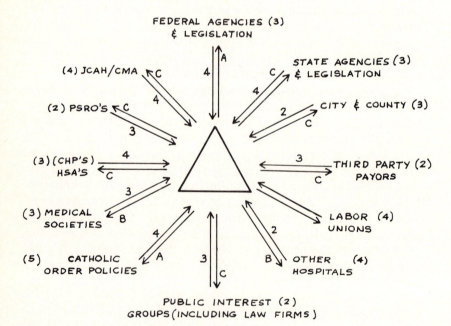

Figure 13-1   Sample map of hospital task environment.

cedures to major modifications that alter the organization's mission, clientele, or relationship with its environment.

Adjustment was measured in two ways. During the pilot study, a list of 20 organizational adjustments frequently made by hospitals was compiled. This list included adjustments in each of the five categories shown in Figure 13-2. At the beginning of the first interview, each administrator was asked whether or not any of these adjustments had occurred in his hospital within the preceding 12 months. We asked, for example, "Has a new department been created or an existing department eliminated? Have budget allocations among departments changed in any important ways?" From the administrator's descriptions of those adjustments which had taken place, an adjustment index for the previous year was constructed. This index thus reflected both the frequency and the scope of organizational adjustment. The adjustment index was complemented by two questionnaire items that elicited administrators' perceptions concerning (1) how useful each of the five types of adjustment would be for maintaining or improving the hospital's performance over the next 3 years, and (2) the probability that such adjustments would actually occur within a 3-year period.

(1)	(2)	(3)	(4)	(5)
		Intra-departmental structure and process	Inter-departmental structure and process	Macro- or extra-organizational
Procedural adjustments	Work group adjustments	adjustments	adjustments	adjustments
Management-determined changes in rules, work procedures, information flow, scheduling, etc.	Changes in the amount or type of participation in group decisions, changes in job design, changes in training programs, etc.	Changes in relationships among work groups, work flow, involvement in scheduling and quality control, supervisory relationships, communication patterns, etc.	Changes in degree of centralization of major decisions, mechanisms for interdepartmental coordination, creation or elimination of a department, etc.	Changes in basic product or service offered or clientele, type of ownership, merger or acquisition, dissolution, etc.

Figure 13-2 Types of organizational adjustment. (*Adapted from R.E. Miles*, Theories of Management, *McGraw-Hill, New York, 1975, Figure 13-1.*)

Decision influence refers to the extent to which various units or groups within the organization affect the outcomes of hospital decision making. Previous research had indicated that organizations differ in the total amount of influence exercised as well as in the distribution of influence among various managerial and employee groups (Tannenbaum, 1968, 1974).

Determining the amount and distribution of influence within any complex organization is difficult. However, measurement problems are especially acute in hospitals because professional members such as physicians, nurses, and dieticians are able to influence decisions on the basis of both their organizational role and their professional expertise. These groups are exempt from many of the control mechanisms employed in other organizations. Furthermore, decision influence may vary widely from issue to issue. For example, the medical staff normally exercises great influence when the hospital administration decides what type of medical equipment to purchase, but it may have little desire to influence a change in accounting procedures. Given these circumstances, simply asking administrators to judge the overall decision-making influence of various subgroups would be unlikely to yield valid data.

We chose to measure decision influence with questionnaire items concerning five specific hospital decision issues, following the approach used by Hinings et al. (1974). These five decision issues were offered by pilot study respondents as recurring and important hospital decisions: (1) changes in personnel training and development programs, (2) decisions concerning medical evaluation programs, (3) the development of new services and programs, (4) changes in work rules for members of the hospital's nonprofessional staff, and (5) capital budgeting decisions. For each of the decisions, administrators indicated on a five-point scale ranging from "little or no influence" to "a very great deal of influence" the amount of influence typically exercised by each of the following hospital subgroups: board of trustees, chief administrator and his or her immediate subordinates, medical staff (doctors), fiscal staff (controller, accountants, purchasing agents, etc.), professional staff (nurses, dieticians, therapists, etc.), and nonprofessional staff (housekeeping and maintenance personnel and other ancillary employees).[3] From these data, scores indicating the total amount and the distribution (centralization) of decision influence in the hospital were computed.

Management theory consists of three basic components: (1) a set of assumptions about employees (specifically, the extent to which managers

---

[3]Respondents in the pilot study indicated that this breakdown would encompass both hierarchical and professional groupings in voluntary hospitals.

believe that employees possess certain traits and capabilities), (2) a related set of policies concerning how a manager ought to direct and control subordinates, and (3) expectations about performance and satisfaction resulting from the application of these policies (Miles, 1965).

Each of the administrators in the sample of hospitals completed a lengthy questionnaire designed to measure various dimensions of management theory (Miles, 1964). Based on previous research, three factors were considered most critical to the present study: (1) subordinates' relative capability, which is the difference between administrators' average rating of their own capabilities across 10 characteristics and the ratings given to their immediate subordinates, (2) employees' relative capability, or the difference between administrators' ratings of their own capabilities and those given rank-and-file employees, and (3) expectations about performance, that is, the extent to which administrators agreed with statements indicating that participative managerial policies will lead to improved job performance.

Hypotheses

This study investigated the major variables included in the theoretical framework of this book: organization strategy, adaptation task-environment perceptions, decision influence, and management theory. More specifically, the hypotheses examined can be summarized as follows:

Hospitals identified as Prospectors and Analyzers will make more frequent and more substantial adjustments to environmental conditions. The administrators of these hospitals will regard internal decision making as more contingent on the task environment. They will perceive in their hospitals a large total amount of decision influence, which is decentralized among hospital subgroups.

Hospitals identified as Defenders and Reactors will make fewer and less substantial adjustments to environmental conditions. The administrators of these hospitals will regard internal decision making as less contingent on the task environment. They will perceive in their hospitals a small total amount of decision influence, which is centralized at the top-management level.

Finally, relationships between strategic type and management theory were explored with the expectation that Prospector and Analyzer administrators would be more inclined to endorse the Human Resources model of management, and Defender and Reactor administrators would tend to endorse the Traditional or Human Relations model. (See Chapter 8 for a discussion of these models.)

RESEARCH FINDINGS

The results presented in Table 13-1 provide considerable support for our hypotheses. That is, Prospectors and Analyzers generally engaged in more substantial organizational adjustments, perceived more task-environmental contingencies, permitted more influence in decision making by organization members, and were more likely to endorse Human Resources management than Defenders and Reactors. Five of the correlations were significant at the .05 level or better, and only two did not fall in the predicted direction.

Thus, generally speaking, these results conformed to the predictions. Prospectors and Analyzers had readily altered hospital structure and process; during the preceding year these organizations had typically adjusted to the task environment more extensively and more frequently than Reactors or Defenders. The chief administrators of Prospectors and Analyzers tended to view the adjustment process as somewhat more helpful in maintaining and improving the performance of the hospital in the near future, although they regarded adjustment as only slightly more likely to occur. The task-environment perceptions of Prospector and Analyzer administrators suggest that they may have enacted task environments that were more dynamic than those of the other types and that therefore demanded the extensive adjustment observed. These administrators believed that the agencies, groups, and other organizations comprising the hospital task environment typically behaved in a less predictable fashion. They also regarded task-environmental elements as less susceptible to the hospital's influence. Consequently, organizational decision making in Prospectors and Analyzers was more contingent on the task environment. Moreover, administrators indicated that members of the organization directly exerted a larger quantity of influence upon hospital decisions. The managerial attitudes of these administrators appeared to conform with the Human Resources model. They endorsed the use of participative managerial policies in their hospitals and were more certain that such policies would lead to improved performance. These administrators also regarded their immediate subordinates as more capable members of the organization than did their counterparts in Defender and Reactor hospitals.

On the other hand, Defender and Reactor hospitals had implemented fewer and less substantial adjustments during the previous year, and administrators of these hospitals expected future adjustments to be less effective in maintaining and improving organizational performance. Defender and Reactor administrators viewed organizational decision making as less contingent on the task environment and indicated that the

Table 13-1 Relationships Among Organization Strategy, Organizational Adjustments, Task-Environment Perceptions, Decision Influence, and Management Theory

		Mean Prospector score	Mean Analyzer score	Mean Reactor score	Mean Defender score	Correlation with strategy[1]
Organizational adjustments	Adjustments last year	31.3	20.5	9.5	13.3	.57 (p<.01)
	Utility of future adjustments	45.1	34.8	26.8	25.8	.43 (p<.03)
	Probability of future adjustments	38.2	34.1	30.5	32.3	.06 (p<.29)
Task-environment perceptions	Task-environment contingency index	3.41	3.23	3.23	3.04	.43 (p<.03)
	Environmental impact	3.77	3.41	3.50	3.47	.05 (p<.30)
	Environmental predictability	3.17	3.26	3.20	3.59	-.34 (p<.06)
	Influence over the environment	2.36	2.46	2.60	2.76	-.26 (p<.12)
Decision influence	Total influence	100.6	87.0	78.0	76.3	.67 (p<.01)
	Centralization of influence	3.15	3.60	2.60	3.58	.06 (p<.29)*
Management theory	Subordinates' relative capabilities[2]	.35	.90	1.00	.95	-.41 (p<.04)
	Employees' relative capabilities[2]	2.70	3.28	3.00	3.20	.22 (p<.16)*
	Performance expectations	4.14	4.11	3.70	3.57	.49 (p<.01)

[1] Because the strategic typology is a classificatory scale, all relationships involving this variable were determined by dichotomizing scores at the median and calculating the contingency coefficient C. Positive signs on the correlations indicate that Prospectors and Analyzers typically score higher on the organization variable. Negative signs mean that Defenders and Reactors typically score higher. Level of significance was determined by Fisher's exact test (one-tailed).

[2] Since these measures are difference scores, small values reflect the view that the capabilities of subordinates or rank-and-file employees are relatively high.

* Relationships that did not occur in the predicted direction.

various subgroups collectively exercised less influence on hospital decision making. Although Defender and Reactor administrators expressed general support for participative policies, they nevertheless expected less improvement in performance to result and viewed their immediate subordinates as less capable relative to themselves than did administrators in Prospector and Analyzer hospitals. These managerial attitudes appeared to be consistent with the Human Relations model, which advocates participation to promote morale rather than performance.

Unexpected Findings

Although the pattern of results presented in Table 13-1 generally supported our hypotheses, several pieces did not fall neatly into place. To illustrate this point, Table 13-2 shows the full set of relationships (whether hypothesized or not) among several of the key variables in this study. The more ambiguous correlations are shown in boldface type.

Several intriguing patterns were apparent in this matrix. First, the modest intercorrelations among the three measures of management theory—subordinates' capabilities, rank-and-file employees' capabilities, and performance expectations—suggested that administrators who accepted one component of management theory did not necessarily accept the others.

Second, the pattern of correlations between these same components of management theory and the two dimensions of decision influence (total influence and centralization of influence) was puzzling. The finding that a large amount of total influence was associated with the managerial view that participation improves performance was logical. However, it was surprising to find that a large amount of total influence was not associated with managerial perceptions that immediate subordinates and rank-and-file employees are more capable. That is, it seemed curious that some administrators who reported that various hospital subgroups exercised more influence in hospital decision making and who tended to believe that such participation improves performance did not also hold their subordinates' and employees' capabilities in higher esteem.

We were also interested to note that this pattern was reversed in the correlations involving management theory and the centralization of decision influence. As we had anticipated, administrators who regarded their own subordinates and rank-and-file employees as more capable individuals tended to indicate that decision influence was decentralized in their organizations. However, contrary to our expectations, administrators who believed that participative management would improve perfor-

Table 13-2 Correlations among Organization Strategy, Decision Influence, and Management Theory

	Total decision influence	Centralization of decision influence	Performance expectations	Subordinates' relative capability*	Employees' relative capability*	Organization strategy†
Total decision influence	—					
Centralization of decision influence	-.06 (p<.36)	—				
Performance expectations	.34 (p<.03)	.09 (p<.31)	—			
Subordinates' relative capability	-.13 (p<.23)	.23 (p<.09)	-.08 (p<.32)	—		
Employees' relative capability	.22 (p<.11)	.30 (p<.04)	-.03 (p<.42)	.12 (p<.25)	—	
Organization strategy	.67 (p<.01)	.06 (p<.29)	.49 (p<.01)	-.41 (p<.04)	.22 (p<.16)	—

*Correlations involving organization strategy were determined by calculating the contingency coefficient C. All other correlations shown in this table are Kendall's rank-correlation coefficient τ.

†Since these measures are difference scores, small values reflect the view that capabilities of immediate subordinates or rank-and-file employees are relatively high.

†Correlations involving organization strategy were determined by calculating the contingency coefficient C. All other correlations shown in this table are Kendall's rank-correlation coefficient τ. Where appropriate, product-moment correlations were also calculated for these data. No differences in direction or significance were found.

mance did not uniformly report that decision influence was decentralized. This finding is not consistent with the widely accepted idea that participation involves sharing power with subordinates.

Finally, the pattern of relationships between strategic type and both management theory and decision influence was not easy to interpret. As anticipated, Prospector and Analyzer administrators reported that a significantly larger amount of influence was exercised in their hospitals. However, we were surprised to find that the distribution (centralization) of this influence was not systematically related to organization strategy. Nor was it apparent why the strong association observed between strategic type and two of the dimensions of management theory—performance expectations and subordinates' capabilities—was not also present for the third dimension, employees' capabilities. To aid in bringing these relationships into sharper focus, Table 13-3 shows the relative number of Prospector, Analyzer, Defender, and Reactor hospitals that scored near the top and near the bottom of the ranked scores measuring management theory and decision influence.

As described in Chapter 8, management theory may be classified according to three general models—the Traditional, Human Relations, and Human Resources models. A Traditional administrator would be expected to regard the capabilities of immediate subordinates and rank-and-file employees as relatively low and to believe that participative policies are not apt to positively affect either morale or performance. A Human Relations administrator also would be expected to regard the capabilities of subordinates and employees as relatively low but to believe that participative policies, while likely to enhance morale, do not directly improve performance. A Human Resources administrator would be expected to regard the capabilities of subordinates and employees as relatively high and to believe that participative policies lead directly to higher performance.

With respect to these expectations, Table 13-3 suggests that it is possible for "pure" Human Resources management to exist within a Defender, Analyzer, or Prospector hospital. That is, members of each of these stable strategic categories scored near the top of each dimension of management theory. However, it also appears that there was no instance within this sample of "pure" Traditional management within a Prospector hospital. It is particularly interesting that no administrators in Prospector organizations rated their subordinates' capabilities as low relative to their own, for previous research had indicated that subordinates' relative capability is a powerful variable in management theory (Ritchie and Miles, 1970).

In the same vein, we expected an organization's strategic type to be

Table 13-3 Number of Organizations by Strategic Type Scoring High and Low on Dimensions of Management Theory and Decision Influence

| Strategic type* | Management theory | | | | | | Decision influence | | | |
| | Performance expectations | | Subordinates' relative capabilities | | Employees' relative capabilities | | Total decision influence | | Centralization of influence | |
	High (Top 7)	Low (bottom 7)	High (top 7)	Low (bottom 7)	High (top 7)	Low (bottom 7)	High (top 7)	Low (bottom 7)	High (top 7)	Low (bottom 7)
Prospectors	3	1	3	0	2	2	4	0	2	2
Analyzers	3	0	2	2	1	3	3	1	3	2
Defenders	1	4	2	4	3	2	0	4½†	2	⅔
Reactors	0	2	0	1	1	0	0	1½	0	2⅓

* Based upon questionnaire data from four Prospectors, five Analyzers, six Defenders, and three Reactors.
† Fractional entries resulted from tied rankings.

227

associated with a decision influence configuration appropriate to that type. The characteristics our theoretical framework ascribed to the Prospector suggested a larger and more dispersed pattern of influence, while those ascribed to the Defender suggested a smaller and more centralized pattern of influence. Accordingly, in Table 13-3, Prospectors uniformly scored near the top of the total decision influence measure, while Defenders uniformly scored near the bottom. However, in terms of the centralization of influence, no systematic differences were observed among the types.

Collectively, the findings discussed above seemed to suggest that organization strategy, management theory, and decision influence must be related in a more intricate fashion than originally envisioned (unless, of course, faulty measurement and/or the size of the sample were distorting the findings). We turned, therefore, to the data from the field interviews to help decipher the questionnaire results.

Interview Findings

The interview comments of hospital administrators suggested, as was inferred from Table 13-3, that the relationship between organization strategy and management theory may be constrained in one direction. That is, while it is unlikely that a Traditional or Human Relations manager can function effectively at the helm of a Prospector organization, it *is* possible for a Human Resources manager to successfully lead a Defender organization. However, the best support we can currently muster for this proposition consists of anecdotal evidence from two of the sample hospitals.[4] The first example highlights some of the problems encountered by a Traditional manager who goes prospecting.

Canyon General Hospital specializes in nonacute care, that is, in the treatment of chronic illnesses such as cancer and heart disease. During the 8-year tenure of the current chief administrator, a new building was erected, increasing the number of patient beds from 72 to 160. Several years ago, Canyon embarked on an ambitious program to acquire the capabilities needed to provide acute care. New hospital-based specialists were recruited, and substantial sums were invested in the necessary medical equipment. Recently, the move toward acute care has encountered some major obstacles. The most persistent problem is low occupancy, which has led to a reduced cash flow, underutilization of equipment, and the departure of several of the new specialists. The administrator

---

[4]In these examples and those which follow, certain characteristics have been disguised in order to protect respondents' anonymity.

commented, "We're losing some of our fast-response capability," and that "fire fighting" is consuming too much of his time.

Although Canyon's administrator expressed dissatisfaction with certain personal and professional characteristics of some members of the hospital's medical staff, he indicated that he can control their behavior to a considerable degree. He also maintained that he is more powerful than the board of directors, who seldom become involved in the internal operation of the hospital. The pattern of the administrator's remarks led us to believe that he was a rather Traditional manager—an impression that was generally reinforced when we subsequently examined his questionnaire responses.

Approximately one month later, at the conclusion of the second interview, we gave the same administrator short written descriptions of the Defender, Reactor, Analyzer, and Prospector strategies and asked him to classify a list of local voluntary hospitals according to this typology. Most of his judgments were consistent with those we received from health professionals and other administrators. However, Canyon's administrator described his own hospital as a Prospector—a view that was incongruent with the opinions of most other raters. Overall, these other raters classified Canyon as a Defender by a 63 percent majority, and only 13 percent believed that the hospital was a Prospector.

Our own observations also suggest that Canyon can best be described as a Defender. We have noted that growth typically occurs through market penetration in Defenders but through diversification in Prospectors. While Canyon's past record of expansion has been quite impressive, the hospital has been more successful in adding beds than in developing new services and programs. Other Defender-like characteristics emerged from Canyon's environmental map and questionnaire data. The task environment of only one sample hospital was perceived to be more predictable, only two reported a smaller total amount of decision influence, and only three implemented a more modest set of adjustments during the last year.

In our view, Canyon's aggressive administrator is largely responsible for the hospital's impressive growth. However, given his managerial style, he may find it difficult to change his organization's strategic type from a Defender to a Prospector. An administrator who endorses the Traditional model of management is rarely able to develop the surveillance mechanisms or willing to permit the decision decentralization necessary to operate a diversified, innovative hospital. In our experience, most administrators of successful Prospectors devote the bulk of their time to external activities, and only under exceptional circumstances do they become personally involved in close supervision of day-to-day internal operations. Adapting to such a leadership role is likely to prove difficult for Canyon's administrator.

The second half of the one-way constraint argument, that it is possible for a Human Resources manager to successfully lead a Defender, is supported by the following example.

Pioneer Hospital was classified as a Defender by 75 percent of those who rated it, and in most respects it is an archetypical specimen of the Defender strategy. Pioneer's narrow service domain, the provision of a limited range of primary medical care, is preserved by immediately referring to other hospitals cases that are esoteric or highly complex, or that require sophisticated medical equipment. The chief administrator commented, "We'll remove your gall bladder, but don't expect to get a kidney transplant here." Environmental surveillance is minimal: the administrator devotes an estimated 90 percent of his time to internal operations and discourages external scanning by other hospital personnel. High-level administrative turnover is low, as evidenced by the respective 12- and 7-year tenures of the chief administrator and controller.

The controller is a party to virtually all major decisions, and he described the hospital as "a lean and hungry organization." As a consequence of the emphasis on cost efficiency, the ratio of hospital employees to the average daily patient census has declined in recent years, and it was among the lowest in our sample during the year the study was conducted. Pioneer has maintained a relatively high occupancy rate, and by consistently operating in the black the hospital has accumulated comfortable financial reserves.

The responses of Pioneer's administrator and controller to our management theory questionnaire suggested a Human Resources management approach. Both individuals saw absolutely no differences between their capabilities and those of their subordinates, and both regarded rank-and-file employees as only moderately less capable.[5]

Pioneer's administrator described his hospital as "a Theory Y organization." There is one less tier in Pioneer's administrative hierarchy than in most hospitals of its size. Furthermore, all administrative positions encompass large areas of responsibility and are designed around the principle that "everybody here does some bench work." Accordingly, no administrator or department head has an assistant or a personal secretary, and nursing supervisors are periodically rotated to perform patient-care responsibilities.

Pioneer's somewhat unorthodox combination of extensive delegation, structural stability, and narrowly defined domain

[5]We were initially surprised to find that both respondents clearly did *not* expect participative policies to lead to better performance. We will return to this point later.

produces substantial cost savings and hence profitability. The hospital is a system of carefully defined positions and work units, each enjoying considerable autonomy within its own sphere of operations. Perhaps this well-conceived organizational and managerial system is the reason why Pioneer's administrator claims that "about 60 percent of the 'work' done in other hospitals is nonessential."

In our view, the well-entrenched Human Resources approach used by Pioneer's chief administrator and controller has minimized interdependence and largely eliminated the need for costly interdepartmental coordination mechanisms. Most of the problems presented by Pioneer's stable domain are familiar, allowing employees to channel their creativity into streamlining internal operations and containing costs.

DISCUSSION

As indicated, the findings of this study were generally consistent with the hypotheses derived from the theoretical framework. Prospectors and Analyzers tended to exhibit more frequent and substantial organizational adjustments, perceived more task-environmental contingencies, allowed organization members more influence in decision making, and used more Human Resources managerial practices than Defenders and Reactors. However, we also indicated that the relationship among organization strategy, management theory, and decision influence was more complex than we had originally envisioned. This particular relationship deserves elaboration.

Although both the data and our interpretation are clearly tentative at this point, from our interviews within Canyon, Pioneer, and other sample hospitals we gleaned three insights that shed considerable light on the anomalous correlations presented in Table 13-2. First, the interviews suggested that, despite the logical linkages between the managerial assumption that subordinates and employees are highly capable and the expectation that participative managerial policies will enhance performance, either of these two ideas may receive greater emphasis within a given organization. Second, the interviews suggested that each of these two components of management theory has unique implications for the configuration of decision influence. Finally, the interviews seemed to indicate that the relationship between management theory and decision influence is moderated by organization strategy.

As indicated earlier, although the administrator and controller of Pioneer Hospital considered the capabilities of subordinates and employees near their own, both of these individuals felt that the hospital would *not* benefit from the application of participative managerial policies. Conversely, we had interviewed other administrators who felt certain that participative policies would improve performance but nonetheless saw a substantial discrepancy between their own capabilities and those of other hospital members. These inverted patterns of emphasis within management theory appeared to be associated with different decision-making processes.

A hospital administrator whose preeminent belief is that the capabilities of other members are near his or her own may choose to relinquish decision-making prerogatives by delegating them down the hierarchy, as was the case in Pioneer Hospital. Extensive delegation of this sort distributes decision influence widely but may have little effect on the total amount that is exercised. Recall that in Table 13-2, the relative capabilities of both subordinates and employees were strongly correlated with the centralization of influence but weakly correlated with total influence. On the other hand, an administrator whose preeminent belief is that participation will produce superior decisions and performance need not abdicate his own role as a decision maker but may instead draw the medical staff, trustees, and other groups into the decision process. Such collaboration increases total decision influence but has little effect on its relative distribution. Again, recall that Table 13-2 showed that performance expectations were strongly correlated with total influence but weakly correlated with the centralization of influence. Thus, linkages among the different dimensions of management theory and decision influence may have been responsible for the "anomalous" correlations obtained.

If, as suggested, the configuration of decision influence is linked to the more salient dimension of management theory, under what conditions does each pattern tend to occur? Our current belief is that organization strategy moderates the relationship between management theory and the amount and distribution of decision influence (see Figure 13-3). In the case of a Prospector hospital, performance is largely based on the ability to develop new services and clientele. Such efforts entail frequent changes in domain and technology, requiring the development of flexible structures and sophisticated forms of coordination to accommodate decisions that regularly cut across organizational subunits. Under these conditions, a de facto variant of the Human Resources approach emphasizing broad participation is likely to result even if this management philosophy was not deliberately adopted and even if top management initially had limited confidence in the capabilities of others. That is, product and market development necessitate collaborative decision making, and thus there is likely to be a large amount of decision influence

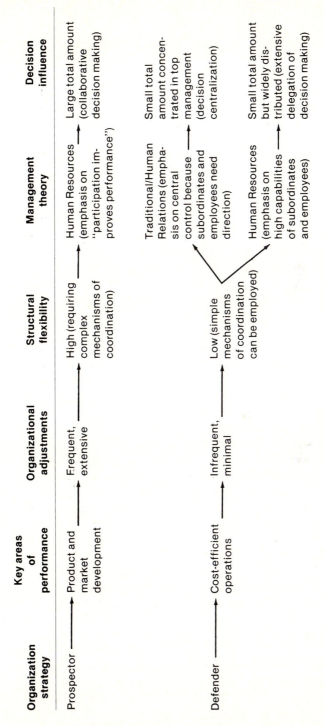

Organization strategy	Key areas of performance	Organizational adjustments	Structural flexibility	Management theory	Decision influence
Prospector →	Product and market development →	Frequent, extensive →	High (requiring complex mechanisms of coordination) →	Human Resources (emphasis on "participation improves performance") →	Large total amount (collaborative decision making)
Defender →	Cost-efficient operations →	Infrequent, minimal →	Low (simple mechanisms of coordination can be employed) →	Traditional/Human Relations (emphasis on central control because subordinates and employees need direction) →	Small total amount concentrated in top management (decision centralization)
			→	Human Resources (emphasis on high capabilities of subordinates and employees) →	Small total amount but widely distributed (extensive delegation of decision making)

Figure 13-3 Proposed linkages among organization strategy, management theory, and decision influence.

present in the organization. In sum, the Prospector's performance orientation encourages, and perhaps demands, widespread participation in decision making.

Conversely, the Defender's performance orientation is toward cost efficiency. Such an orientation requires the development of a stable domain and technology, which in turn limit structural flexibility and coordination requirements. However, the pursuit of a Defender strategy does not require a particular management approach. A Defender guided by a Traditional administrator can enjoy dramatic growth through market penetration, as demonstrated by the Canyon Hospital example. Both the Traditional and the Human Relations models prescribe centralized decision making and control, which result in a small amount of aggregate decision influence and limited decentralization of influence within the organization. Thus, the Defender strategy is compatible with Traditional or Human Relations management since organizational stability usually permits key decisions to be made near the top of the organization.

But while the Defender strategy is compatible with decision centralization, cost efficiency can alternatively be pursued through extensive delegation, as was the case at Pioneer Hospital. If the dominant coalition's beliefs about the capabilities of subordinates and employees are consistent with the Human Resources model, then substantial decision influence may be delegated to lower-level organization members. Unlike the Prospector that uses Human Resources management, however, the Defender's total amount of decision influence will be relatively small. Given the Defender's overall stability, the need for mutual adjustment among departments is minimal. Instead of practicing collaborative decision making with middle managers, top management simply delegates selected decisions to this group. Since the majority of these decisions are focused on cost containment and procedural efficiency within a stable overall system, they can be delegated provided top management has confidence in the abilities of subordinates. Thus, the Defender strategy does not require a particular management system; it permits the use of the Traditional, Human Relations, or Human Resources approach.

THE PREDICTION OF ORGANIZATIONAL ADAPTATION

Although this study was designed primarily to describe and explain relationships among strategy, adaptation, management theory, and decision influence, two important developments occurred in health care during the course of the study that allowed us to explore the predictive capabilities of the theoretical framework. These developments were a month-long physicians' strike precipitated by a rate increase in malpractice insurance and the passage of a federal law requiring the creation of regional health-planning agencies. In this section, we compare the responses of Prospectors, Analyzers, Reactors, and Defenders to these developments.

In the spring of 1975, the Argonaut Insurance Company, the second largest malpractice insurer in the nation, terminated its group coverage of 4,000 northern California physicians—and then offered to reinsure individual doctors at a 384 percent rate increase (Bodenheimer, 1975). Some physicians elected to pay the rate increase; others chose to continue practicing without insurance. Some older physicians opted for early retirement. However, with a tenacity provoked by the highest rates facing any group of physicians, anesthesiologists went on strike for a period of 1 month in the hopes of prompting government intervention. Nonemergency surgery and hospital occupancy levels dropped precipitously across the hospitals in our sample, producing alarming cash-flow declines in many instances. The net loss of several local hospitals exceeded half a million dollars, and although no major hospital went bankrupt as a direct result of the strike, financial reserves were depleted, and there are indications that the crisis may have long-term effects on censuses, surgical volume, and employment in the industry.

Of course, a sudden and unprecedented crisis of this sort is likely to produce a variety of responses from the hospitals affected. However, every hospital in the region was simultaneously responding to another development that had emerged more predictably. In January 1975, President Ford signed into law the National Health Planning and Resources Development Act, hailed as the most significant piece of federal health legislation since Medicare and the potential forerunner of national health insurance. The law was intended to contain spiraling health costs and to correct a pattern of proliferation and uneven distribution of facilities, beds, and expensive medical equipment in the nation's hospitals. It authorized the U.S. Department of Health, Education and Welfare to establish and supervise a network of approximately 200 regional planning bodies called Health Systems Agencies (HSAs). Each HSA would develop a long-range health plan and approve or disapprove applications for federal funding by local providers of health care. The law also directed each state to establish a Health Planning and Development Agency, which must approve all health facilities construction projects as well as the initiation of costly new hospital services and programs.

The ultimate consequence of this legislation for individual hospitals is uncertain. The intent of the statute is ambiguous in places and thus subject to different interpretations. Some observers expect HSAs to erode hospital autonomy seriously. Others point to the tremendous complexity of the administrative machinery created by the law and to the conspicuous inability of previous health-planning experiments to accomplish their purposes. Nonetheless, administrators in most of the sample hospitals were obviously concerned about the law, and many were developing responses to the impending arrival of HSAs.

Hospital Adjustment by Strategic Type

These two environmental developments provided focal points for the specific comparison of organizational adjustment. Data concerning responses to the doctors' strike and the health-planning legislation were obtained from 17 hospitals during the second field interview with chief administrators. These were open-ended interviews, and respondents were asked to direct their comments to concrete actions taken or planned by the organization and to avoid a general analysis of the two developments.

The logic of the theoretical framework suggested that the following five questions concerning adjustment behavior should be related to organization strategy: (1) Was the process of adjustment initiated before the primary impact of the external development (proactive) or after the primary impact (reactive)? (2) In general, were adjustments intended to reduce costs or to increase organizational effectiveness? (3) Did adjustments take the form of limited and temporary response to a short-term situation, or did the adjustment process lead to more extensive and permanent change (usually manifested in the reallocation of organizational resources)? (4) Were adjustments undertaken through the collaboration of various organizational groups, or were they unilaterally chosen and implemented by top administrators? (5) Was the primary target of adjustment internal organizational change or change in external actors and conditions?

Based upon notes from the second field interview, comments related to these five questions with respect to the doctors' strike and the HSA law are summarized in Figure 13-4. While some administrators did not address these questions directly, in most instances the answers were apparent from their descriptions of the adjustments undertaken by the hospital.

(1) Timing of Adjustment Behavior A majority of the Prospectors and Analyzers interviewed indicated that the hospital had anticipated the anesthesiologists' walkout by 2 to 4 weeks—a sufficient margin to allow some advance preparation, which typically involved communication with hospital employees and contingency planning by department heads. Similarly, Prospectors and Analyzers tended to take a proactive adjustment posture with respect to HSAs. Most of these hospitals reported that specific adjustments to the HSA legislation were already under way,

despite the fact that members of the HSA board still had not been selected when the interviews were concluded.

On the other hand, most Defenders and Reactors failed to anticipate
the occurrence of the doctors' strike and thus did not prepare for its impact. Although all of these hospitals were aware of the imminent establishment of HSAs, only one Defender had begun to make substantive
adjustments.

(2) Efficiency versus Effectiveness   The adjustment behavior of
each Prospector hospital was clearly oriented toward enhancing effectiveness. For instance, in negotiations following the doctors' strike, one
hospital agreed to begin paying anesthesiologists' malpractice premiums
in exchange for the promise of uninterrupted service and certain other
concessions. The surveillance system of the same Prospector predicted
passage of the HSA statute 2 years before it occurred, and despite a
recognized need for the administrative consolidation and integration of
previous entrepreneurial activity, the hospital postponed such internal
adjustment in order to continue the further development of new
programs and services (which could be curtailed when HSAs become
operational).

Conversely, the overriding objective of Defenders and Reactors in
adjusting to the doctors' strike was to improve their cash flow by cutting
costs. Similarly, Defender responses to HSAs primarily involved efforts
to reduce health-care costs by increasing hospital efficiency and thus
avoid the sanctions of HSAs. (In the case of the Reactor hospitals, this
question and others simply did not apply, because these hospitals reported making absolutely no substantive adjustments.)

(3) Extent and Longevity of Adjustments   Although notable differences among strategic types were not apparent in terms of the permanence of adjustment to the doctors' strike, Prospector hospitals described the allocation of substantially greater organizational resources
for adjustment to HSAs than other types. These resources included the
creation of new administrative positions and the involvement of trustees
and members of the medical staff in regional planning activities. (The
administrator of one Prospector described his medical staff and trustees
as "scarce and valuable resources," and said that the timing and target-
ing of their involvement presented an important issue.)

(4) Participation in Adjustment   Prospectors and Analyzers unanimously reported that members of the administration, medical staff,
trustees, and employee groups had collaborated in adjusting to both

Characteristics of adjustment	Hospital				
	P1	P2	P3	P4	A1
	Doctors' Strike				
(1) Did the hospital anticipate the strike? [YES–NO]	YES	YES	NO	N.E.[1]	N.E.
(2) Were adjustments aimed at cost reduction or increased effectiveness? [COST–EFF]	EFF	EFF/COST	EFF	EFF	COST
(3) Did any long-run organizational changes result? [YES–NO]	YES	NO	YES	NO	NO
(4) Was the adjustment process collaborative or unilateral? [COL–UNI]	COL	COL	N.E.	COL	COL
(5) Were adjustment targets internal or external? [IN–EX]	EX/IN	IN/EX	EX/IN	EX	IN
	Health Systems Agencies (HSAs)				
(1) Was the hospital's posture proactive or reactive? [PRO–REA]	PRO	PRO	PRO	REA	PRO
(2) Were adjustments aimed at cost reduction or increased effectiveness? [COST–EFF]	EFF	EFF	EFF	EFF	EFF
(3) Were substantial resources allocated? [YES–NO]	YES	YES	YES	NO	NO
(4) Was the adjustment process collaborative or unilateral? [COL–UNI]	COL	COL	COL	N.E.	COL
(5) Were adjustment targets internal or external? [IN–EX]	EX	EX/IN	EX/IN	N.E.	EX/IN

[1]No evidence (the respondent failed to address this issue).
[2]Not applicable (because there was no substantive adjustment).

Figure 13-4 Strategic type and characteristics of hospital adjustment to doctors' strike and HSAs.

developments. Although collaboration was also reported by several Defenders and one Reactor, in other hospitals of these types it appeared that the chief administrator had selected and instigated adjustments unilaterally.

(5) Adjustment Targets The interview findings clearly suggested that Prospector hospitals were more prone to attempts to manipulate conditions and actors in the hospital's task environment than the other strategic types. These externally targeted adjustments included attempts

Hospital											
A2	A3	A4	A5	D1	D2	D3	D4	D5	R1	R2	R3
Doctors' strike											
YES	N.E.	YES	N.E.	YES	NO	NO	NO	NO	YES	NO	NO
COST	N.E.	COST	COST	COST/EFF	COST	COST	COST	COST	COST	COST	COST
NO	NO	NO	NO	YES	NO	NO	NO	YES	NO	NO	NO
COL	COL	COL	COL	COL	UNI	COL	UNI	COL	UNI	COL	UNI
IN	IN	IN/EX	IN	IN	IN	IN	IN	IN	IN	IN	IN
Health Systems Agencies (HSA)											
PRO	PRO	REA	REA	PRO	REA	REA	PRO	REA	REA	REA	REA
N.E.	EFF	COST	COST	EFF	COST	COST	COST	COST	N.A.[2]	N.A.	N.A.
NO	YES	NO	NO	NO	NO	NO	YES	NO	NO	NO	NO
COL	COL	COL	COL	COL	UNI	COL	COL	COL	N.A.	N.A.	N.A.
IN	IN	IN	IN	IN	IN	IN	EX/IN	IN	N.A.	N.A.	N.A.

to educate or politicize the public, to bring direct influence to bear upon selected organizations or political entities, and to develop shared services or forge other permanent linkages with other hospitals.

Adjustment in Four Hospitals

Although the interview findings summarized above appear to be highly consistent with the logic and the implications of the theoretical framework, it would be inappropriate to use these categorizations in systematic, detailed analyses. As indicated, they were based upon the notes of relatively unstructured and open-ended interviews, and were subsequently coded by the researchers. Although we attempted to do this in an objective manner, some of the evidence was contradictory, and some of the categorizations were difficult. Consequently, these findings should be viewed with caution.

Having called for interpretative caution, we nevertheless feel it is useful to offer one final, more detailed picture of the comparative behavior of strategic types with regard to the doctors' strike and the HSA legislation. Below we present the actual descriptions given by the administrators of an illustrative Prospector, Analyzer, Reactor, and Defender hospital.[6]

The Prospector   The Prospector is a rapidly growing community hospital which has broken new ground in developing outpatient surgical clinics and other innovative methods of delivering primary health care.

Response to the doctors' strike: First, you should understand how [this hospital] is organized. Many of the normal duties of a chief administrator are delegated to the department head level. We anticipated the strike by 65 or 70 days—the signs were clear. I not only supported the strike, I encouraged it because I thought it was critical to call attention to the malpractice problem.

We started by making a set of very pessimistic assumptions: the loss of most if not all surgical patients and half the medical patients, a very restricted definition of surgical emergency (patients who would be critically damaged by transportation), a drop in hospital occupancy to 40 or 50 percent of normal levels, and a 50 percent increase in the utilization of our outpatient services.

Forty-five days prior to the strike, this scenario was presented to all department heads. They were told to submit formal projections of the impact on departmental utilization and written plans for action by April 15.

When the strike began on May 1, occupancy quickly fell to 40 percent. No more than 15 operations were performed for the duration of the strike. Departmental contingency plans were implemented with little or no alteration. Cost cutting was highly effective. In fact, the hospital netted $10,000 during the course of the strike. This is pretty good, since we lost $50,000 in May of 1974.

Layoffs were extensive—over half of our employees. There were three stages. A lot of people volunteered, especially in cases where the

---

[6]These descriptions were condensed from administrators' verbatim statements. They have been edited for reasons of brevity and to conceal respondents' identity. Certain details have also been altered to preserve anonymity.

family had a second source of income. Then we reduced everyone's hours. Finally, new employees were laid off according to seniority, although this policy was modified for low-income employees.

There was a policy of full disclosure of relevant information at all times. We issued weekly bulletins to all personnel, and our employees were unexpectedly supportive. When the strike was over, we had no difficulty getting people back to work. Occupancy climbed back to normal levels, and we suffered no other long-term consequences.

The strike was a real learning experience, a good experiment. We learned that given sufficient warning, we could adapt to almost anything—including a drastic drop in our patient load.

Response to the HSA law: The most fundamental strategy with respect to HSA is to create a totally acceptable plan, one that would be approved by any agency that might come along. For years, [this hospital] has had a sophisticated master plan. It begins with the community's needs and develops services accordingly. We don't just present a schedule of facility expansion.

I'm also trying to influence the appointment of people who understand my problems. [Members of the regional board were then being selected.] I sat on the county CHP [Comprehensive Health Planning] board for several years, and my prediction is that in the final analysis, the same people will be doing the planning under HSA who have always done it.

The Analyzer The Analyzer is a community-oriented general hospital, which is organized into three administrative units. Two of these units perform comparatively stable activities: one is responsible for nursing and other aspects of patient care, while the other provides supportive services including medical records, pharmacy, plant maintenance, and housekeeping. The third unit functions in more innovative areas. It operates the hospital's laboratories, medical equipment, and several specialty clinics.

Response to the doctors' strike: Comparatively speaking, [this hospital] wasn't hit too hard by the strike. This was in part a consequence of our pattern of medical specialization. Although we did lose most of our surgery, other important areas were relatively unaffected. We have a large outpatient component, a psychiatric clinic, and a hemodialysis unit, all of which continued operating at roughly normal levels. This definitely dampened the effect of the anesthesiologists' walkout.

We're on a flexible staffing plan, so no fundamentally innovative response was necessary. We maintain routine contingency plans that specify responses to different kinds and rates of decline in our census. A number of employees took time off voluntarily, and few layoffs were necessary. Frankly, I don't know why the impact wasn't more severe. I'd like to think it was partly due to a history of cooperative relations with the medical staff and the community.

Response to the HSA law: We're trying to stay well informed. We've sent at least one member of the administration to every hearing or meeting concerning HSAs. We have also attempted to get some representation on the [HSA] board, but I don't know if this gambit will succeed.

In my judgment, HSA's most significant impact will be in the area of rate setting. They will have authority to compile data on the cost of comparable services across hospitals and to discourage rates that are grossly in excess of the mean. Our future strategy will be to move into areas of specialization that are being less actively pursued by other hospitals and develop efficient techniques for delivering these services. This hospital won't blaze many trails, but we won't sit back, either.

The Reactor   The Reactor was the first hospital established in its service area. In recent years, the hospital has faced mounting financial deficits and declining occupancy as newer hospitals have made inroads into its clientele.

Response to the doctors' strike: Our first action was to reassure people and let them know what was happening to the hospital. We informed our employees, and through our public information office we assured our current patients that the hospital would continue to meet their needs. I also held meetings with the joint conference committee of the medical staff and the board of directors.

Our patient population dropped by almost 100 percent. The reason we were affected so severely is that the medical community in [this area] took the situation very seriously. Our chief pathologist's attitude was, "We'll show 'em" [the insurance companies]. He built up a spirit of cooperation and solidarity among the doctors that led to an almost total boycott of the hospital. At many other hospitals there was only fragmentary support for the strike.

At first, we asked employees to use their accumulated vacation time during the strike. This reduced the number of people coming to work, but since we had to continue paying salaries, it aggravated our cash-flow problem. Later, we were forced to drop the vacation policy and reduce staff through layoffs according to seniority.

Occupancy still isn't back to normal [9 months later]. Our average patient stay has fallen from 7.2 days before the strike to just 4.8 days. Doctors are avoiding complex cases and practicing more conservative medicine because they're concerned about malpractice lawsuits.

Response to the HSA law: I'm not very well informed. I've tried to become involved but really haven't kept up to date. We're not doing much at the moment. HSAs are going through "fumbleitis" looking for leadership. I'd be really worried about the consequences [for our hospital] if we hadn't just completed a substantial expansion of facilities. We didn't see the law coming, we were just lucky. Perhaps we should have taken a stronger leadership role. I did attend several breakfast meetings with an ad hoc group of [local] hospital administrators. But all I got out of them was high cholesterol.

The Defender The Defender is a medium-sized hospital that admits a large number of low-income patients. In 1974, the hospital completed an extensive and costly construction project undertaken to replace or renovate its antiquated facilities.

Response to the doctors' strike: The malpractice crisis took us by surprise, and it caught us when our financial reserves were very low. Nearly all surgery was lost, and occupancy fell about 30 percent. The only thing that held occupancy that high was the OB [obstetrics] department. The immediate need was to cut expenses, which meant payroll since this amounts to nearly 70 percent of our operating expenses.

The doctors went out on Monday, and the management team met that afternoon. Each division head was charged with the responsibility of evaluating how the strike would affect cash flows within his or her specific area and how expenses could be cut to guarantee the hospital's survival. We met again Tuesday. Plans were quickly approved and implementation got under way.

This fast response was possible because we're a closely knit group with good working relationships—also because division heads are accustomed to exercising authority and being held accountable for performance.

Actually, we came out of the strike in better shape than we went in. For some time we had been attempting to reduce the level of staffing in the hospital, but resistance from the unions and other employee groups was strong. By nearly pushing us over the edge, the strike provided the leverage we needed to cut costs. We learned that we could cut back or discontinue many services without damage to the hospital. When the strike ended, we rehired selectively. Fortunately, a number of our laid-off employees had found other jobs or left the area. Our staff is 10 percent smaller today than it was before the strike. A subsequent strike would be less traumatic. This is because of what we learned the last time and because our staffing is much more efficient now.

Response to the HSA law: The feeling here is that HSA won't be all that effective. The law could have a large impact if the feds fund it heavily. In that case, we would respond—and the malpractice crisis demonstrated our ability to move rapidly. In the meantime, we have a healthy crop of concrete internal problems to occupy our attention. Right now, for example, I'm trying to set up a joint purchasing arrangement with a nearby hospital that should reduce supply costs for both of us. It's hard enough just to stay on top of your own responsibilities without trying to prepare for future crises that probably won't occur.

General Comments The adjustment behavior of these four hospitals was generally consistent with our theoretical framework. We have maintained that each of the three stable strategic types exhibits unique capabilities or distinctive competences. Accordingly, the Prospector hospital (whose capabilities include environmental surveillance, contingency planning, and structural flexibility) anticipated the malpractice insurance crisis, accurately predicted its impact on the hospital, and adjusted internal operations with such dexterity that the hospital made money during the strike. Furthermore, the Prospector's penchant for shaping emerging environmental events was illustrated by this hospital's proactive efforts to influence the composition of the HSA board. In the Analyzer hospital, whose distinctive competence lies in the ability to develop new services and programs while continuing to serve traditional clients, the impact of the doctors' strike was cushioned by the uninterrupted operation of the hospital's adaptive component and by the advance preparation of contingency plans. Moreover, this hospital's approach to the impending HSA law reflects the Analyzer's dual emphasis on efficiency and flexibility. The hospital was preparing to develop in those areas where it could presumably create delivery systems efficient enough to satisfy HSA's projected emphasis on reduced hospital rates. For the Defender, whose strength lies in continuously improving health care efficiency, the doctors' strike provided an opportunity to cut costs by permanently reducing the level of staffing. In addition, the Defender's commitment to its present domain and its heavy focus on internal operations were reflected in the hospital's small concern with the future consequences of HSAs.

We noted earlier that Reactor organizations are characterized by the lack of a well-articulated distinctive competence. Their human resources, however capable individually, are not as sharply targeted as those in the other types. Lacking a clear external orientation, Reactors display varying degrees of internal inconsistency and consequently may find it difficult to adjust in a timely and efficient manner. These characteristics appear to have been borne out, at least in part, by the adjustment behavior of the Reactor hospital. The protracted effects of the malpractice insurance crisis and the ambivalence expressed concerning HSAs suggest that this hospital lacks a consistent strategy and an appropriate set of mechanisms for responding to environmental change.

CONCLUSIONS

The basic purpose of this study was to test the ability of the model of strategic types to both explain and predict different configurations among managerial perceptions, organizational adaptation, management theory, and decision influence. We used a combination of field interviews and questionnaires to collect data in a homogeneous sample of 19 voluntary hospitals. Our findings suggested that most of these organization variables were systematically related to organization strategy.

One of the study's most significant implications is that the perceptions and choices of the dominant coalition concerning both the organization itself and external conditions can play a crucial role in linking the organization to its environment. The hospitals in our sample are situated within the same physical and social environment and provide many of the same health care services. Nevertheless, among these hospitals we observed differences in enacted task environments, administrative structures and processes, and types of organizational adjustment. Our research suggests that the concept of organization strategy can be a powerful tool in the comprehension and, to some extent, in the prediction of these differences.

The studies described in Chapters 11, 12, and 13 represent a first phase in the development and exploration of a theoretical paradigm using the organization as a unit of observation and analysis. In no sense do we consider or offer these studies as "proof" of the validity of our conceptual framework. It is our hope that the utility of this approach for understanding intra-industry variations in environmental enactment and internal organizational characteristics will be examined in a variety of other settings. We believe this approach will prove useful and that it should, at least, provide the raw material for more advanced conceptualizations.

Part Three

Overview
of the Literature

Chapter 14

Prior Theory and Research

This chapter is intended for those readers who desire a more detailed discussion of the literature on organization-environment relations. Throughout the book, we have referred to concepts appropriate to the analysis of organizations and their environments, such as environmental change and uncertainty, strategy, technology, structure, and process. The purpose of this chapter is to describe and discuss these concepts in more depth and to cite studies that have investigated aspects of the organization-environment relationship. The discussion is not meant to be exhaustive; rather, it is intended to provide an overview that highlights the key features of the literature.

The discussion centers primarily on those areas of the Organizational Behavior and Business Policy literature which pertain to organizational adaptation to the environment. In our opinion, however, theory and research in both of these fields have concentrated overwhelmingly on simple specification and description of existing relationships between organizations and their environments but have largely ignored the processes by which these relationships came about. Although the literature on organization-environment relations is growing rapidly, it is still in search of theoretical paradigms that can fully portray the complexities and dynamics of the behavior of total organizational systems.

The chapter is divided into three major sections. In the first section, we discuss briefly some of the early perspectives on organizations. Invariably, these approaches excluded, or at least deemphasized, environmental factors as important influences on the organization. The environment first began to receive the serious attention of organizational analysts with the appearance of the contingency approach, which is the subject of the second section. In the final section, we discuss theory and research related to what might be called the neocontingency perspective. This approach is not yet fully developed, but it focuses on the role of managerial choice in organizational adaptation, a variable that is excluded from most contingency models.

EARLY PERSPECTIVES

For the first half of this century, management and organization theorists tended to ignore the environment, or at least to hold it constant, as they sought universalistic principles of structure, planning, control, and the like. Weber (1947), who first articulated the characteristics of a bureaucracy (clearly defined hierarchy, positions, and rules) was aware of some of the dysfunctions of bureaucratic structures and processes, but he nevertheless implied that bureaucracy was appropriate for all organizational settings. Similarly, Taylor (1911) viewed his principles of scientific management as universally applicable, and he treated environmental demands and organizational objectives as fixed in his search for the "one best way" to manage job performance at the worker level. Finally, more recent proponents of administrative principles, such as Brown (1945), Fayol (1949), Mooney (1947), and Urwick (1943), enlarged the focus to include the upper reaches of the organization. But these theorists paid little attention to environmental differences, even though they were attempting to integrate experiences from the church, the military, and business into a common set of practical recommendations for the design and management of organizations.

Economists, on the other hand, were concerned with organizational adjustments to the environment, but by and large these adjustments were treated simply as formal exercises in profit-maximizing logic. In economic models, market forces set the prices for goods and services, and the entire organization was characterized by a production function whose blend of capital and labor was dictated by the quest for productive efficiency. Entrepreneurial and marketing decisions were viewed as important, but few attempts were made to extend the implications of these decisions to organizational structure and processes. Organizations were viewed as monolithic entities headed by a single entrepreneur who made all major adjustment decisions—a portrayal that bore scant resemblance to the realities of organizational behavior.

Each of these early perspectives—Weber's bureaucratic model, Taylor's scientific management, and the various administrative principles—emphasized nonhuman elements of the organization such as goals, structure, policies, and procedures, and the theorists of this period implied that their models were applicable under all types of environmental conditions. Although these universalistic models had a sizable impact on managerial practice, they gave way fairly quickly to perspectives that were more realistic but also more complicated.

Attacks on universalistic, and usually prescriptive, organization and management theories began in the thirties and forties and became more heated in the fifties. The primary criticism concerned the alleged inability of bureaucracies to adapt to the needs of individuals and to changes in the environment. Gouldner (1954) provided case-study evidence suggesting that bureaucratization could be efficacious in one setting (an office) but damaging in another (a mine). Burns and Stalker (1961) extended this notion of contingent organizational forms by noting that successful firms in a stable environment tended to have mechanistic or highly bureaucratized structures and processes, while successful firms in changing and uncertain environments tended to have organic or flexible structures and processes. The impact of Burns and Stalker's findings was enhanced by the growing acceptance of the "systems" view of organizations, which portrayed them as sociotechnical mechanisms that draw resources from the environment, transform them, and then export goods and services back into the environment (von Bertalanffy, 1968; Churchman, 1968; Simon, 1969). Thus, with the advent of the contingency perspective, environmental factors came to be viewed as an important influence on the behavior of organizations.

CONTINGENCY PERSPECTIVES

Through the late fifties and the sixties, a series of increasingly elaborate contingency models portraying the linkages among environment, technology, structure, and process were developed. Essentially, the contingency approach argues that "it depends," and the recent thrust of conceptualization in the area of organization theory has been toward the identification and description of the major contingency variables upon which organizational behavior depends. Unlike the early theorists, who tended to treat structure and process as independent variables that could be manipulated by managers, contingency theorists viewed many internal aspects of the organization as dependent variables, whose form was largely determined by forces originating in the organization's environment.

Organizational Environments

It is usually taken for granted that there is some boundary separating the organization from its environment. However, Starbuck (1976) has compared the problem of locating an organization's boundary to that of finding the boundary of a cloud. In defining a cloud, one can measure the density of its moisture and, by selecting some specific level of density, determine what properly "belongs" to the cloud and what "belongs" to its environment. But with organizations the boundary problem is more difficult. If, for example, one wishes to measure the density of member interaction and involvement, he or she must specify the decisions or issues that are concerned. Clearly, interaction patterns and degree of involvement of various individuals and groups (e.g., stockholders, unions, suppliers, etc.) vary depending upon whether the concern is with long-range planning, wage and salary issues, or the imminent bankruptcy of the firm. Thus, while the density of interaction and involvement can be measured, it changes over time and across decision areas, thereby changing the determination of what is "in" the organization and what is "in" the environment.

Conceptualizing the Environment The difficulty of specifying where the organization ends and the environment begins suggested that models that included external variables might provide a more complete understanding of behavior within the organization. However, theorists are still attempting to develop descriptions of the environment that are flexible enough to permit meaningful comparison of different kinds of organizations and yet precise enough to be analytically useful. The first widely recognized typology presented four types of environment based on the degree of interconnectedness and the extent of change in the environment (Emery and Trist, 1965). Arranged in ascending order of change and uncertainty, these environments are: (1) placid-randomized, (2) placid-clustered, (3) disturbed-reactive, and (4) turbulent field. Emery and Trist argued that each type of environment required a different form of organization structure, although they did not specify these contingent structural forms.

Hall (1972) distinguished the *general* environment, which affects all organizations (technological, legal, economic, demographic, and cultural conditions), from the *specific* environment, which consists of those external entities that interact directly with the focal organization. Evan (1966) has called the specific environment the *organization set*—that collection of persons, groups, and other organizations which supplies inputs to or receives outputs from the focal organization. Similar concepts proposed by other theorists include Thompson's (1967) *task environment* and Dill's (1958, p. 410) *relevant environment,* both referring to those external actors or conditions "relevant or potentially relevant to goal setting and goal attainment."

Most theorists have settled upon the task environment as the primary set of forces to which the organization must respond. Task environments, in turn, have been investigated with respect to a number of potentially important dimensions. Many researchers have focused on change as a key environmental dimension, arguing that the more variable and unpredictable the task environment, the more flexible organizational structure and process must be (Dill, 1958; Burns and Stalker, 1961; Thompson, 1967; Lawrence and Lorsch, 1967; Duncan, 1972; and Osborn and Hunt, 1974). But some of these investigators have not distinguished between rate of environmental change and degree of uncertainty (that is, unpredictable change) and have therefore implicitly equated the two. It is possible to have rapid but largely predictable change in the environment, and under such circumstances the organization does not actually confront uncertainty, as managers feel reasonably confident about the sort of environmental conditions they will face in the future. A related problem involves treating the environment and the organization as global entities, as though a monolithic environment somehow produces uniform responses across the entire organization. However, examples are readily available of organizations with a stable technology that face volatile credit and money market conditions, and of organizations with a flexible structure that meet constant customer demand for uniform products. Recent research has attempted to refine the conceptualization of environmental uncertainty (Tosi et al., 1973; Pennings, 1975), and current thinking is that uncertainty *perceived* by managers influences organizational responses more directly than does "objectively" determined uncertainty (e.g., Downey et al., 1975).

Other theorists (particularly Thompson, 1967; Perrow, 1967; and Duncan, 1972) have stressed the heterogeneity of the environment. They argued that complex and diverse environments are likely to require more highly differentiated organizational structures than are simple and homogeneous environments. Once again, however, some confusion develops. Thompson treats the dimensions of heterogeneity and change as independent, while Duncan views both as components of environmental uncertainty. Other dimensions of the environment that have been investigated include: (1) concentration-dispersion of resources, (2) environmental capacity (rich-lean), (3) domain consensus-dissensus, and (4) environmental mutability-immutability (Aldrich, 1972).

Environmental Uncertainty Although theory and research on organizational environments have employed numerous dimensions, the uncertainty dimension has received by far the most attention. March and Simon (1958) suggested that uncertainty absorption is one of the most fundamental functions of an organization. Weick (1969) and Galbraith (1973) argued that organization structure largely arises from attempts to remove equivocality from external information and to process this information during the performance of internal tasks. Finally, Thompson (1967, p. 159) claimed: "Uncertainty appears as the fundamental problem for complex organizations and coping with uncertainty, as the essence of the administrative process."

Research findings have suggested that many facets of the organization may be contingent upon environmental uncertainty. Lawrence and Lorsch (1967) reported that organizational success in uncertain environments required high differentiation between functional subunits and the use of elaborate integrative mechanisms to coordinate subunit activities. Conversely, they found that success in more certain environments required less differentiation and less elaborate integrative mechanisms. Other studies have found that relatively uncertain environments are associated with : (1) extensive participation in organizational decision making, less formalized job design, and rapid program innovation (Hage and Aiken, 1967); (2) greater lateral communication, self-contained tasks, and extensive environmental surveillance (Thompson, 1967; Galbraith, 1973); and (3) lower task specialization, less internal consensus, and more organizational slack (March and Simon, 1958). Thompson (1967) has suggested that some organizations create specialized uncertainty-absorbing subunits located at their boundaries, and it has been found that the ability to absorb uncertainty is related to the distribution of power among subunits (Hinings et al., 1974). On the other hand, it appears that relatively certain or predictable environments are associated with more bureaucratized, stable, centralized, homogeneous, and introspective organizational systems.

In sum, the concept of uncertainty has emerged as a primary variable linking a great number of organizational characteristics to conditions in the environment. However, little is known about the process through which uncertainty leads to internal change in the organization. Most studies have undertaken little beyond establishing statistical associations between uncertainty and organization variables. These studies generally adopt the most straightforward causal assumption—that uncertainty determines the observed organizational characteristics. However, as Child noted (1972, p. 2), "The 'fact' of a statistically established relationship does not 'speak for itself.' At the very least, it may mask a more complex set of direct and indirect relationships."

Manipulating the Environment

In addition to adjusting the internal system, organizations can act to effect change in the environment itself. Attempts to shape the environment to make it conform more closely to the organization's preferences have been documented at both the industry and organization level. For example, Hirsch (1975) showed that firms within the same industry can collaborate to make their environments more manageable. He noted that despite similar technologies and other organizational features, the typical pharmaceutical manufacturing firm was far more profitable than the typical phonograph record company. Hirsch attributed this discrepancy in profitability to the ability of pharmaceutical firms to (1) control prices and channels of distribution, (2) negotiate favorable legislation in the areas of patents and copyrights, and (3) coopt important opinion leaders in the industry (e.g., doctors versus radio station executives). In each of these three areas, record companies were neither as active nor as successful in shaping the environment to fit their needs. Similar attempts to shape the environment along desired lines involve working with trade associations, coordinating groups (Litwak and Hylton, 1962), government agencies (Stigler, 1971), and exchanging executives across firms (Pfeffer and Leblebici, 1973).

At the organizational level, additional mechanisms are available for regulating environmental uncertainty and interdependence. One set of mechanisms involves direct interaction with the groups or organizations concerned, using such means as long-term contracts (Guetzkow, 1966), joint ventures (Aiken and Hage, 1968), cooptation (Selznick, 1949), or merger (Pfeffer, 1972). Another approach is less clear-cut. Perrow (1970) has described instances where corporations "willingly suspended" competition in the short run because of strong industry norms concerning how business relations ought to be conducted. Finally, if factors prove difficult to manage, the organization has the option of choosing another domain, that is, avoiding uncertainty or dependence by getting into a new line of activity. Consequently, diversification is another way of coping with the environment (Pitts, 1977b).

In sum, these and other studies have indicated that organizations engage in a variety of tactics to stabilize conditions in their environments. However, as was the case in research concerning uncertainty-related changes in internal characteristics, this literature typically does not address the process by which organizations select and implement externally directed adjustments. Consequently, it is not known why specific responses are employed by some organizations but not others. Furthermore, there is little research evidence pertaining to the impact of these responses on either the organization or the environment. Of particular interest would be data suggesting the relative contribution of different forms of adjustment to organizational effectiveness.

Technology and Structure

Other theorists have regarded technology as the contingency variable that has the most pervasive impact upon organization structure. Broadly defined, technology is the combination of skills, equipment, and relevant technical knowledge needed to bring about desired transformations in materials, information, or people (Davis, 1971). Structure, which exists to control and coordinate the technology as well as buffer it from environmental disturbances, refers to the characteristics of organizational subunits and the relationships among them.

Types of Technology Woodward (1965), the first to introduce technology as an important organizational variable, constructed a technological scale ranging from unit or small-batch production, through large-batch or mass production, to continuous-process production. Each of these technologies differs in the degree to which it is labor or capital intensive and particularly in the extent to which it permits specialized handling. Other typologies have been offered (e.g., Perrow, 1967; Thompson, 1967; Hickson et al., 1969), but Woodward's scheme permits some broad comparisons to be made across different types.

The unit or small-batch production technology is labor intensive and highly adaptable. Thus, it is suitable for custom products but less appropriate for standardized products and long production runs. This type of technology can operate at low output levels and tolerate considerable fluctuation in output. A unit technology is usually accompanied by a flexible organization structure that has a small administrative component (relative to the number of employees), few hierarchical levels, and a moderately broad span of supervisory control. Most of the employees who operate this type of technology have general as opposed to specialized skills, and the unit technology may be adjusted with comparative ease to permit experimentation with new products and work processes.

Mass-production technologies usually operate at intermediate levels of both labor and capital intensity. Because they typically employ expensive, limited-purpose equipment, mass-production technologies are far less flexible than unit technologies and require a very high volume of output to be economical. Due to requirements for precise scheduling, even small fluctuations in output are costly within this type of system. The organization structure appropriate for a mass-production technology tends to be highly formalized and to have a larger administrative component with a wider span of control than does a unit technology. Standardized procedures are utilized to control employees whose specialized skills may be relatively interchangeable within the system but cannot be easily adapted to new methods and processes.

Finally, continuous-process technology is highly capital intensive and requires a large output volume. Although this type of technology often allows the manufacture of a considerable range of related products, the technology itself is quite rigid—it can be adapted to produce different products only at great cost. The structure compatible with a continuous-process technology has the largest administrative component, the most hierarchical levels, and the narrowest span of control. Continuous-process technology requires comparatively few individuals to monitor the machinery, but such employees must have high levels of judgment and technical skill.

Control, Coordination, and Technology Woodward (1970) and others (e.g., Thompson, 1967; Perrow, 1967; Comstock and Scott, 1977) have suggested that the structure of an organization does not respond directly to technology but rather to the different demands for control and coordination imposed by different types of technology. For example, Reeves and Woodward (1970) found that as technology moves from unit to mass production and then to continuous-process, there is an increase in mechanical over personal forms of control. At the same time, as one moves through the technology classification, control systems tend to be unitary in unit technologies (applied throughout the organization), fragmented in mass-production technologies (with different control standards and mechanisms for each major organizational subunit), and unitary once again in continuous-process technologies. Thus, Reeves and Woodward argued, the different technologies require different forms of control, and these in turn create some demand for, but do not precisely determine, a particular organization structure (e.g., unitary control can be achieved either by formalized rules or by centralized decision making).

Similarly, each type of technology must be coordinated differently, and these different coordination demands must be accommodated by the organization's structure. Van de Ven et al. (1976) found that different coordination mechanisms were used depending upon the degree of task uncertainty, work flow interdependence, and subunit size. As tasks increased in uncertainty, coordination by mutual adjustment through lateral communications and group meetings was used in lieu of coordination through the formal hierarchy or through impersonal rules and plans. As work flow interdependence increased, more use was made of all types of coordinating mechanisms—impersonal modes as well as personal and group modes. Finally, increases in subunit size had an impersonalizing effect on coordination, with more frequent use of hierarchical rules, plans, and policies.

In sum, contingency approaches emphasizing technology have indicated that this variable may be related to numerous aspects of organization structure, primarily through the control and coordination requirements associated with different types of technology. However, reviews of the literature on technology, size, and structure have concluded that: (1) the definition and measurement of both technology and structure have not been consistent across studies, rendering comparison difficult; (2) studies across several types of organizations may reflect interindustry differences and their impact on structure rather than the specific influence of technology; (3) a single organization may operate more than one technology, making the dominant technological influence difficult to ascertain; (4) organization size often appears to be a stronger determinant of structure than does technology; and (5) because technology and size together explain such a small amount of the variance in organization structure, other predictors of structure need to be investigated (Mohr, 1971; Child and Mansfield, 1972; Jelinek, 1977).

Recently, it has been noted that few investigators have isolated technology's distinct effects at different organizational levels such as individual, work group, subunit, and total organization (Hrebiniak, 1974; Gillespie and Mileti, 1977), and these distinctions appear to be important. For example, Comstock and Scott (1977) showed that technology is most closely associated with the characteristics of individual members when it is measured as a set of discrete tasks, but when aspects of the work flow are measured, technology is most closely associated with structural characteristics of the entire subunit. In addition, many technology theorists have implied that structure is caused, or at least greatly constrained, by technology. However, it seems likely that in some cases, technology is a consequence of structure rather than its cause. At the work group level, for example, if decentralization and group autonomy are deeply entrenched structural characteristics, new tasks that might have been standardized may actually be performed in a nonroutine fashion. Similarly, at the organizational level, a system that is organized by functional departments is likely to adopt and capitalize upon mass-production technologies more readily than a system organized by product divisions.

Limitations of the Contingency Perspective

The contingency models discussed above arose from a growing dissatisfaction with universalistic theories of organization and management. Today, universalistic approaches are rarely advanced, as most theorists give at least passing recognition to the need for situational modifications of whatever models they are advocating. Recently, however, theorists have begun to point out limitations of the contingency approach as well. Two major limitations can be identified: (1) the predominant emphasis of contingency models on individual and situational differences rather than similarities and (2) a strong deterministic bias that largely ignores the important variable of managerial choice.

Ultimately, the notion that "every situation is different" becomes an atheoretical point of view that provides even less guidance than did the universalistic assumption that "every situation is the same." As models accumulate, each typically relating variables drawn from only the environment or technology to a similarly restricted set of organizational characteristics, the collective result is a maze of disjointed contingency variables and relationships. To escape from this labyrinth is a herculean task, for theorists have yet to provide useful maps—that is, models that aggregate variables to depict the operation of entire sociotechnical systems in interaction with their environments. Such models might utilize a set of core concepts to describe and, more important, to explain broad patterns of organizational behavior.

The second limitation, the deterministic bias present in many contingency approaches, has had at least two important consequences. First, determinism has masked the complexity with which environmental, organizational, and technological variables are related. Correlational evidence, even when collected on a longitudinal basis, leaves underlying organizational and managerial processes to be inferred. Consequently, less is known about these processes than about the surface characteristics that they generate, and causal effects have been attributed to variables that are, in fact, only indirectly related. Second, the presumption that organizational forms are dependent upon prior causes has justified attempts to predict these forms without reference to the organizations' power-holders, who decide upon strategic courses of action. It has been frequently noted that organizations adopt a variety of forms in response to apparently similar environmental demands (Miles et al., 1974; Anderson and Paine, 1975). Thus, there is evidence to refute a "functional imperative" of organizational structure and behavior. However, relatively few studies have focused on the top-management group and how managers' choices affect the direction, the shape, and the actions of the organization. Another important but largely unexplored question is how today's managerial decisions affect the organization's ability to respond to the environment of tomorrow.

To date, Thompson (1967) has presented the most useful synthesis of the contingency approach in the form of an integrated model, which suggests how the dynamic organization, through the actions of its dominant coalition, develops structures and processes that take both environment and technology into account. Generally speaking, Thompson argued that organizations try to identify homogeneous segments of the environment and establish specialized structural units to deal with each. They endeavor to seal off their core technologies from environmental disturbances, largely by deploying input and output subunits around the technology. When it is possible to isolate the technological core from boundary-spanning activities, the organization is usually centralized and functionally organized. However, when these two kinds of activity are reciprocally interdependent, a structure that approximates a matrix is more likely. In addition, the more uncertainty the organization faces, the more bases for power are present, and the larger the dominant coalition is apt to be.

In essence, Thompson suggests that the organization in a stable environment is not obliged to invest heavily in environmental scanning and, subject to technological constraints, is able to achieve coordination and control through standardized rules and centralized decision making. As the environment becomes more unpredictable, scanning activities become more important, and the organization must decentralize decision making and resort to increasingly sophisticated and costly coordination mechanisms. Thompson concluded that the basic function of management is to insure the survival of the organization by maintaining an effective coalignment among three dynamic elements: environment, technology, and organization structure.

NEOCONTINGENCY PERSPECTIVE:
THE ROLE OF MANAGERIAL CHOICE

Following Thompson (1967), other theorists have recently disagreed with the view that organizational characteristics are fully preordained by technological considerations or environmental conditions (e.g., Child, 1972; Miles et al., 1974; Anderson and Paine, 1975). They have emphasized instead the importance of the decision makers who serve as the link between the organization and its environment. Although this neocontingency perspective has not been developed fully, it clearly rejects the environmental determinism implicit in most contingency theories of organization. Adherents of this approach view an organization's domain of activity as the result of managerial choice. Weick (1977), for example, argues that organizational environments are acts of managerial invention rather than discovery, and thus the theorist's basic task is to investigate how and why managers focus their attention on a particular portion of the environment, how they gather information about this area of concern, and how they interpret this information for decision-making purposes. This process of creating an organizational environment is a never-ending one, involving the coalignment of the organization with a continually evolving network of environmental constraints and opportunities. Several theorists have concluded that the coalignment process is best studied by observing the strategies that organizations develop to cope with their environments.

Organizational Strategy

The concept of organizational strategy was advanced by the Harvard Business School in the late fifties to embrace the major decisions that serve to match organizational resources with environmental opportunities and constraints (Andrews, 1960). Chandler (1962, p. 13) was one of the most influential early proponents of strategy, which he defined as "the determination of the basic long-term goals and objectives of the enterprise and the adoption of courses of action and the allocation of resources necessary for carrying out these goals."

Strategy was initially treated as a highly situational art, an imaginative act of integrating numerous complex decisions. Consequently, early theories of strategy offered prescriptions based principally on the analysis of single organizations (although these were embedded in widely differing environments). Recently, however, organizational strategy has been investigated more systematically, and some progress has been made toward the development of a theory of the strategy formulation *process* (Hofer, 1975). Studies of the strategic process have examined: (1) the influence of long-range planning on organizational performance (Warren, 1966; Steiner, 1969; Thune and House, 1970; Rue and Fulmer, 1972); (2) the impact of an incremental approach to policy making on budgeting (Wildavsky, 1964; Wildavsky and Hammond, 1965); (3) strategic decision-making activity among members of the dominant coalition (Aguilar, 1967; Bower, 1970; Mintzberg et al., 1976); and (4) the relationship between managers' personal values and strategy (Guth and

Tagiuri, 1965; Hage and Dewar, 1973). On the other hand, there is only a limited body of theory and even less research that treats strategy as an outcome and addresses the *content* of strategies (Ansoff, 1965; Rumelt, 1974; Schoeffler et al., 1974; Anderson and Paine, 1975; Cook, 1975; Hofer, 1975; Miller, 1975).

Specialists in Business Policy have often viewed strategy in a comparatively narrow sense. Many have restricted the definition of strategy to the means that enable the organization to attain its objectives with respect to the environment, excluding the processes through which those objectives are chosen. The policy field has generally treated the development of strategy as a discrete activity (Saunders, 1973), seldom specifying how strategy is linked to structure, process, and past and current organizational performance. Similarly, theorists have generally assumed that strategy is developed consciously and purposefully. Mintzberg (1976) pointed out, however, that this assumption forces the researcher to deal only with the more abstract and normative aspects of strategy.

These characteristics of the policy approach, in conjunction with the tendency of organization theorists to view the organization as a mechanical system largely determined by lawful processes, have led both groups to disregard the complementarity between organization theory and policy theory.

Strategy as Coalignment

Recently, several theorists have suggested that an expanded concept of organization strategy can best depict the coalignment process that links the organization to environment and technology (e.g., Miles et al., 1974; Anderson and Paine, 1975; Lawrence, 1975). Mintzberg (1976) has conceived strategy as a *pattern* in an ongoing stream of organizational decisions. This definition encompasses both deliberate or premeditated strategies and unintended strategies that emerge from the ongoing behavior of the organization. In other words, "the strategy maker may *formulate* his strategy through a conscious process, or strategy may *form* gradually as he makes decisions one by one" (Mintzberg, 1976, p. 3). The important advantage of this approach is that strategy becomes a tangible and researchable phenomenon, an observable product of the decision stream. This view of strategy emphasizes the dynamics of organizational behavior, admits the possibility of multiple causation among organizational characteristics and environmental conditions, and focuses attention on the role of managerial choice in achieving coalignment—qualities conspicuously absent in present contingency theories.

CONCLUSIONS

We have argued that theory and research concerning organization-environment relations can be characterized using three alternative perspectives. The early, universalistic perspective introduced a number of useful concepts of organizational structure and process, but these were rarely linked to the environment. The alternative organizational designs offered (which were few) tended to ignore the impact of the environment on organizational behavior.

With the advent of the contingency approach, environmental constraints and opportunities were explicitly introduced into models that linked various aspects of environment, technology, structure, and process. However, as we have pointed out, contingency models (1) have emphasized the differences rather than the similarities of organizational behavior, and (2) have focused on environmental determination rather than managerial choice as the primary cause of organizational characteristics. In their search for uniqueness, contingency theorists have made dramatic strides in isolating major contingency variables and demonstrating the relationships among them. However, few contingency theorists have attempted to resynthesize these relationships back into the larger whole from which they were derived.

Attempts at synthesis and elaboration appear to be the province of the neocontingency theorists, although we should hasten to add that this perspective has not taken a fully definitive shape nor can its adherents be clearly identified. We have characterized the neocontingency perspective as one that (1) views managerial or strategic choice as the primary link between the organization and its environment; (2) focuses on management's ability to create, learn about, and manage the organization's environment; and (3) encompasses the multiple ways that organizations respond to environmental conditions. As the neocontingency approach develops, it must give increased attention to the relationships among strategic choice and such important variables as technology, structure, and managerial ideology or philosophy, and to detecting and displaying for managers the implications of their current decisions for the long-run adjustment capabilities of their organizations.

Bibliography

Aguilar, Francis J.: *Scanning the Business Environment,* Macmillan, New York, 1967.

Aiken, Michael, and Jerald Hage: "Organizational Interdependence and Intra-organizational Structure," *American Sociological Review,* vol. 33, pp. 912–930, December 1968.

Alchian, Armen A.: "Uncertainty, Evolution, and Economic Theory," *Journal of Political Economy,* vol. 58, pp. 211–221, June 1960.

Aldrich, Howard: *An Organizational-Environment Perspective on Cooperation and Conflict Between Organizations in the Manpower Training System,* New York State School of Industrial and Labor Relations Reprint Series, New York, 1972.

Anderson, Carl R., and Frank T. Paine: "Managerial Perceptions and Strategic Behavior," *Academy of Management Journal,* vol. 18, pp. 811–823, December 1975.

Andrews, Kenneth R.: *The Concept of Corporate Strategy,* Irwin, Homewood, Ill., 1960.

Ansoff, H. Igor: *Corporate Strategy,* McGraw-Hill, New York, 1965.

———, and John M. Stewart: "Strategies for a Technology-Based Business," *Harvard Business Review,* vol. 45, pp. 71–83, November-December 1967.

Argyris, Chris: "On Organizations of the Future," *Administrative and Policy Study Series,* vol. 1, no. 03-006, Sage Publications, Beverly Hills, Calif., 1973.

————: "Double Loop Learning in Organizations," *Harvard Business Review,* vol. 55, pp. 115–125, September–October 1977.

Beer, Michael, and Stanley M. Davis: "Creating a Global Organization: Failures Along the Way," *Columbia Journal of World Business,* vol. 11, pp. 72–84, Summer 1976.

Biller, Robert P.: "On Tolerating Policy and Organizational Termination: Some Design Considerations," *Policy Sciences,* vol. 7, pp. 133–149, June 1976.

Bodenheimer, Tom: "The Malpractice Blow-up," *Health Policy Advisory Center Bulletin,* no. 64, pp. 12–15, May-June 1975.

Bower, Joseph L.: *Managing the Resource Allocation Process,* Harvard Graduate School of Business Administration, Boston, 1970.

Brown, A.: *Organization,* Hibbert, New York, 1945.

Burns, Tom, and G. M. Stalker: *The Management of Innovation,* Tavistock, London, 1961.

Chandler, Alfred D., Jr.: *Strategy and Structure,* Doubleday, Garden City, N.Y., 1962.

Child, John: "Organizational Structure, Environment, and Performance—The Role of Strategic Choice," *Sociology,* vol. 6, pp. 1–22, January 1972.

————, and Roger Mansfield: "Technology, Size, and Organization Structure," *Sociology,* vol. 6, pp. 369–393, September 1972.

Churchman, C. West: *The Systems Approach,* Dell, New York, 1968.

Cohen, Michael D., James G. March, and Johan P. Olsen: "A Garbage Can Model of Organizational Choice," *Administrative Science Quarterly,* vol. 17, pp. 1–25, March 1972.

Comstock, Donald E., and W. Richard Scott: "Technology and the Structure of Subunits: Distinguishing Individual and Workgroup Effects," *Administrative Science Quarterly,* vol. 22, pp. 177–202, June 1977.

Cook, Curtis W.: "Corporate Strategy Change Contingencies," *Academy of Management Proceedings,* August 1975.

Cyert, Richard, and James G. March: *A Behavioral Theory of the Firm,* Prentice-Hall, Englewood Cliffs, N.J., 1963.

Darran, Douglas C., Raymond E. Miles, and Charles C. Snow: "Organizational Adjustment to the Environment: A Review," *American Institute for Decision Sciences Proceedings,* November 1975.

Davis, Louis E.: "Job Satisfaction Research: The Post-Industrial View," *Industrial Relations,* vol. 10, pp. 176–193, May 1971.

Davis, Stanley M.: "Two Models of Organization: Unity of Command Versus Balance of Power," *Sloan Management Review,* vol. 16, pp. 29–40, Fall 1974.

————: "Trends in the Organization of Multinational Corporations," *Columbia Journal of World Business,* vol. 11, pp. 59–71, Summer 1976.

Dill, William R.: "Environment as an Influence on Managerial Autonomy," *Administrative Science Quarterly,* vol. 2, pp. 404–443, March 1958.

Donnelly, John F.: "Participative Management at Work," an interview with John F. Donnelly, *Harvard Business Review,* vol. 55, pp. 117–127, January-February 1977.

Downey, H. Kirk, Don Hellriegel, and John W. Slocum, Jr.: "Environmental Uncertainty: The Construct and Its Application," *Administrative Science Quarterly,* vol. 20, pp. 613–629, December 1975.

Drucker, Peter F.: *The Practice of Management,* Harper & Brothers, New York, 1954.

_____: *Management: Tasks, Responsibilities, Practices,* Harper & Row, New York, 1974a.

_____: "New Templates for Today's Organizations," *Harvard Business Review,* vol. 52, pp. 45–53, January-February 1974b.

Duncan, Robert B.: "Characteristics of Organizational Environments and Perceived Environmental Uncertainty," *Administrative Science Quarterly,* vol. 17, pp. 313–327, September 1972.

Emery, Fred E., and Eric L. Trist: "The Causal Texture of Organizational Environments," *Human Relations,* vol. 18, pp. 21–32, February 1965.

Evan, William M.: "The Organization-Set," in James D. Thompson (ed.), *Approaches to Organizational Design,* University of Pittsburgh Press, Pittsburgh, 1966, pp. 173–191.

Fayol, Henri: *General and Industrial Management,* translated by Constance Stours, Pitman, London, 1949.

Forrester, Jay W.: "A New Corporate Design," *Industrial Management Review,* vol. 7, pp. 5–18, Fall 1965.

Fouraker, L.E., and J.M. Stopford: "Organization Structure and the Multinational Strategy," *Administrative Science Quarterly,* vol. 13, pp. 47–64 June 1968.

Galbraith, Jay: *Designing Complex Organizations,* Addison-Wesley, Reading, Mass., 1973.

Gillespie, David F., and Dennis S. Mileti: "Technology and the Study of Organizations: An Overview and Appraisal," *Academy of Management Review,* vol. 2, pp. 7–16, January 1977.

Gouldner, Alvin W.: *Patterns of Industrial Bureaucracy,* Free Press, New York, 1954.

Guetzkow, Harold: "Relations Among Organizations," in Raymond V. Bowers (ed.), *Studies on Behavior in Organizations,* University of Georgia Press, Athens, Ga., 1966, pp. 13–44.

Guth, William, and Renato Tagiuri: "Personal Values and Corporate Strategy," *Harvard Business Review,* vol. 43, pp. 123–132, September-October 1965.

Hage, Jerald, and Michael Aiken: "Relationship of Centralization to Other Structural Properties," *Administrative Science Quarterly,* vol. 12, pp. 72–92, June 1967.

_____, and Robert Dewar: "Elite Values Versus Organizational Structure in Predicting Innovation," *Administrative Science Quarterly,* vol. 18, pp. 279–290, September 1973.

Hall, Richard H.: *Organizations: Structure and Process,* Prentice-Hall, Englewood Cliffs, N.J., 1972.

Hickson, David J., D.S. Pugh, and Diana C. Pheysey: "Operations Technology and Structure: An Empirical Reappraisal," *Administrative Science Quarterly,* vol. 14, pp. 378–397, September 1969.

Hinings, C.R., D.J. Hickson, J.M. Pennings, and R.E. Schneck: "Structural Conditions of Intraorganizational Power,"*Administrative Science Quarterly,* vol. 18, pp. 22–44, March 1974.

Hirsch, Paul M.: "Organizational Effectiveness and the Institutional Environment," *Administrative Science Quarterly,* vol. 20, pp. 327–344, September 1975.

Hofer, Charles W.: "Toward a Contingency Theory of Business Strategy," *Academy of Management Journal,* vol. 18, pp. 784–810, December 1975.

Hrebiniak, Lawrence G.: "Job Technology, Supervision, and Work Group Structure," *Administrative Science Quarterly,* vol. 19, pp. 395–410, September 1974.

Hutchinson, John: "Evolving Organizational Forms," *Columbia Journal of World Business,* vol. 11, pp. 48–58, Summer 1976.

Jelinek, Mariann: "Technology, Organizations, and Contingency," *Academy of Management Review,* vol. 2, pp. 17–26, January 1977.

Lawrence, Paul: "Strategy: A New Conceptualization," *Seminars on Organizations at Stanford University,* vol. 11, pp. 38–40, Autumn 1975.

_____, and Jay W. Lorsch: *Organization and Environment,* Harvard Graduate School of Business Administration, Boston, 1967.

Likert, Rensis: *The Human Organization,* McGraw-Hill, New York, 1967.

Litwak, Eugene, and Lydia F. Hylton: "Interorganizational Analysis: A Hypothesis on Co-ordinating Agencies," *Administrative Science Quarterly,* vol. 6, pp. 395–420, March 1962.

Mace, Myles: *Directors: Myth and Reality,* Harvard University Press, Cambridge, 1971.

March, James G.: "The Technology of Foolishness," reprinted in Michael D. Cohen and James G. March, *Leadership and Ambiguity: The College President,* McGraw-Hill, New York, 1974, pp. 216–229.

_____, and Herbert Simon: *Organizations,* Wiley, New York, 1958.

McGregor, Douglas: *The Human Side of Enterprise,* McGraw-Hill, New York, 1960.

Miles, Raymond E.: "Conflicting Elements in Managerial Ideologies," *Industrial Relations,* vol. 4, pp. 77–91, October 1964.

_____: "Human Relations or Human Resources?" *Harvard Business Review,* vol. 43, pp. 148–163, July-August 1965.

_____: *Theories of Management,* McGraw-Hill, New York, 1975.

_____, Charles C. Snow, and Jeffrey Pfeffer: "Organization-Environment: Concepts and Issues," *Industrial Relations,* vol. 13, pp. 244–264, October 1974.

Miller, Danny: "Towards a Contingency Theory of Strategy Formulation," *Academy of Management Proceedings,* August 1975.

Mintzberg, Henry: "Patterns in Strategy Formation," Faculty of Management Working Paper, McGill University, Montreal, 1976. (Mimeographed.)

_____, Duru Raisinghani, and Andre Théorêt: "The Structure of 'Unstructured' Decision Processes," *Administrative Science Quarterly,* vol. 21, pp. 246–275, June 1976.

Mohr, Lawrence B.: "Organizational Technology and Organizational Structure," *Administrative Science Quarterly,* vol. 16, pp. 444–459, December 1971.

Mooney, James: *Principles of Organization,* Harper, New York, 1947.

Osborn, Richard N., and James G. Hunt: "Environment and Organizational Effectiveness," *Administrative Science Quarterly,* vol. 19, pp. 231–246, June 1974.

Pennings, Johannes M.: "The Relevance of the Structural-Contingency Model for Organizational Effectiveness," *Administrative Science Quarterly,* vol. 20, pp. 393–410, September 1975.

Perrow, Charles: "A Framework for the Comparative Analysis of Organizations," *American Sociological Review,* vol. 32, pp. 195–208, April 1967.

_____: *Organizational Analysis: A Sociological View,* Wadsworth, Belmont, Calif., 1970.

Pfeffer, Jeffrey: "Merger as a Response to Organizational Interdependence," *Administrative Science Quarterly,* vol. 17, pp. 382–394, September 1972.

_____, and Huseyin Leblebici: "Executive Recruitment and the Development of Interfirm Organizations," *Administrative Science Quarterly,* vol. 18, pp. 449–461, December 1973.

_____, and Gerald R. Salancik: "Organizational Decision Making as a Political Process: The Case of a University Budget," *Administrative Science Quarterly,* vol. 19, pp. 135–151, June 1974.

Pitts, Robert A.: "Incentive Compensation and Organization Design," *Personnel Journal,* vol. 53, pp. 338–348, May 1974.

_____: "Unshackle Your 'Comers,'" *Harvard Business Review,* vol. 55, pp. 127–136, May-June 1977a.

_____: "Strategies and Structures for Diversification," *Academy of Management Journal,* vol. 20, pp. 197–208, June 1977b.

Prahalad, C.K.: "Strategic Choices in Diversified MNCs," *Harvard Business Review,* vol. 54, pp. 67–78, July-August 1976.

Reeves, T. Kynaston, and Joan Woodward: "The Study of Managerial Control," in Joan Woodward (ed.), *Industrial Organization: Behaviour and Control,* Oxford University Press, London, 1970, pp. 37–56.

Ritchie, J.B., and Raymond E. Miles: "An Analysis of Quantity and Quality of Participation as Mediating Variables in the Participative Decision Making Process," *Personnel Psychology,* vol. 23, pp. 347–359, Autumn 1970.

Ritti, R. Richard: "Underemployment of Engineers," *Industrial Relations,* vol. 9, pp. 437–452, October 1970.

Rogers, Everett M.: *Communication of Innovations: A Cross-Cultural Approach,* 2nd ed., Free Press, New York, 1971.

Rue, Leslie, and Robert Fulmer: "Is Long Range Planning Profitable?" *Academy of Management Proceedings,* August 1972.

Rumelt, Richard P.: *Strategy, Structure, and Economic Performance,* Harvard Graduate School of Business Administration, Boston, 1974.

Salter, Malcolm: "Stages of Corporate Development," *Journal of Business Policy,* vol. 1, pp. 23–37, Autumn 1970.

Saunders, Charles B.: "What Should We Know about Strategy Formulation?" *Academy of Management Proceedings,* August 1973.

Sayles, Leonard R.: "Matrix Management: The Structure with a Future," *Organizational Dynamics,* vol. 5, pp. 2–17, Autumn 1976.

Schoeffler, Sidney, Robert D. Buzzell, and Donald F. Heany: "Impact of Strategic Planning on Profit Performance," *Harvard Business Review,* vol. 52, pp. 137–145, March-April 1974.

Scott, Bruce: "Stages of Corporate Development—Parts I and II," Working Paper, Harvard Business School, Boston, 1970. (Mimeographed.)

Segal, Morley: "Organization and Environment: A Typology of Adaptability and Structure," *Public Administration Review,* vol. 35, pp. 212–220, May-June 1974.

Selznick, Philip: *TVA and the Grass Roots: A Study in the Sociology of Formal Organization,* University of California Press, Berkeley, 1949.

Simon, Herbert A.: "The Architecture of Complexity," in Joseph A. Litterer (ed.), *Organizations: Systems Control and Adaptation,* vol. 2, Wiley, New York, 1969, pp. 98–114.

Sloan, Alfred P., Jr.: *My Years with General Motors,* Doubleday, New York, 1964.

Snow, Charles C.: "The Role of Managerial Perceptions in Organizational Adaptation: An Exploratory Study," *Academy of Management Proceedings,* August 1976.

Starbuck, William H.: "Organizations and Their Environments," in Marvin D. Dunnette (ed.), *Handbook of Industrial and Organizational Psychology,* Rand McNally, Chicago, 1976, pp. 1069–1123.

Steiner, George A.: *Top Management Planning,* Macmillan, New York, 1969.

Stigler, George J.: "The Theory of Economic Regulation," *Bell Journal of Economics and Management Science,* vol. 2, pp. 3–21, Spring 1971.

Stinchcombe, Arthur: "Social Structure and Organizations," in James G. March (ed.), *Handbook of Organizations,* Rand McNally, Chicago, 1965, pp. 451–533.

Tannenbaum, Arnold S.: *Control in Organizations,* McGraw-Hill, New York, 1968.

————, Bogdan Kavcic, Menachem Rosner, Mino Vianello, and Georg Wieser: *Hierarchy in Organizations: An International Comparison,* Jossey-Bass, San Francisco, 1974.

Taylor, Frederick: *The Principles of Scientific Management,* Harper & Brothers, New York, 1911.

Thain, Donald H.: "Stages of Corporate Development," *Business Quarterly,* vol. 34, pp. 33–45, Winter 1969.

Thompson, James D.: *Organizations in Action,* McGraw-Hill, New York, 1967.

Thune, Stanley, and Robert House: "Where Long Range Planning Pays Off," *Business Horizons,* vol. 13, pp. 81–87, August 1970.

Tiryakian, Edward A.: "Typologies," *International Encyclopedia of the Social Sciences,* vol. 16, Macmillan, New York, 1968, pp. 177–186.

Tosi, Henry, Ramon Aldag, and Ronald Storey: "On the Measurement of the Environment: An Assessment of the Lawrence and Lorsch Environmental Uncertainty Questionnaire," *Administrative Science Quarterly,* vol. 18, pp. 27–36, March 1973.

Urwick, Lyndall F.: *The Elements of Administration,* Harper, New York, 1943.

Van de Ven, Andrew H., Andre L. Delbecq, and Richard Koenig, Jr.: "Determinants of Coordination Modes Within Organizations," *American Sociological Review,* vol. 41, pp. 322–338, April 1976.

von Bertalanffy, Ludwig: *General System Theory,* Braziller, New York, 1968.

Warren, Kirby E.: *Long Range Planning: The Executive Viewpoint,* Prentice-Hall, Englewood Cliffs, N.J., 1966.

Weber, Max: *The Theory of Social and Economic Organization,* translated by A.M. Henderson and Talcott Parsons, Free Press, New York, 1947.

Weick, Karl E.: *The Social Psychology of Organizing,* Addison-Wesley, Reading, Mass., 1969.

_____: "Enactment Processes in Organizations," in Barry M. Staw and Gerald R. Salancik (eds.), *New Directions in Organizational Behavior,* St. Clair Press, Chicago, 1977, pp. 267–300.

Wildavsky, Aaron: *The Politics of the Budgetary Process,* Little, Brown, Boston, 1964.

_____, and Arthur Hammond: "Comprehensive Versus Incremental Budgeting in the Department of Agriculture," *Administrative Science Quarterly,* vol. 10, pp. 321–346, December 1965.

Woodward, Joan: *Industrial Organization: Theory and Practice,* Oxford University Press, London, England, 1965.

_____, ed.: *Industrial Organization: Behaviour and Control,* Oxford University Press, London, 1970.

Worthy, James C.: "Organizational Structure and Employee Morale," *American Sociological Review,* vol. 15, pp. 169–179, April 1950.

Index

Page numbers in *italic* indicate illustrations or tables.